# The Complete Idiot's Reference Card

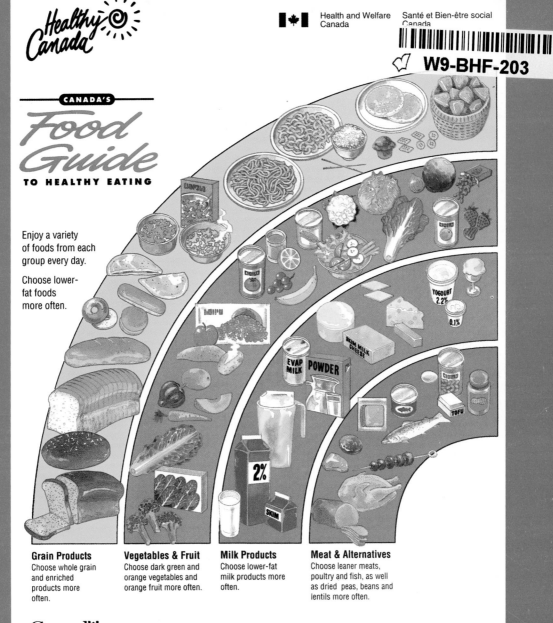

Healthy Canada

Health and Welfare Canada

Santé et Bien-être social Canada

W9-BHF-203

CANADA'S

Food Guide

TO HEALTHY EATING

Enjoy a variety
of foods from each
group every day.

Choose lower-
fat foods
more often.

YOGOURT
2.2%

0.1%

SKIM MILK CHEESE

EVAP MILK  POWDER

TOFU

2%

SKIM

**Grain Products**
Choose whole grain
and enriched
products more
often.

**Vegetables & Fruit**
Choose dark green and
orange vegetables and
orange fruit more often.

**Milk Products**
Choose lower-fat
milk products more
often.

**Meat & Alternatives**
Choose leaner meats,
poultry and fish, as well
as dried peas, beans and
lentils more often.

Canada

**PUTTING BREAD FIRST**

Bread is front and centre in the
Grain Products Group.
Recommended servings per day
from this group are now 5 to 12.
That's good news you can sink
your teeth into!

**PREPARATION TIPS**

■ Frozen bread toasts just as fast as fresh bread.
■ Busy day? Make a hot sandwich for dinner. Try a quick'n
easy tuna melt, or use leftovers for a hot turkey or beef sandwich.
■ Allow frozen bread to thaw at room temperature *inside* its
plastic bag. The moisture will then be re-absorbed into the
bread.

■ For a complete protein *without* cholesterol, have bread
with beans, peanut butter, lentils or peas.
■ French toast can be made ahead and stored in your
freezer. Just pop it into the toaster for a great start to a
weekday morning.
■ For bread crumbs and croutons, use fresh or leftover
bread.

Bakery Council of Canada

alpha
books

# Different People Need Different Amounts of Food

The amount of food you need every day from the 4 food groups and other foods depends on your age, body size, activity level, whether you are male or female and if you are pregnant or breast-feeding. That's why the Food Guide gives a lower and higher number of servings for each food group. For example, young children can choose the lower number of servings, while male teenagers can go to the higher number. Most other people can choose servings somewhere in between.

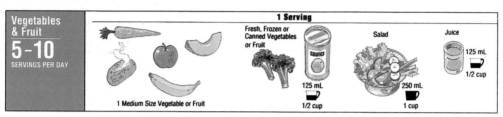

## Grain Products
### 5-12
**SERVINGS PER DAY**

**1 Serving**
- 1 Slice
- Cold Cereal 30 g
- Hot Cereal 175 mL 3/4 cup

**2 Servings**
- 1 Bagel, Pita or Bun
- Pasta or Rice 250 mL 1 cup

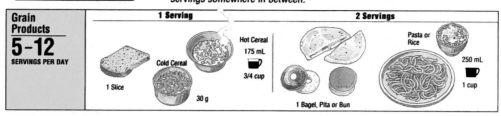

## Vegetables & Fruit
### 5-10
**SERVINGS PER DAY**

**1 Serving**
- 1 Medium Size Vegetable or Fruit
- Fresh, Frozen or Canned Vegetables or Fruit 125 mL 1/2 cup
- Salad 250 mL 1 cup
- Juice 125 mL 1/2 cup

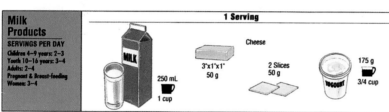

## Milk Products
**SERVINGS PER DAY**
Children 4–9 years: 2–3
Youth 10–16 years: 3–4
Adults: 2–4
Pregnant & Breast-feeding Women: 3–4

**1 Serving**
- MILK 250 mL 1 cup
- Cheese 3"x1"x1" 50 g
- 2 Slices 50 g
- Yogourt 175 g 3/4 cup

## Other Foods

Taste and enjoyment can also come from other foods and beverages that are not part of the 4 food groups. Some of these foods are higher in fat or Calories, so use these foods in moderation.

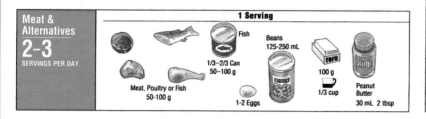

## Meat & Alternatives
### 2-3
**SERVINGS PER DAY**

**1 Serving**
- Meat, Poultry or Fish 50-100 g
- Fish 1/3–2/3 Can 50–100 g
- 1-2 Eggs
- Beans 125-250 mL
- TOFU 100 g 1/3 cup
- Peanut Butter 30 mL 2 tbsp

*Enjoy eating well, being active and feeling good about yourself. That's* VITALITÉ

### GOOD NEWS

Now more than ever, you can enjoy a lot more bread in all its different shapes and textures each and every day.

### NUTRITION TIPS

- All bread is low in fat. One slice (one serving from the Grain Products group) averages just 75 calories.
- Fibre is great for people who want to eat less. Bread's fibre helps satisfy your hunger without adding many extra calories.
- When you have a sandwich, the bread provides you with 9 essential nutrients: thiamin, riboflavin, niacin, folacin, pantothenic acid, phosphorus, magnesium, iron and zinc.
- All white flour in Canada is enriched. So *all* bread contains B vitamins and iron.

Bakery Council of Canada

# THE COMPLETE IDIOT'S GUIDE® TO

# Low-fat Cooking

## Canadian-Style

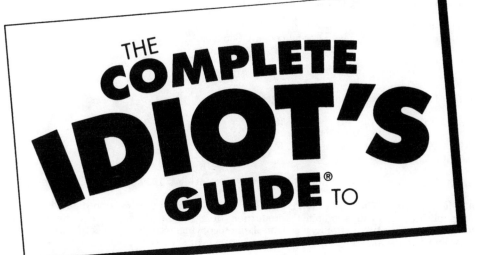

THE
# COMPLETE IDIOT'S GUIDE® TO

# Low-fat Cooking
## Canadian-Style

*by Pamela Steel and Brigit Légère Binns*

Prentice Hall Canada

A Pearson Company
Toronto

alpha books

**Canadian Cataloguing in Publication Data**

Steel, Pamela
   The complete idiot's guide to low-fat cooking Canadian-style

Includes index.
ISBN 0-13-086710-1

1. Low-fat diet-Recipes. I. Binns, Brigit Legere. II. Title.

RM237.7.S73 2000              641.5'638              C00-930119-4

ISBN 0-13-086710-1

Editorial Director, Trade Division: Andrea Crozier
Acquisitions Editor: Nicole de Montbrun
Copy Editor: Madeline Koch
Production Editor: Lori McLellan
Art Direction: Mary Opper
Cover Image: © 1999 PhotoDisc
Interior Design: Nathan Clement
Production Manager: Kathrine Pummell
Page Layout: Quadratone
Illustrator: Kevin Spear

1 2 3 4 5 WC 04 03 02 01 00

*Printed and bound in Canada.*

Visit the Prentice Hall Canada Web site! Send us your comments, browse our catalogues, and more. **www.phcanada.com**.

A Pearson Company
Toronto

# Contents at a Glance

# Contents

# Foreword

By now, I think just about everyone is aware of the importance of a lowfat diet. We all know that too much fat can contribute excess calories leading to weight gain, not to mention leaving you feeling sluggish after a meal. More serious is the fact that too much fat, especially if it's the wrong kind of fat, can lead to heart disease and certain kinds of cancer. We've known these things for a long time and they've been the focus of many books written by doctors, dietitians (myself among them), and self-proclaimed diet gurus.

Yet there has remained a gap between the experts who proclaim the health benefits of a lowfat diet and the cooking professionals who disdain cooking with less fat as impossible to prepare tastefully. I once heard Julia Child admit that we should use less fat (after her husband suffered a debilitating stroke) and follow that quickly with the comment that there's nothing wrong with a "little bit of butter." Although it's true, she neglected to give the reader concrete advice about *how much* fat is "a little" and how you can use various techniques as well as ingredients to add flavour to make lowfat food taste as good, if not better than its original counterpart.

This book bridges that gap. It tells readers not only why a lowfat diet is beneficial, but *how to put it in to practice* in an easy, clear, step-by-step way. Whether you want to grill, steam, roast, braise, or eat food raw, the book gives you enough information on lowfat cooking techniques to make you a verifiable healthy-cooking expert on the above-mentioned subjects. Tips to help you stock your pantry with the right foods and the equipment will make it easy for you to evolve toward this new style of eating. You'll never want to go back to your old ways of cooking. What's more, you won't feel like you're giving up a thing. In fact, you're gaining a great style of eating and better health to boot.

The approach is simple. By paying attention to how much fat you eat on a daily basis and then averaging it over the course of a week, this book shows you how you can mix and match nonfat and lowfat foods with an occasional high-fat indulgence and still end of with a diet that meets the 20% to 30% fat guidelines. But you won't need a pencil or a calculator and you won't need to embark on yet another "diet." Just follow the tips and recipes, all of which make a lowfat diet not only accessible and easy, but also, above all, taste great. In fact, when I got my advanced copy, I ended up employing certain tips with my clients who are battling their weight and trying to cook in a healthy and satisfying manner. This book tells you how to increase the flavour without the fat and tells you which herbs and spices go with which dishes.

I recommend this book to health-conscious people who love to eat great food and don't want it to interfere with their weight or their health, to professional chefs who are trying to please the growing number of health-conscious customers who frequent their restaurants, and to gourmet food lovers who are ready to move on to today's cuisine that sacrifices nothing in flavour yet gives everything in good nutrition.

To all of you trying to evolve your diet toward a delicious and nutritionally sound, low-fat one without requiring that you give up your favourite foods, *bon appetit*!

—Mary Donkersloot

Mary Donkersloot, RD, is a Beverly Hills-based nutrition therapist who treats clients dealing with eating disorders, weight control, and fitness and nutrition issues. She is the author of *Simply Gourmet Diabetes Cookbook*.

# Introduction

North Americans are consumed (excuse the pun) with weight loss. From phenomenally successful magazines that target the lighter approach to cooking, to fat-free frozen dinners, popcorn, and cookies, the nation's retailers reflect the continuing concern over bulging bellies. Fad diets may come and go, but dieting in itself is not a fad—for many people, it's a way of life. And every day, as baby boomers begin to age and don't much like it, more recruits join the hordes that are "watching their weight." Converts range from gourmet cooks who once swore never to touch a "low-cal" dish with a ten-foot pole, to blue-collar folks whose families are waving statistics on heart disease. The lowfat bandwagon not only has many followers, but also it extends across cultural, economic, and age gaps more than any other trend or fad, arguably, in history.

Many diet books attempt to re-invent the wheel, whereas lowfat cooking is really just a matter of using your head. Certainly, maintaining the ideal weight is not easy—most of us have tried and failed at least a few times in our lives. But it's not rocket science, either. Understanding your favourite ingredients, knowing how the body reacts to them, and learning how to combine them to create a tasty and diverse "diet" will make you an expert in no time at all. Then it's simply a matter of motivation, and here is the all-time best answer to that traditional stumbling block: Look in the mirror!

This book answers the questions:

• Why cook with less fat?

• Is it OK to splurge?

• Do I still have to exercise?

• How can I make my favourite dishes lower in fat?

• What can I cook tonight that will be good for my family?

and more.

It's a book that will appeal both to the perpetual dieter and the newcomer to lowfat eating. There is extensive nutritional information, including charts and tables indispensable for everyday use. A few diet fads are even shot down.

The recipes are simple to prepare, and range from the everyday to the slightly more sophisticated. Each recipe has been analyzed for nutritional content per serving, in an easy-to-read format that includes fat grams (broken down in saturated, polyunsaturated, and monounsaturated); calories, carbohydrates, protein, cholesterol, fibre, vitamins, iron, potassium, sodium, and zinc. Thus, whatever the experts may say next, the reader will still be able to assess his or her daily intake of nutrients.

# How to Use This Book

This is much more than just a book of recipes, though the recipes are pretty great on their own. If that's all you want, flip to Part 4. Maybe that's what you'll do the first few times you open the book, especially if you're a busy person with just one thing in mind—to get a healthy dinner on the table. But don't pass up the other parts of the book, such as:

**Part 1: Why Cook with Less Fat?** examines the motivation behind a desire for cutting down on fat, and how to make sure that motivation is something you can keep for years to come. Also explained: how to use all the charts, Health Canada's Food Guide Rainbow and Nutrition Information labels as tools in your quest. There is an exhaustive overview of basic nutrition (including some information about essential vitamins and minerals). The sometimes confusing world of nutrition research is examined, including an interview with a nutritionist and a dietitian that may surprise you. There's a chapter on how to make your new, healthy way of dining a painless part of your life for the rest of your life. The question of wine as part of a healthy diet is discussed, and you may be happy to learn that wine in moderation may be good for you, for several different reasons.

**Part 2: Fat-Free Is NOT Flavour-Free** reveals ingenious ways to add flavour and excitement to your food without adding fat, and explores in detail spices, flavouring pastes, and various condiments that can raise a bland dish to great heights. There's a chapter on stocking your pantry full of ingredients that will make lowfat cooking quick and easy, with lots of goodies that aren't even perishable. There's a chapter on dining out and how you can make it work for you within your new awareness of fat. Some popular ethnic cuisines are examined separately and in-depth, with recommendations for what to search out and what to avoid. If you eat out frequently, this chapter is a must.

**Part 3: Lowfat-Friendly Cooking Methods Explained** takes you step by step through steaming, grilling, roasting, braising, paper-baking, and eating foods raw. Each cooking method is explained clearly, so you can understand not just how it works but how it can help you cut down on fat. The grilling chapter alone could make a comprehensive book on the subject that is so close to many of our hearts! There are lists of ingredients that are suitable for each method, and cooking times for all. There's a chapter on garnishing that will let you create your own colourful and healthy dishes simply by combining one of the cooking methods with one or two of the garnishes. Lastly, every tool and piece of equipment a lowfat kitchen could ever require is identified and discussed.

**Part 4: Recipes to Live With (and Live On, and On, and . . .)** provides a wealth of simple, delicious recipes, all tested in our kitchens and all clearly and concisely written. From soups to breakfasts to desserts, these are recipes that will become a part of your daily life and stay there. There are lots of meat, fish, and fowl recipes for keeping your protein intake high, if desired. And plenty of grain, vegetable, and legume dishes for versatile side dishes and for those who choose not to eat meat. There are elegant appetizers and quick snacks. A few reworked classics and lots of modern, light food from all over the world are included as well.

## Extras

Sprinkled judiciously throughout the book you'll find sidebars of four different types. These highlight important facts that are worthy of special notice.

### Toothsome Tips

Advice that will make your cooking more delicious!

### Watch Out!

Possible pitfalls to keep an eye out for.

### Tidbits!

Extra or little-known bits of information about the main subject.

### What's the Skinny?

Definitions of terms that you may not be familiar with.

# Acknowledgments

I am grateful first and foremost to Brigit Légère Binns for writing the excellent American edition of this book. Her knowledge of food and nutrition makes this an excellent handbook to lowfat cooking. Thanks also to my friend Rosie Schwartz, RD. Her advice and input as a dietitian and food specialist were invaluable. Many thanks to all the great people at Health Canada who lent their knowledge to the project, most notably to Stephanie Charron, Educational Services Consultant with the Health Protection Branch of Health Canada, and to Susan Close from the Health and Nutrition Branch of the Health Department. Many thanks to Dr. Donna Woolcott, the Chair of the Family Relations and Applied Nutrition Department at the University of Guelph and to the staff at McGill University's School of Dietetics and Human Nutrition. Many thanks to Nicole de Montbrun and Madeline Koch and the whole team at Prentice Hall.

And, saving the best for last, as always a million thanks to Bill Coke, my chef husband, for his stunning and creative input, his educated palate, and his patience.

—Pamela Steel


I am eternally indebted to my friend and compatriot Mary Donkersloot, RD, a registered dietitian and prominent Los Angeles nutrition therapist. She found time in her hectic schedule to (a) warn me that I had better "get it right" or nutritionists all over the country would have me for dinner, (b) read through the technical information on nutrition in Chapter 3, and (c) offer herself as an interviewee for "What About the Latest Study That Says . . ." in Chapter 4.

For her advice on current thinking in the world of exercise and fitness, I am grateful to my friend Coquina Kinzler. Coqui has managed to keep her exquisite form intact even after her marriage to a classically trained French chef.

For preliminary editing, injections of humour, and expressions of occasional disbelief, my thanks to Christopher Pelham, a talented writer and, conveniently, a virtual member of the extended Binns family.

As ever, thanks to Maureen and Eric Lasher, who have become much more than just my agents. They are friends, fellow Apple/Mac voyagers, and possessors of some of the most irreverent humour this side of the Mississippi. This book would not exist without them.

To Jim Willhite, who inherited this project unexpectedly, thanks for making it your own under less-than-relaxed or perfect circumstances.

For his help at the hectic, bitter end of the testing process, I thank Greg Cowan, a talented cook who at first doubted my lowfat recipes could be delicious. He graciously acknowledged his error after following them religiously and tasting the results.

My husband Greg has again proved his ability to taste and comment wisely on whatever eclectic style of cooking should be consuming our kitchen at a given time. Because of him, many of the dishes in this book have become staples of our cooking repertoire. He lost 10 pounds while I was writing this book.

—Brigit Légère Binns

# Part 1
# Why Cook with Less Fat?

# Chapter 1

# Looking Good Equals Feeling Good—Let's Get Started

> ### In This Chapter
>
> ➤ What's my motivation?
>
> ➤ How painful is this going to be, anyway?
>
> ➤ Rework yourself inside and out and get ready to reap the benefits

If you're reading this book, you're probably concerned about your health. Maybe you need to lose weight. Perhaps you have a high cholesterol count and your family is worried about you. Or maybe you're just resolved to live a healthier lifestyle. Whatever the reason, you've taken the plunge and admitted you need to cut some of the fat out of your diet. Note that we said *some* of the fat—a diet without any fat at all would cause serious problems, like loss of skin elasticity or malnutrition, to name two big ones.

If you're a perpetual dieter who is looking for the next cure-all diet—one that will somehow work better than the last three you tried—you're out of luck. This book does not offer a cure-all diet. There is no such thing. This book is about common sense, following your heart (as long as your heart doesn't tell you to eat jelly doughnuts), eating delicious, fresh, and healthy food, and keeping the joy in your cooking. Whether you eat only to live, or live for the chance to eat, there is a way to cut fat from your diet.

You are your own boss, and your decisions will affect the quality of your life and perhaps even the length of it. Your choices can also directly affect your family, especially if you prepare the meals. These are weighty issues. Life-altering decisions must be made. But it isn't rocket science. After much research, we've discovered it's easier if you don't dwell too much on what the experts say (which changes every 6 months anyway). When foods contain nutrition labels, it helps to make sound

### Tidbits

Fat is good for you. Don't be alarmed—and don't order an extra-large deep-dish pizza with extra cheese, either. A little fat in the diet is essential for good health. Without it, you would quickly lose energy and have trouble absorbing the important nutrients and vitamins from food. But too much fat is definitely bad, and can cause heart disease, obesity, and other nasty problems.

decisions about your diet without slavishly following someone else's regime. Currently, food labelling in Canada is voluntary, and it's not surprising that 93 percent of Canadians want standardized labelling of all food products. Food producers tend to listen to their market so we can expect more and more well-labelled products, but in the meantime, pay attention to the labels that are already in place and use a good calorie/fat-counting reference book to work out the rest. Some common sense, a little knowledge, and balance are the qualities you need to create a new, better lifestyle—one you can stick with over the long term.

## Food Must Be Fun

For most of us, food is pleasing, and if we remove all the pleasure from our food, life would become miserable. Besides that, taking the joy out of eating and cooking can lead to instant diet-failure, so the goal is to keep yourself happy and healthy at the same time.

Many people don't watch their diets because they just can't accept the thought of never again having a steak, or a baked potato smothered in butter, or a cheesy Caesar salad. But the truth is that you *can* have all those things—you just can't have them very often. Examine your diet and identify the high-fat culprits. Use them as rewards when you have kept a sensible, lowfat regime for a certain amount of time. After a week or 10 days, celebrate! Reward yourself with one of your favourite high-fat culprits, and then move on. It's back to the lowfat regime, but you'll feel better now, because you have the memory of that slice of chocolate cake to last until you deserve another reward.

Over time, you'll develop different eating habits, which is the true goal. Surprisingly, you may find that you don't want richer, heavier foods, because they'll make you feel heavy and sluggish, and perhaps even a bit guilty. But don't expect that to happen immediately. You can't build Rome in a day; you just have to chip away at it. By the way, there is one more reward—not an edible one—that you can look forward to after a reasonable period of time: it's your image in the mirror (or your next blood-cholesterol test)!

## Do I Have to Use the Recipes in This Book Forever?

You are embarking on a long-term project here. We believe strongly that diets don't work. You must evolve a way of living and eating that does work for you over the long haul. The recipes in this book are just a guideline; in fact the most important information here is probably the detailed description of lowfat cooking methods in Part 3.

Soon you should be able to browse through the market and pick up whatever looks good, knowing that you'll be able, quickly and easily, to turn those items into a lowfat meal. Turn to the steaming and grilling chapters for generic and specific information on ingredients. Then, visit your pantry, which should be well stocked with flavourful condiments and spices that will bring excitement to dinner without much fat. Sure, it's easy to make a sauce for pasta taste good if you use butter, cream, and cheese. What you'll learn from this book is another way to make pasta taste good, just as easily, with about 85 percent less fat.

## Self-esteem and You

If you've tried to diet in the past, or you've hesitated to try because you felt you would fail, then you probably feel pretty bad about yourself. Feeling bad, you might be tempted to go to the corner for a cheeseburger with everything on it— that should make you feel better, right? When you get home, you'll look in the mirror and know you've failed again. That person in the mirror will look back and shake a finger at you. "You're just a failure!" that person will seem to say. Do you see where this scenario is leading? Failure reinforces failure and you can end up feeling pretty sorry for yourself.

### What's the Skinny?

If you're like a lot of people, you hear the word "lowfat" and your mind fills with the image of pale, sticklike people who will recommend that you eat mung beans and gravel or graze in the backyard. You'll expect ghastly recipes attempting to mimic real food that feature inedible-sounding ingredients. Setting out to make a pizza, you'll end up with something that tastes like handballs melted on cardboard. We used to think like that, too. But we've discovered that lowfat food is still "real" food. Common sense and a few techniques will allow you to create real *good* food that's good for you, too.

### Toothsome Tips

Don't feel too bad if your favourite food is apple pie, potato chips, or ice cream. There are no "good" or "bad" foods, just foods that must be kept to a minimum if you are trying to limit your fat intake. For most people, a healthy diet should include from 40 to 50 grams of fat per day, and that means your favourites can *occasionally* return!

**Watch Out!**

Don't ever give up just because you've broken your "diet." Just start again. As with any program of self-improvement, like exercise or even learning a language, skipping one workout session or lesson, or eating something completely inappropriate does *not* mean failure. You'd hardly be human if you didn't mess up once in a while. Just pick up where you left off and try not to make it *too* much of a habit.

This is a great reason not to pursue a promotion at work, not to mend the hole in the pocket of your overcoat, not to ask the cutie in accounting out for a date—in general, not to try to improve your life, because you'll probably just mess it up. On the other hand, success breeds success. Say you eat reasonably healthy meals, cooking at home and saving money, for about a month. You feel lighter, quicker, more, well, *successful.*

Suddenly that promotion seems like a piece of cake (excuse the reference), and it's only a matter of moments to grab a needle and thread and mend the hole in your pocket, the one your keys have been falling out of for the last 6 months. You'll feel like an attractive, confident person. Using this model, you can see that the sky's the limit, and there's much more than weight loss on your horizon if you master and stick with a new way of eating.

# Is Dropping a Size or Two Really That Important?

We all have our own strengths, and our own weaknesses. Usually, we know what they are, either because we are particularly intuitive, or because our friends tell us about them ad nauseam. When it comes to self-image, though, it can be harder to get at the truth. In fact, we can sometimes be blind to the obvious, or have so many excuses lined up that the problem vanishes into thin air. Statistics abound, reminding us what the ideal weight is for our sex, height, weight, and age, but they mean little because every body in the world is different, thank goodness. Big bones, small bones, heredity, frequency of exercise—these are some of the factors that affect how we may vary from the weight guidelines offered by our government and other helpful institutions.

Have you had a girlfriend who looks like Kate Moss complaining bitterly about her abdominal bulge? Or a guy friend who has suddenly gone from wearing medium to extra, extra-large swimming trunks, and claims it doesn't affect his sex appeal one little bit? It's enough to make you scream, right?

In the end, it is you and you alone, not your friends or the media, who can decide to change your diet, and thereby change your life. For many of us, dropping a dress or trouser size or two would rank somewhere up there with winning a small lottery. But there's more to be gained from healthy eating than improved self-image. There are the side effects, too, like an increased life span due to squeaky-clean arteries, and increased energy and enthusiasm for life—neither of which is anything to sneeze at.

# Can I Still Eat in Restaurants?

There are many places that sell prepared food, from McDonalds (a Big Mac clocks in at 560 calories, 52 percent of which are from fat), to your local sandwich counter (lean ham in a pita pocket with sprouts and mustard carries only 187 calories, 14 percent of them from fat). Once you become familiar with common foods and their fat and calorie content, it's pretty easy to order wisely in a restaurant or at a sandwich counter. But for most people, economic reasons mean eating out is an occasional, not an everyday affair.

Cooking your own is not only a safe option (you have complete control over what goes on the plate), but it's a pleasant, nurturing choice as well. Nothing is better at showing your family or friends you care than producing a delicious meal with your own hands. And if you've managed to make it taste great and still be good for them, that shows the ultimate concern.

## What's the Skinny?

Keeping up with current dietary advice can sometimes seem like playing basketball in a blindfold: first, all fat is bad; then no, just some fats are bad. Butter is bad. No, now margarine is worse. Carbo-loading is a good weight-loss gambit; no, high-protein diets are better. The truth is that good common sense is worth more than any fad, trend, or revelation from the pundits. This regime is something you have to live with for a long time, not a momentary fad. It had better be a sensible and trustworthy one.

## Table 1.1: Fat and Calorie Content of Various Foods

| Food Item | Portion | Calories | % fat |
|---|---|---|---|
| Baked chicken breast, without skin | 3 oz (90 g) | 142 | 21 |
| Baked chicken breast, with skin | 3.5 oz (105 g) | 193 | 35 |
| Tabbouleh (grain salad) | 1/2 cup (125 mL) | 112 | 32 |
| Warm German Potato Salad | 1/2 cup (125 mL) | 139 | 35 |
| Coleslaw, with mayonnaise-style dressing | 1/2 cup (125 mL) | 103 | 85 |
| 9-inch (23-cm) Single-Crust Strawberry Pie | 1 slice (1/8) | 184 | 36 |
| 9-inch (23-cm) Single-Crust Pecan Pie | 1 slice (1/8) | 431 | 49 |

*Source*: Adapted from *Health Counts* (John Wiley & Sons, 1991).

**Tidbits**

The latest figures from Health Canada show that 46 percent of Canadians are somewhat overweight and 31 percent are overweight to the point of possible health risk. And we thought the nation was "switched on" to good health! In Canada, 76 percent of women and 60 percent of men are concerned about the amount of fat they are consuming. Supermarket shelves are flooded with lowfat claims, but it appears many Canadians still don't know how to take that excess weight off for good. Of the people who successfully lose weight on a regimented diet, about 75 percent of them gain all the weight back within 2 years.

# Do I Need to Calculate the Fat Content of Every Bite I Take?

If you are seriously overweight, or you have a significant heart or cholesterol problem, you might want to start your lowfat program by keeping a food diary for a few weeks, noting down everything you eat every day. Then, sit down with a calorie and fat chart to fill in the numbers and find out if you are on or near the target of about 25 percent of calories from fat.

Remember, your goal is to keep fat down to 25 to 30 percent of your *total* calorie intake per day. Not every dish needs to derive 30 percent of its calories from fat; it's the average of the day that you're after. For that matter, it's the average per *week*. This is what can keep you going. It allows you to splurge a little bit once in a while, knowing that you will toe the line afterwards to make up for it. This type of dieting is much more realistic than a stricter, regimented approach, and therefore, in our experience, more likely to succeed.

# Using Nutrition Information Labels to Help Lose Weight

Although food labelling is still voluntary in Canada, many companies are meeting consumer needs by printing Nutrition Information panels on their packages. These panels make it easy to see exactly how many grams of fat are in each serving size, and, sometimes, how much of that fat is saturated. Contrary to many dieters' beliefs, however, it's not just the fat in food that matters: it's also the calories. If you eat more calories than you should, whether those calories are made up of carbohydrates, proteins, *or* fats, you will gain weight. A big bowl full of plain pasta adds up to about 400 calories. Though it has almost no fat, it still counts as part of your daily calorie intake, almost 20 percent for an 1,800/day limit. What are you going to eat for the rest of the day? Carrots?

We can expect to see more labels on food products only if you exercise your power as a consumer and choose foods that make it clear what you are eating by breaking it down for you right there on the package. You may still need to do a little arithmetic, but the labels do make some things easier:

1. Instant choices: while shopping, you can compare products, making your decision based on the relative fat, fibre, and nutrient levels of each.

2. Calculating calories for a food diary: it's a good idea to try this when you are starting out, so you can get some idea of your good and bad habits. The labels make it easy to count fat grams and total calories so you can easily compute your percentage of calories derived from fat and keep it under 30 percent. After a few weeks you'll get the hang of it and shouldn't need the diary.

Before you begin, you'll need to determine your total daily intake of calories. There are a number or different methods for calculating the best daily calorie intake for your age, sex, height, and weight. It's best to ask your family doctor or a qualified dietitian to set healthy goals for weight loss. NEVER CONSUME LESS THAN 1,200 CALORIES PER DAY UNLESS A PHYSICIAN ADVISES YOU TO DO SO.

**Watch Out!**

Label watching is an easy way to watch fat intake—but beware: some products are labelled by weight and not by calories. Keep this in mind or the information may be misleading. A product labelled 80 percent fat-free can mean the fat content is 20 percent of the weight, not of the calories. So when you calculate the percentage of calories from fat you come up with 72 percent! Not so good after all.

## Table 1.2: Recommended Energy Intake Based on Age and Sex

| Age | Cal/day |
| --- | --- |
| **Females** | |
| 10–12 | 2,200 |
| 13–15 | 2,200 |
| 16–24 | 2,100 |
| 25–49 | 1,900 |
| 50–74 | 1,800 |
| 75+ | 1,700 |
| **Males** | |
| 10–12 | 2,500 |
| 13–15 | 2,800 |
| 16–18 | 3,200 |
| 19–24 | 3,000 |
| 25–49 | 2,700 |
| 50–74 | 2,300 |
| 75+ | 2,000 |

*Source*: Health Canada

## Watch Out!

Many foods which are low in fat can be very high in salt (sodium) or sugar. That's how they make up for the flavour that fat would provide. Excess sodium intake can aggravate high blood pressure and cause water retention. And beware of eating too much sugar—empty carbohydrates. Solid nutrition is more than just cutting out the fat.

# What's the Deal with Fat?

A new study by the McGill University School of Dietetics and Human Nutrition shows that most Canadians are watching their fat intake. In the early 1970s, fat intake was around 40 percent of calories, but has dropped to 30 percent with only 10 percent of calories coming from saturated fats. This is right in line with recommendations by Health Canada. That means, for instance, that a healthy adult female who consumes 1,800 calories per day probably consumes about 54 grams of fat daily. This is excellent news for the health of Canadians because if we really are keeping our fat and calorie intake within recommended parameters, then we will begin to lose weight. According to Health Canada, the 31 percent of Canadians who are currently obese are in danger of many health risks, like heart disease and many types of cancer. As we begin to lose weight, we will improve our health and our overall well-being. This is not deprivation. And it is NOT a diet. Diets don't work long term, but changing your ways permanently, i.e., for GOOD, does work. The average is what is important, not each and every dish at each and every meal. And many nutritionists suggest limiting your intake of fat to 25 percent of your daily calorie intake—now you are losing weight.

## The Least You Need to Know

➤ Fat is not a villain. We all need some fat in our diets. Otherwise we would be unable to manufacture the nutrients that help keep us alive. We'd also lose energy, have dull, lackluster hair, and lose skin tone.

➤ Diets that make you feel deprived just don't work. A lifestyle you can live with is more likely to stick.

➤ Averaging your daily calorie and fat intake is what's important, not slavishly consuming the same amount at every meal. This method is what allows occasional splurging.

➤ Watching calories is just as important as watching fat. Too many calories will cause weight gain just as fast as too much fat.

➤ Motivation is a strong factor in the success of any lifestyle change. Visualize how much better your life will be if you stick to your new regime. Reward yourself. Make it fun.

# Chapter 2

# The Relationship between Fat and Cholesterol: Your Arteries and You

## In This Chapter

➤ Too much fat means more than just extra pounds

➤ Your arteries and you

➤ Listen to your ancestors

There is more to losing weight than just looking better and increasing your self-esteem, even though those are pretty attractive goals. By eliminating excess weight you'll also be giving your heart a better chance to do its work efficiently, easing the strain on this sensitive and important muscle.

Most people who are overweight also have high cholesterol, which can lead to a buildup in and blockage of the critical arteries that supply blood to your heart. When arteries become seriously clogged, heart disease and eventual heart attack are the likely results. Other factors can contribute to the likelihood of developing heart disease. Some, like genetics, sex, and age, you can't do much about; others, like high blood pressure, cigarette smoking, and exercise, are things you most definitely *can* change.

Changing your eating habits and adopting a diet low in fat—more particularly, low in *saturated* fat—may increase your life span. A little knowledge is a wonderful weapon in the fight against excess weight and excess cholesterol.

### What's the Skinny?

There are two kinds of cholesterol: (1) dietary (in other words, what you eat), and (2) blood cholesterol. Blood cholesterol is determined by your genetic background (blame it on your parents!) combined with the amount of cholesterol you consume. For proper nutrition, the body must consume a small amount of fat—otherwise vitamins and minerals will not be absorbed efficiently—but the body needs *no added cholesterol.* Although your body requires some cholesterol to run smoothly, it can make its own.

# What Is Cholesterol?

Cholesterol is a soft, waxy, odourless substance found in every part of your body, from your brain to your bones. It is an important factor in the manufacture of hormones and Vitamin D, among other things, but your body is quite capable of producing as much cholesterol as it needs. Even if you never, ever consumed any saturated fat or dietary cholesterol, your body would still provide enough for its needs. Any cholesterol that is eaten simply increases the overall level of blood cholesterol, often leading to dangerously high levels if your diet is high in saturated fats. Saturated fats are the worst of the three kinds of fat—they raise cholesterol levels, clog arteries, and can lead to heart disease—whereas monounsaturated fat can actually *decrease* blood cholesterol. This is why olive oil, a mono-unsaturated fat, is so much better for you than butter, a saturated fat.

# What Constitutes a "High" Cholesterol Level? (Or Blinding Me with Science . . .)

To find out if you have high cholesterol, you must have a blood test by a medical professional. A small amount of your blood will be analyzed, and you will be told the results. A total blood cholesterol of 240 mg/dl (240 milligrams per decilitre of blood, if you must know) is considered high. Any level between 200 and 239 is labelled "Borderline High." Under 200 is considered to be good.

There is a little more to understand, however. Your total blood cholesterol should be broken down into two types, the "good," or HDL cholesterol, and the "bad," or LDL cholesterol. Your HDL cholesterol should be at least 35 mg/dl, and your LDL level should be less than 130 mg/dl. An LDL level of 130 to 159 mg/dl is borderline, and above 159 mg/dl is high risk.

So there is more to reading the results of your cholesterol test than meets the eye. To be fully informed, you must know the LDL and the HDL levels that go into making up that total.

# I've Got High Cholesterol; Is That Bad?

Those in the high-risk category have bad news and good news. The bad news is that high LDL cholesterol will almost certainly lead to coronary heart disease, the leading cause of death for both men and women worldwide (according to Health Canada's Laboratory Centre for Disease Control). In Canada, 48 percent of men and 43 percent of women have elevated cholesterol levels. For men, levels rise rapidly from age 18 to 44; obviously, it's never too soon to start thinking low fat! Women's cholesterol levels rise more slowly until age 44 and by the age of 55, they exceed the rate of similarly aged men.

# So What's the Good News?

There's a little. Changing one's habits and, if necessary, taking certain drugs can bring down cholesterol levels, but the drugs are only a last resort. It's imperative to start by changing your habits. We didn't say it was great news. Just good.

# Some Causes of High Cholesterol

To bring cholesterol levels down, you must first understand what makes it high in the first place.

1. Diet. Of the things you can change to lower your cholesterol (as opposed to your genes or gender), diet is the most important. Saturated fat and dietary cholesterol raise blood cholesterol levels more than anything else you can consume.

2. Weight. It's a vicious circle: overweight people tend to have high cholesterol, thus putting themselves at risk of heart disease. They also place more strain on their hearts because running a heavier body demands more effort from the heart muscle. Losing weight is one way to reduce blood cholesterol levels and also reduce strain on the heart muscle.

3. Physical Activity/Exercise. Experts aren't yet sure if exercise can reduce the buildup of cholesterol in your arteries, but they do know exercise can control weight, lower blood pressure, and increase your "good," or HDL, cholesterol levels. If you live a sedentary lifestyle, you place yourself at high risk.

4. Genetic Factors. This is a tough one, because there's nothing much you can do about it. Investigate back as far as family records will go and see how many of your forebears perished from heart attacks. Listen to what your ancestors can tell you. It can be a sobering experience. If you find that heart disease runs in your family, that is another big factor in placing you in the high-risk category.

**Watch Out!**

Doing a little genetic research is easier than it may sound, unless, of course, you are adopted. Ask your parents, grandparents, aunts, uncles—anyone with a good memory—about the family mortality rates. Or look in the county record books, which can usually be found in the reference section of your local library. You may find out some amusing or surprising facts about your family while you're at it, but try not to get sidetracked. You want to know how many of your relatives died from heart disease.

5. Sex/Age. As we have seen, cardiovascular disease is the leading killer worldwide. In Canada, 38 percent of all deaths are due to cardiovascular disease. Men are at much greater risk until women hit menopause. Then women's risk levels rise sharply, probably due to lower estrogen levels; 41 percent of all deaths in Canadian women are due to cardiovascular disease.

6. Alcohol. Countless studies show that moderate alcohol consumption can increase the "good" HDL cholesterol level, thereby reducing the risk of developing heart disease. However, because of the other health risks associated with alcohol, such as stroke, liver disease, and accidents, experts have stopped short of actually recommending it as a definitive way to lower cholesterol. Keep in mind that the positive effects of alcohol have mainly been associated only with red wine, and that benefits drop off rapidly if consumption rises above 2 glasses a day. Recently, the Scientific Review Committee from Health and Welfare Canada compiled a paper outlining new Nutrition Recommendations for Canadians. It states that, "The Canadian diet should include no more than 5 percent of total energy as alcohol, or 2 drinks daily, whichever is less." Nondrinkers can benefit from the heart-healthy compounds in red wine, too—they are called flavonoids, and are present in nonalcoholic red grape juice and peanuts.

7. Stress and High Blood Pressure. Again, experts aren't sure if stress raises cholesterol levels, or if we just eat more fatty foods when we are experiencing high stress; however, high stress and high cholesterol levels often go hand in hand. High blood pressure is a more serious condition associated with stress, and must be brought down with the help of your doctor, who may or may not prescribe medication.

This is a long list, and some things are impossible for you to change. So focus on the things you can change, like watching out for excess fat in your diet and increasing your level of physical activity. Every little bit helps. If you find that not just a few, but many of these factors apply to you, then it should give you an extra jolt of motivation in the fight to cut down on fat.

# The Three Types of Fat

There are three types of fat: monounsaturated and polyunsaturated fat, and saturated fat. Monounsaturated fat is the best of the three, and since your body does need to some fat to function efficiently, it's best to stick with this one.

1. Monounsaturated fats are oils like olive, fish, canola, grapeseed, avocado, and walnut. These are considered the *good* fats, although you should still keep fat down to around 25 percent of your daily calorie intake, or 50 grams in a 2,000 cal/day diet. One tablespoon (15 mL) of olive oil contains 10.3 grams of monounsaturated fat.

2. Polyunsaturated fats like corn, soybean, and peanut oil are generally considered OK, because they can lower "bad" cholesterol levels. But they are not as effective as the monounsaturated fats. Most margarine is made with these fats, but recently it has been discovered that the process that solidifies margarine (to make it look more like butter) also produces the very undesirable trans-fatty acids, which have been implicated in increased risk for heart disease. Olive oil is by far the better choice.

3. Saturated fats are the bad guys of the three. These fats are generally solid at room temperature, and are mostly found in meat, poultry, and full-fat dairy products. Certain vegetable oils, such as palm and coconut oil, are also high in saturated fat. Recently corn oil has been suspected of being a saturated fat culprit. As recently as 5 years ago, corn oil was considered a "good" oil!

**Tidbits**

Canada's Food Guide recommends that Canadians cut fat to 30 percent of their daily calories, but many doctors and nutritionists don't think this is good enough. They'd like to see fat at 25 percent or 20 percent daily. The Food Guide is currently under review and one of the reasons for this is that it was compiled in the spirit of ensuring nutritional adequacy. Today, obesity and related illnesses like heart disease and cancer, born of overindulgence in certain foods, have led health officials to recognize that the greatest threat to our health stems from excessive food and nutrient intake.

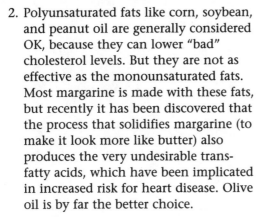

**Watch Out!**

Be aware if you see the word "hydrogenation" on a label! In order to make polyunsaturated fats like corn and safflower oil more attractive (i.e., to make them look and act like butter), these fats are often hydrogenated or processed to make the liquid oils solid. Margarine is the most obvious example, but hydrogenated fats also appear in other packaged foods. The process creates "trans-fatty acids," which experts now believe cause heart disease and raise levels of "bad" LDL cholesterol. This is a relatively new development in the study of health and nutrition. Butter is now considered better for you than margarine, even though it does contain the "bad" saturated fat. (We suspected butter was better all the time.)

## Table 2.1: Common Fat and Oils Ranked from Lowest to Highest Saturated Fat Content

Canola oil †
Safflower oil
Sunflower oil
Corn oil
Olive oil †
Soft margarine
Stick margarine
Soybean oil
Peanut oil †
Cottonseed oil
Fish oil
Shortening
Poultry fat
Pork fat
Lard (processed, usually hydrogenated, pork fat)
Beef fat
Cheese, Cream, Butter
Palm oil
Coconut oil

*† Primarily monounsaturated*

### The Least You Need to Know

➤ Many people who are overweight also have high cholesterol, which causes heart disease, the number-one killer of adults worldwide. Both body fat and blood cholesterol basically come from the same source: saturated fats.

➤ Some fats are not as bad for you as others, and monounsaturated fats like olive oil can even help reduce levels of "bad" cholesterol. This doesn't mean you can eat as much olive oil as you want—it just means you're better off drizzling a little olive oil on a baked potato than smearing on a large pat of butter. Saturated fats (which come from dairy and animal fat) should be kept to 10 percent of your fat calories per day, since they are the real villains. But a steak once in a while is not out of the question. It's all a matter of balance.

➤ Even if weight loss is your only goal, it's worth having a blood cholesterol test. If you find that you have high or borderline-high cholesterol, it will provide added motivation for your program of lowfat dining. Two reasons are always better than one when you decide to improve your habits. We have always felt that increasing life expectancy is a fairly worthy goal.

# Chapter 3

# A Few Bytes on Nutrition

---

## In This Chapter

➤ The Complete Idiot's Guide to Nutrition

➤ The Food Guide Rainbow explained

➤ Finding fibre

---

Gather a group of nutrition "experts" and you'll get a dizzying range of opinions on every subject from the correct percentage of fat in the diet to the dangers of consuming too much sodium (salt). Luckily, almost all qualified nutritionists and doctors agree on the most important issues, so it's easy to map out a lifestyle that will reap the rewards of good health and longevity. Understanding the basics of nutrition will let you make your own smart choices about fuelling your body in a sensible, simple, and "diet-free" way. There are tomes on nutrition that can rival an encyclopedia, but the essence of nutrition is simple: we eat food (calories) to fuel our bodies, and if our energy intake is more than our energy output (i.e., physical activity), we gain weight.

Understanding the role of calories in our diet is the first and most important step; understanding fat is secondary but still crucial, particularly for those with high cholesterol. Eating healthfully, however, requires more than watching calorie and fat intake. Lack of calcium in the diet may cause bone weakness and osteoporosis; lack of iron can cause anemia. It's only by maintaining a healthy, balanced diet that includes all the vital nutrients, vitamins, and minerals in roughly the correct amounts that you will function at the height of perfect, radiant health.

Health Canada has created a cute food chart in the shape of a rainbow to help us simple-minded folks follow a healthy diet without taking remedial biology courses.

### What's the Skinny?

Calorie-counting books are handy, as is food labelling where it exists. Use a counting method for planning a menu and making a shopping list, though, to insure that temptation doesn't win at the market. Calories are abbreviated as cal, and grams usually as g. Don't make the mistake of getting them mixed up, however. There's a big difference between the 9.6 *grams* of fat contained in a 3¹/₂-ounce (105-g) piece of roasted pork loin and the 209 *calories* it carries.

But the food rainbow has a few problems: (1) the serving sizes can seem confusing and unrealistic; (2) it does not fully take into account the difference in calorie requirements for a 20-year-old student and a 35-year-old manual labourer; and (3) it doesn't tell you how to make food fun. Science aside, food should be something we look forward to and enjoy without guilt. A few facts, some common sense, and you can plan your lifelong program of good health.

# Calories and Energy

Our food is made up of three different groups: protein, carbohydrates, and fats. Everything we eat falls into one of these categories, and each carries a different number of calories. Carbohydrates range from very few (lettuce = .13 cal per gram) to lots (pasta = 3.58 cal per gram); proteins have a bit more (4 cal per gram); and fats are sky-high in calories (9 cal per gram). To survive, we need to eat some of each group, and the daily combination adds up to our total calorie intake.

Each person has a different daily calorie requirement, depending on his or her height, weight, age, and level of physical activity. If you take in more calories than your body needs, you will gain weight. If you expend more calories than you consume, you will lose weight. For instance, if your recommended calorie intake is 1,900 per day and you regularly consume 2,000, you will gain about 10 pounds (4.5 kg) in a year. By increasing your energy output, or exercise, by 30 minutes a day, you would lose the same amount in a year. But make sure you don't eat more to reward yourself for exercising, or the effect of the exercise will be lost.

## Those Sneaky Pounds

If you have attempted to follow a program of exercise and found yourself gaining weight, there may be another reason: muscle tissue weighs more than fat. So if you replace fat tissue with lean muscle, you'll weigh more. Many a new visitor to a health club has sighed when the scale reads the same after 3 months of exercise. Just remember, muscle will burn fat, so it's a better *kind* of weight than you had before, and the mirror will likely confirm that fact!

## It's a Matter of Balance

Weight control is simply a matter of balancing energy output with energy intake. And the key to success is to look at your food consumption as a matter of balance, too. Don't eat all your allowed calories every day—save some till the end of the week and blow them on a piece of chocolate cake. Enjoy! Try to look at your calorie intake as an average, not a daily target. This is where crash diets go wrong. Joy is not balanced with hardship, and the dieter is so disappointed by the inevitable failure to keep up the strict regime that the diet is usually abandoned. Who wants to fail all the time?

## Counting Calories: Is It Necessary?

Unless you are a math whiz and carry a notebook and a calculator in your back pocket, counting calories will probably be a bit time-consuming. Unfortunately, if you plan to follow the "honour system" diet that involves no rules but lots of common sense, you'll need to have some idea of what you are eating.

This doesn't mean you'll be a calorie-nerd for the rest of your life. It just means that as you ease into this fairly liberal way of creating a healthy diet for yourself, yes, you will have to keep track. If you follow the recipes in this book, you'll have the calorie and fat count spelled out for you. Write it down, start a chart—it's not forever. Food labelling can make it easy to count calories from many prepared foods, but how will you know how many calories are in that baked potato you ordered (yogurt topping, please) at a restaurant? And as we know there's no nutrition label on fresh fruits and vegetables.

This is where it's helpful to have a calorie-counting guide on hand. There are some excellent ones available, but we've had good results with *Health Counts*, from Kaiser Permanente (John Wiley & Sons, 1991). It even has pages at the front that you can copy and use as a calorie-counting chart. As soon as you've figured out what you like to eat, what you should be eating, and, most importantly, what portion sizes make sense for your new regime, you can abandon this practice (it took Brigit about 3 weeks to get comfortable enough to stop keeping the chart).

### Watch Out!

Losing weight sounds so simple when you put it into scientific terms: 30 minutes of moderate exercise per day will strip 10 pounds (4.5 kg) per year from the average adult. The problem comes *after* you exercise, when your body craves more calories to compensate for those burned. It's a vicious circle: if you then consume an extra 100 calories (say, 2 slices of bread), you'll cancel any possible weight-loss benefit from the exercise (of course, the exercise is still good for your heart).

# Protein: We Are What We Eat

Protein is the most basic and most crucial fuel that the human body requires for survival. Take away the 99 percent of our bodies that is water, and what's left over is protein. Enzymes, antibodies, hemoglobin, and insulin are all protein—without these the body would quickly cease to function. These crucial proteins are gradually worn away as they are used, and the only way to replenish them is with dietary protein. Protein is highest in animal foods, so vegetarians must find their protein from grains, nuts, and legumes, but each of those are deficient in certain *types* of protein, specifically amino acids. This is why, back in the 1970s, many practitioners of the Zen macrobiotic (all-grain) diet ended up in the hospital with malnutrition. Luckily, plant-based proteins tend to be complementary—what one lacks, the others can provide. This is why vegetarians must be careful to balance grains with beans, nuts, and fresh vegetables in order to obtain the necessary protein for survival.

Proteins are made up of a combination of up to 20 amino acids, and are considered either "complete" or "incomplete." Complete proteins come only from animal sources (meat, eggs, and dairy products); all plant proteins start out incomplete, but by our own manipulations we can turn wheat into "wheat germ" and soybeans into "soy protein," both of which are nearly complete proteins. Health Canada advises the average woman to consume from 47 to 55 grams of protein per day, depending on her age, while the average man should consume from 58 to 64 grams, and a 6-year-old child should have 19 grams. Consuming too much protein shoots up calorie levels, as well as making the kidneys work harder to process waste byproducts.

## Table 3.1: Protein Levels of Various Foods

| Product | Serving Size | Grams of Protein |
|---|---|---|
| Beef sirloin | (3$^1$/$_2$ ounces or 100 mL) | 30 g |
| Lamb loin | (3$^1$/$_2$ ounces or 100 mL) | 30 g |
| Pork loin | (3$^1$/$_2$ ounces or 100 mL) | 28.6 g |
| Cheddar cheese | (1 ounces or 30 mL) | 6 g |
| Lowfat cottage cheese | (1 cup or 250 mL) | 28 g |
| Eggs | (1) | 6.3 g |
| Egg Beaters | ($^1$/$_4$ cup or 50 mL) | 5 g |
| Dried beans, cooked | (1 cup or 250 mL) | 15 g |
| Spaghetti, cooked | (1 cup or 250 mL) | 6.7 g |
| Long grain brown rice | (1 cup or 250 mL) | 5 g |
| Whole wheat bread | (2 slices) | 5.4 g |
| Broccoli, cooked | (1 cup or 250 mL) | 4.6 g |
| Lettuce, shredded | (1 cup or 250 mL) | 1 g |

### Toothsome Tips

Don't try to build Rome in a day—it takes time. If you don't like the taste of nonfat or skim milk, try 2 percent first, then ease yourself into nonfat and other lowfat or nonfat dairy products. There is no need to eliminate the high-fat culprits in your regular diet; you just need to reduce them quite a bit. Feelings of deprivation can lead to diet failure, so remember that portion control is all-important in the lowfat lifestyle.

# Fat, A Necessary Evil

We all need some fat in order to live, contrary to what some high-profile no-fat exponents might have us believe. It is a medical fact that without fat, our cell walls would weaken and we would be unable to absorb and metabolize certain essential vitamins and amino acids. Our systems are incapable of synthesizing these essential fatty acids from inside the body, so it must be consumed as part of our diet. According to Health Canada's Recommended Nutrient Intakes, you need from 8.1 grams to 11.6 grams of essential fatty acids daily, depending on your age and sex, with extra allowances for pregnant and nursing women. It is wise not to limit fat intake severely, and consuming monounsaturated fats and polyunsaturated fats is not just good for you, it's essential. From family experience, Brigit has seen what happens to strict followers of a completely nonfat diet, such as the Pritikin program, over the long term. Skin elasticity is lost, energy is very low, and hair takes on the appearance of steel wool.

Health Canada has another piece of advice that is of interest: we should limit fat to 30 percent of our daily calories—but many doctors and nutritionists agree that 30 percent is too much; many experts feel that 25 percent is a more admirable goal. One thing everyone does agree on is that saturated fat (the kind that comes from animal fat and butter) should be restricted to 10 percent of your calorie intake. See the calorie intake chart on page 22 and compute your fat and saturated fat gram intake using the table below.

## Fat and Cholesterol

The relationship of dietary fat to cholesterol levels is explored more fully in Chapter 2. This is something you need to understand if cholesterol is a problem for you. Ask your doctor how often you should have your cholesterol checked—likely at least once every 5 years, more if you have a history of high blood cholesterol. But there is another important fact to keep in mind: even if your main reason for wanting to cut down on fat in your diet is a high cholesterol level, you should still closely watch your calorie intake.

## Table 3.2: Fat Grams as a Percentage of Calorie Intake

| Total Daily Calories | Total Grams of Fat Daily | | | Saturated Fat |
|---|---|---|---|---|
| | 30% | 25% | 20% | 10% max |
| 1,200 | 40 | 33 | 27 | 13 g |
| 1,500 | 50 | 42 | 33 | 17 g |
| 2,000 | 67 | 66 | 44 | 22 g |
| 2,500 | 83 | 69 | 56 | 28 g |
| 3,000 | 100 | 83 | 67 | 33 g |

As we've seen, consuming more calories than you expend means weight gain, and weight gain means more work for your heart. If your heart is weakened by a high level of blood cholesterol, it will have to struggle harder to power an overweight body. It's a recipe for coronary heart disease, which causes 38 percent of all deaths in Canada.

Almost all fat falls into one of the following three groups:

1. Saturated fats such as animal fat, dairy fat, and palm and coconut oils interfere with the blood stream's ability to clear out cholesterol. They also increase the production of "bad" LDL cholesterol. Saturated fat should make up less than 10 percent of the total caloric intake.

2. Polyunsaturated fats are mostly vegetable oils, such as canola, sunflower, safflower, soybean, and peanut oil, listed according to percentage of saturated fat content (i.e., canola has the least saturated fat, peanut oil has the most). These fats are better for you than saturated fat, and can lower "bad" LDL cholesterol levels.

3. Monounsaturated fats consist of olive oil, canola oil, and avocado oil. These "good" fats have been shown to increase the "good" HDL cholesterol and lower the "bad"

### Toothsome Tips

There is one kind of fat that's really good for you: Omega-3 fatty acids, found in fatty fish like salmon and tuna. Studies show these fatty acids may reduce the risk of breast cancer, and research suggests that even one serving of salmon per week can cut the risk of heart disease by up to 75 percent. It's still a fat, so you have to limit consumption in line with your own personal guidelines, but it's probably the best protein and fat source you can choose.

LDL cholesterol. Of all the choices for your required daily fat intake, olive oil is the best. There is much research being done into the Mediterranean diet, which appears to be high in monounsaturated fats, largely from olive oil; people who live around the Mediterranean are often heart healthier people.

Note: Fats and oils are placed in these groups based on the highest level of one of these particular fats; most have a little of all three, but are predominately made up of one (this is why canola oil appears in both the polyunsaturated and the monounsaturated groups).

# What's the Deal with Carbohydrates?

Carbohydrates should form the bulk of our diet, and include sugars and starches, as well as vegetables, grains and legumes, and desserts and sweets. The primary role of carbs in the body is to provide energy to our cells—carbs are what we run on.

There are two kinds of carbohydrates: simple and complex. Simple carbohydrates are sugars, present in table sugar and fruit, and sugar alcohols (contained in sweeteners).

### Watch Out!

Don't think you can load up on nonfat calories to your heart's content as long as you keep fat grams low. One study from McGill University suggests that Canadians are counting fat grams and keeping them below the recommended levels. And yet, we're still overweight! Calories, not fat, cause weight gain, and calories are present in proteins, simple and complex carbohydrates, *and* fat. Too much of *any* of the three will cause weight gain (although it's virtually impossible to eat so many vegetables that your calorie count tips the balance, unless you pour Hollandaise sauce on them).

### Toothsome Tips

Vegetarians and those who want to cut down on animal protein and fat should consider adding limited amounts of nuts to their diet. Recent studies show that nut oils are at least as beneficial as monounsaturated fat in lowering "bad" LDL cholesterol. Peanuts and almonds contain almost as much protein per ounce or gram as red meat, and they're full of good vitamins and minerals, too. Don't get excited, though. Nuts are still a fat source and must be controlled (about 180 calories and 18 grams of fat per handful—unless you have a very small hand). Keep your nut intake to 2 tablespoons (25 mL) per day.

Complex carbs are starches such as wheat, bread, pasta, rice, cereals, grains, legumes, and other vegetables.

But these foods carry vastly different *levels* of carbohydrates. Grains and starchy vegetables like potatoes, peas, and corn pack large quantities, while some other vegetable are so low in carbs that they can be eaten with great abandon (lettuce, spinach, mushrooms, and tomatoes . . . mmmm). Confusion abounds about the role that carbohydrates play in weight loss, but all you need to know is that 1 raw tomato has 5.7 grams of carbs (25 cal), while a cup of cooked white rice packs 50 grams (223 cal). It's easy to see which of these can be eaten with almost complete impunity.

# Vitamins, Minerals, and Water

Vitamin and mineral deficiencies were understood by the lay person long before scientists understood what was actually occurring in the body. Sailors on long voyages who never ate fresh fruit or vegetables contracted scurvy, a debilitating disease featuring anemia and infection, among other things. A Scottish doctor discovered that fresh limes eradicated the disease, and in 1840 the British navy ordered that limes be required as shipboard rations (this had two side effects: Brits worldwide inherited the nickname "limeys," and the daily rum ration got a lot tastier).

It wasn't until much later that scientists discovered the need for Vitamin C. A balanced diet that loosely follows the Food Guide Rainbow, paying particular attention to fruits and vegetables, will provide adequate vitamins and minerals. It's only when dietary habits are changed drastically that deficiencies become a problem (like when those sailors went to sea).

**Tidbits**

Eating small amounts several times during the day curbs your hunger and is better for you than one or two large meals, which can drive up insulin levels, causing you to store most of your calorie intake as fat. This is even more important for the middle-aged and the elderly, who lose the ability to burn off fat as quickly. Don't even think about skipping meals, which can lead to out-of-control hunger, cravings, and instant diet failure. Snacking should be restricted to small quantities of lowfat granola, muesli, dried or fresh fruit, or crackers.

## Vitamins

*Vitamin A* comes from dark green and yellow vegetables, milk, butter, cheese, egg yolks, and liver. Vitamin A helps keep our vision clear and maintains the balance of mucous membranes. It also keeps skin, bones, and teeth healthy. Never consume more than the recommended daily amount, as overdoses can be toxic.

*Vitamin B* is a water-soluble vitamin, which means it is easily lost to boiling water, heat, and light. There are eight different substances grouped under the heading of Vitamin B, the most common being B6 and B12. They are available as supplements, or pills, labelled B complex, and unless you are prepared to be very careful about cooking methods and adopt some fairly strenuous habits (like drinking the water in which your grains were cooked), it's easier to take the B vitamins as a supplement. Vitamin B is widely thought to reduce the risk of heart attack, and aids in keeping the metabolism functioning at an efficient level. Consult a dietitian or your doctor, or purchase a copy of the Recommended Nutrient Intakes to find out the appropriate amounts of B vitamins required for your size, sex, and age.

### Tidbits

Overdoses of Vitamin A can be toxic, and a case in England in the 1970s illustrates the point: a food faddist named Basil Brown went on a carrot juice fast, consuming 10 gallons (45 L) a day for 10 days. Carrots are rich in Vitamin A, and he was consuming about 10,000 times the RDA. His skin turned bright, fluorescent yellow, and then he died.

*Vitamin C*, also called ascorbic acid, is another water-soluble vitamin. Most Vitamin C comes from fruits and vegetables, notably currants, strawberries, pineapple, and citrus fruits. Unfortunately, the water-solubility problem means that most of the vitamin is lost within minutes of being cut, juiced, or otherwise exposed to the air. Vitamin C plays a crucial role in maintaining the collagen in our connective tissues. Without this "cement," the body can almost literally fall apart, as happened to the sailors with scurvy. Vitamin C can be synthesized by animals but not by humans, so we need to consume Vitamin C in our diets. How much is a matter of some conjecture and occasional heated argument. Any Vitamin C that is not needed by the body is excreted, so overdose is not generally considered to be a problem, although some studies associate long-term high dosing of Vitamin C with the formation of kidney stones. A recent *New York Times* article reported findings that show our DNA can actually be damaged by overdosing on Vitamin C. This is one nutritional controversy that deserves watching.

*Vitamin D* is mainly found in fortified milk—other sources like eggs, liver, and fish oils don't contain enough to matter. This vitamin can be synthesized by the body when it is exposed to sun, so deficiencies can occur in people who inhabit northern, low-sun climates and don't drink enough milk. Vitamin D is crucial for children for developing bone density, but it is just as important for adults. Older individuals who don't drink enough milk can suffer from "adult rickets," a bowing of the legs. A combined program of Vitamin D and calcium supplements for elderly individuals has been shown to reduce bone fracture rates and counteract the effects of osteoporosis in men.

*Vitamin E* comes from grains and legumes, where the plants synthesize their own to protect the seed coating prior to germination. Vitamin E is thought to be involved in the

**Tidbits**

Vitamin C is notoriously elusive, disappearing within minutes after a fruit is exposed to oxygen. The only way to gain adequate natural Vitamin C from orange juice is to squeeze your own and drink it within 12 minutes. After that, it's just another high-calorie juice.

formation of red blood cells, and it plays an important role in maintaining the immune system particularly for the elderly. In recent studies, doses of up to 200 milligrams have been shown to increase the immune system's response to foreign antigens (the substance that helps the body produce antibodies). It is an antioxidant, which is a group of substances believed to prevent the oxidizing of fats in blood, which then build up on artery walls. Deficiencies are rare, and generally only occur in newborn babies.

*Vitamin K* is a relative newcomer on the scene. Its main function is to aid the blood in clotting efficiently. Recent studies have shown that it may also help prevent the onset of osteoporosis after menopause. Vitamin K is found in leafy vegetables and inside the small intestines of animals, where it is synthesized by a symbiotic bacteria. Luckily, it is also synthesized in laboratories, and this is a more potent source than the other two. Patients who take antibiotics can accidentally kill all the friendly bacteria in their digestive tract, and eradicate Vitamin K in the process. This could cause problems with efficient clotting of blood.

## Minerals

*Sodium chloride,* or salt, was once one of the most valuable commodities on earth. It was used not only as a dietary supplement and to make food taste better, but also to preserve food before the advent of refrigeration. This could mean the difference between death and survival through the winter for many in the Middle Ages and beyond. Salt, along with potassium, maintains stable conditions inside and outside our cells so that imbalances do not build up (it's called *osmotic regulation*—Yikes!). Sodium and potassium are lost through sweat when you exercise, and lack of water to replenish and lubricate muscles can cause those muscles to cramp. If you drink plenty of water and still cramp up, your diet is probably low in sodium. If you consume lots of prepared foods (you shouldn't, but sometimes there's not much choice), your sodium intake will probably be too high. Lowfat prepared foods are big culprits, since manufacturers often use salt to replace the flavour that was lost when the fat was removed. If you prepare all your meals from fresh ingredients, don't be afraid to add salt. Food just doesn't taste like itself without a little bit.

*Calcium* serves to harden our bones and teeth, which is why children need to consume adequate amounts when they are in the process of forming their bone structure. But adults need calcium, too (though less of it), and it goes hand in hand with Vitamin D: if one is deficient, usually the other is, too. Calcium gets used up, and if it's not replaced, the skeleton can actually be weakened. Milk is by far the best source of calcium, though calcium is also present in clams, oysters, and canned salmon (with the bones).

Lack of *iron* is one of the most commonly found mineral deficiencies, principally among women, who lose iron when they menstruate. Iron-rich foods include lean meats, organ meats, leafy green vegetables, whole grains, and legumes. Dairy products are not a good source. We only absorb 10 percent of the iron we consume, and this is why keeping up adequate levels can be difficult. Unfortunately, lack of iron will quickly lead to weakness and anemia.

Our bodies also need *phosphorus, sulphur,* and *magnesium,* which are found in animal foods and grains, and will generally be sufficient in a good, balanced diet. Trace elements like iodine, copper, and fluorine are needed in such small quantities that they are rarely lacking in a normal diet.

*Zinc* deficiencies are fairly rare, but studies have shown that zinc helps repair damaged cells and speeds healing, so those who don't consume much or any animal protein (its principal source) may want to take supplements, especially during the winter cold season. Recent studies in China have shown that children who began to consume 10 milligrams of zinc daily had increased perception, memory, reasoning, and better psychomotor skills such as eye-hand coordination. Pregnant women need zinc in higher levels, and amazingly enough, a pregnant woman's ability to absorb zinc from food increases up to 30 percent during the term of the pregnancy. Recent studies show that taking iron supplements during pregnancy can erase the increased ability to absorb zinc. Nonanimal foods rich in zinc are popcorn, peanuts, and whole-wheat crackers. Beef, liver, and oysters are the richest sources of all.

### Tidbits

Salt has been traded along with gold and gems, it's been stolen, and fought over. The current cheapness of salt and concern over the relationship between sodium and high blood pressure may make us forget, but salt is as essential to our well-being as any of the other nutrients we've discussed. In Roman times, soldiers were given an allotment of salt to keep up their strength in times of battle, called a *salarium,* the root of the word "salary." A good person is "worth his or her salt," or is "the salt of the earth." Although many of us strive to keep salt consumption down, our language reminds us of the value of salt.

# *Water, Water, Water*

There's one thing that every fad diet, expert nutritionist, and respected doctor agree on: the importance of adequate water to maintain health. "Drink 8 glasses of water a day" rings throughout the health and weight-loss media. Water keeps the metabolism functioning, clears impurities out of the system, and transports nutrients and wastes around the system. Don't leave home without it.

Our bodies use up several litres of water every day, even without strenuous exercise. When we exercise, we lose even more. Water stimulates the metabolism, meaning we absorb foods and nutrients more quickly and more efficiently. For weight-loss purposes, this is important because it means we are less likely to store excess nutrients as fat.

Most of our foods, particularly fruits and vegetables, are made up mostly of water, and our bodies can extract the water from them. But it just isn't enough. Coffee, tea, and caffeinated soda act as diuretics, causing the body to shed water, so they don't count as part of recommended water intake. Buy bottled water if you like, or drink tap water if it's good in your area. Keep water with you at all times and drink it as a matter of course. Once you get into the habit it's not difficult to consume 8 glasses a day.

## The Food Guide Rainbow

After costly and exhaustive studies, Health Canada has provided us with a nice, simple drawing that illustrates how we should be eating. On the surface, it looks easy to understand, but get right down to it and it has a few problems.

For one thing, the serving sizes are unrealistic and confusing. We are advised to eat 5 to 12 servings a day from the Grain Products group—which sounds rather overwhelming. That is, until you discover that 1 serving of cold cereal equals 30 grams. Differences of calorie content in different fruits are not taken into account (1 apple, at 81 cal, is equal to 1 banana, at 105). The important things are clear, though: fats, oils, and sweets are to be consumed in small quantities only, and vegetables and grain products should make up the bulk of our diet. The low-carb proponents might disagree with the large quantity of grain products that are recommended (grains = high carbohydrates = high calories = weight gain—*if* over the RNI). What everyone does agree on is that for heart-healthy living, fat consumption should be kept below 30 percent of daily calories.

# *Canada's Food Guide*

Meat and Alternatives: 2 to 3 servings per day

➤ 2 ounces to 3$^1$/$_2$ ounces (50 to 100 g) meat, poultry, or fish

➤ 2 ounces to 3$^1$/$_2$ ounces (50 to 100 g) canned fish

➤ 1 to 2 eggs

➤ $^1$/$_2$ cup to 1 cup (125 to 250 mL) cooked beans

➤ 3$^1$/$_2$ ounces (100 g) tofu

➤ 2 tablespoon (30 mL) peanut butter

Milk Products: Adults, 2 to 4 servings per day

➤ 1 cup (250 mL) milk

➤ 2 ounces (50 g) cheese

➤ 6 ounces (175 g) yogurt

Vegetables and Fruits: 5 to 10 servings per day

➤ 1 medium-sized vegetable or fruit such as a banana, an apple, a carrot, a wedge of melon, or a potato

➤ $^1$/$_2$ cup (125 mL) fresh, frozen, or canned vegetables or fruit

➤ 1 cup (250 mL) salad

➤ $^1$/$_2$ cup (125 mL) juice

Grain Products: 5 to 12 servings per day

➤ 1 slice bread

➤ 1 ounce (30 g) cold cereal

➤ $^3$/$_4$ cup (175 mL) hot cereal

➤ 1 bagel, pita, or bun

➤ 1 cup (250 mL) cooked pasta or rice

Other Foods

➤ Taste and enjoyment can also come from other foods and beverages that are not part of the four food groups. Some of these foods are higher in fat or calories, so use these foods in moderation.

# Fantastic Fibre

Experts actually all agree that a diet high in fibre has many benefits. From improving digestion to protecting against colon cancer, this is truly a wonder nutrient. Experts now believe that a diet with sufficient fibre can even prevent your body from absorbing some of the fat that you consume. It's not a huge amount, so it doesn't mean you can have a cheese omelette for breakfast just because you had bran fibre yesterday. People who eat a diet high in fat generally absorb about 98 percent of dietary fat, but with sufficient fibre present that number drops to 94 percent. Every little bit helps!

Unfortunately, most people find it difficult to consume the recommended amount of fibre (25 to 30 g), even though most fibre-rich foods are also rich in beneficial vitamins and minerals. Beans and legumes (like lentils) are great sources of fibre, and can be jazzed up with all kinds of lowfat flavour enhancers. Rice, beans, and legumes feature quite prominently in the heart-healthy Mediterranean diet, which we'll be discussing throughout this book.

And remember, fibre is more than beans and bran. Use the table below to find a few additional sources of fibre.

## Table 3.3: Fibre Content of Various Foods

| Product | Serving Size | Grams of Fibre |
|---|---|---|
| Five-bean vegetable soup | 1 cup (250 mL) | 13 |
| Dried figs | 3 | 6 |
| All-Bran cereal | $1/3$ cup (75 mL) | 9 |
| Baked beans | 1 cup (250 mL) | 7 |
| Kidney beans, cooked | $1/2$ cup (125 mL) | 9.5 |
| Barley, dry | $1/4$ cup (60 mL) | 7.8 |
| Three-bean chili, canned | 1 cup (250 mL) | 7 |
| Prunes, stewed | $1/2$ cup (125 mL) | 5 |
| Sweet potato, baked | 1 med. | 6.8 |
| Peas and carrots, cooked | 1 cup (250 mL) | 6.2 |
| Spinach, boiled or steamed | $1/2$ cup (125 mL) | 6 |
| Corn on the cob, cooked | 1 med. | 6 |
| Lentils, dried | $1/4$ cup (60 mL) | 6 |
| Chick peas, cooked | $1/2$ cup (125 mL) | 6 |
| Split pea soup | 1 cup (250 mL) | 5 |
| Swiss Muesli | $1/2$ cup (125 mL) | 5 |
| Buckwheat pancake mix | $1/2$ cup (125 mL) | 5 |
| Raisin Bran | $3/4$ cup (185 mL) | 5 |

| Product | Serving Size | Grams of Fibre |
|---|---|---|
| Baked potato with skin | 1 med. | 4.9 |
| Raspberries, fresh | $^1/_2$ cup (125 mL) | 4.5 |
| Artichoke hearts, canned | 5 small | 4.5 |
| Oat bran, dry | $^1/_3$ cup (75 mL) | 4.2 |
| Broccoli, cooked | 1 cup (250 mL) | 4 |
| Oatmeal, cooked | 1 cup (250 mL) | 4 |
| Green beans, cooked | $^1/_2$ cup (125 mL) | 4 |
| Winter squash, baked | $^1/_2$ cup (125 mL) | 3.5 |
| Brown rice, cooked | 1 cup (250 mL) | 3.3 |
| Shredded wheat cereal | 1 biscuit | 3 |
| Spaghetti, cooked | 1 cup (250 mL) | 2.2 |

## To Juice or Not to Juice

Every few years there is a juice fad, and fasting faddists sometimes exist on nothing but juice for days. Juices are a good source of vitamins, but be aware that juices contain just as many calories as bottled and canned pop. And there is another problem. Whole fruits contain fibre; by juicing them you remove the fibre and are left with only the sugars. Fibre slows absorption of sugar into the metabolism, saving it for when it is needed by the body for energy. Without the fibre, these sugars race straight through, and if they are not immediately required for energy, the body will store them as fat.

### Toothsome Tips

Oatmeal has been proven to be heart smart. However, it is high in calories and you have to eat 2 cups (500 mL) of cooked oatmeal (290 cal) to get 8 grams of fibre. Just 3 dried figs, on the other hand, not only taste great but also provide you with 6 grams of lovely fibre with only 143 calories!

## The Least You Need to Know

➤ Nutrition is a complex science, but understanding just a few facts will enable you to make smart choices every day, without having to use a calculator or consult a book.

➤ We fuel our bodies by consuming calories, which are present in all three food groups: protein, carbohydrates, and fats. Each group carries a different number of calories by weight. If we consume more calories than we burn, we will gain weight.

➤ Creating a balanced diet means more than just watching calories and fat grams—it means understanding a little about the role of vitamins and minerals in maintaining good health. Luckily, consuming a balanced diet with lots of fruits and vegetables and plenty of water will provide most of the necessary nutrients.

➤ Getting the recommended amount of fibre in a balanced diet is a little more difficult than keeping vitamins and minerals up to par. Eating fibre will benefit your digestion, rate of fat absorption, and the inside of your arteries. Study the fibre guide and keep a few dried figs on hand at all times.

# Chapter 4

# What About the Latest Study That Says . . .

**In This Chapter**

➤ Why believe the "experts" when they keep changing their minds?

➤ Zoning out on diet fads

➤ Interviews with two dietitians

First the experts say butter is bad, margarine is better. Then, margarine is bad, and olive oil is better. First all fat is bad, then only saturated fat is bad; monounsaturated fat is actually, oddly enough, good.

Confused? We don't blame you, so are we. It seems as if a new study comes out every few months or so that contradicts the last study. Most of us regular mooks are left scratching our heads. We're trying to do the right things, but if we can't figure out what the right things are, how can we get started?

Brigit went to top Los Angeles nutritionist, Mary Donkersloot, RD, to find some answers, and her opinions may shed some light on what can sometimes be a foggy situation. But first, let's examine the problem.

# Who Are the So-Called "Experts," and Why Do They Keep Telling Us What to Do?

Nutrition is a science, based on research that determines certain facts. The problem is that the facts are sometimes conflicting. Studies are done by many different doctors and research institutions, but a system of checks and balances does exist. Health Canada sorts through all the information available and translates hard science into food recommendations that the Canadian public is encouraged to follow. For information from Health Canada, contact your local health department or visit their excellent Web site. But Health Canada is not the only voice we hear. Those of us who are concerned with overall health or weight loss are exposed to many different opinions, some from people who are no more "expert" than Brigit's mother-in-law, who claimed her daily cup of tea was responsible for her low cholesterol level. And there is a new study that says she just may be right—the benefits of both green and black teas are only beginning to be realized.

A great deal of study, the work of many superior minds, and countless research dollars go into providing Canadians with sound nutritional advice like the Food Guide Rainbow. Health Canada has good reason to be so concerned: 46 percent of Canadians are overweight and 31 percent are obese to the point of probable health risk. The Scientific Review Committee told Health Canada that, "The major health concerns facing Canadians today are obesity and diet-related chronic diseases such as heart disease and cancer, in which excessive food and nutrient intake is the issue." And heart disease is a killer, causing 38 percent of all Canadian deaths annually. So it behooves the government to spend generous amounts of time and money on problem-solving research.

# But We *Want* to Change . . .

Canada is a country that is consumed (excuse the pun) with weight loss. From the countless diet books sold every year to fat-free frozen dinners, popcorn, and cookies, the nation's publishers, television producers, and retailers reflect our continuing concern over bulging bellies and chubby thighs.

Fad diets may come and go, but dieting in itself is not a fad—for many people, it's a way of life. And every day, as baby boomers begin to age and don't much like it, more recruits join the hordes that are "watching their weight." Converts range from cynics and die-hard foodies who once swore never to touch a "low-cal" dish with a barge pole, to regular folks whose families are reciting statistics on heart disease. The lowfat bandwagon not only has many followers, but also extends across cultural, economic, and age gaps more than any other trend or fad, arguably, in history.

Answers are sought in fad diets, books, and magazines. There is a persistent belief that some "magic formula" exists that will allow us to have slim, healthy bodies while still eating huge portions of over-processed, chemically enhanced, unhealthy food. The solution is not magic; it's just common sense and some hard work. The longer people follow the lowfat lifestyle, the less work it will be. Eventually, it will become our "normal" lifestyle.

# A Word on Fad Diets

Because so many North Americans want to lose weight, any new diet, no matter how silly, gets attention, sometimes an appalling amount of it. Every year or so a new personality emerges with, supposedly, the "magic bullet" that so many are searching for. High-protein diets, no-carbohydrate diets, no-sugar diets—the list is endless, and yet, isn't nutrition a science? We know that it is.

How can these (often well-qualified) individuals cite facts to prove their theories, often using the same basic facts to prove completely different theories? Why do these people get so much attention? Because people are desperate, and that means there's money to be made. It's pretty easy to manipulate the facts to come up with an original, highly convincing, new magic bullet. Remember the old saying: "There are lies, damned lies, and statistics." Check the credentials before you subscribe to the ideas.

There has been a lot of discussion about the role of insulin in weight gain. Most people used to think of insulin only in relation to diabetes, but some of the most popular recent diet trends have claimed that insulin levels can be kept low through a complex course of eating practices. As a result, they claim, the body is discouraged from putting on fat. The science looks correct, and many people have lost weight. But when you calculate what is actually recommended by this and other similar diets, it turns out it's simply a lowfat, low-calorie eating regime, nothing more.

## Watch Out!

Health Canada's Food Guide Rainbow is a useful tool that has helped many people identify and change their bad eating habits. But a brief glance may not be enough to help you put the guidelines to work. Beware of portion sizes in the Rainbow, since they are considerably smaller than the portions most people eat. We are advised to eat 5 to 12 servings from the grain group, yet a typical sandwich at an over-loading restaurant could count as 5 servings. A bowl of pasta and sauce intended to serve one person might stack up as 5 servings of grains and the entire daily allowance for fat. Many Canadians simply eat too much, and until we learn to eat portions that keep us within our calorie needs we'll continue to be among the fattest people on the globe.

Brigit asked **Mary Donkersloot**, **RD**, to talk a little bit about the brouhaha over insulin and weight loss. The author of *Everyday Gourmet* (Clarkson Potter, 1998), Mary Donkersloot is a Beverly Hills-based consulting nutritionist who treats clients dealing with diabetes, weight control, eating disorders, and fitness and nutrition. She is also the nutrition consultant for numerous American food corporations.

**MD:** "For normal people who don't have diabetes, our pancreas produces the hormone insulin when we eat carbohydrates. And yes, it does encourage fat to deposit. But this only happens if you *over*eat. Low consumption of carbohydrates doesn't trigger the release of excess insulin."

# So, Who Should We Be Listening To?

Conflicting advice bombards us through the media. We wanted to know who we should be listening to, and why the messages change so frequently.

**MD:** "Let's remember that nutrition and health policies are developed by scientists. It's a science, yes, but there is an art involved in interpretation.

"Many different professionals do research. Their results are published and reviewed by their professional peers. Conclusions are eventually made. But sometimes the media gets a hold of the information and releases it before the professional journals and other concerned groups have a chance to duke it out and decide what the findings mean, and how to translate them into recommendations for the public.

"Small studies with only a few people may make headlines because the media knows the consumer is hungry for new facts. This happens even though the findings are preliminary at best and often inconclusive. Research dollars are also a factor, since money for the grants that pay for these studies is scarcer than it used to be. Researchers all need money, and those who make a big, splashy pronouncement may be more likely to receive further grants.

"Professional journals and conferences are, or should be, the proving grounds for all the divergent studies. Letters to the editor, discussion, and debate—these are the processes that produce firm understanding, not a headline about a study in Sweden that turns conventional wisdom on its head.

"There are some giveaways about how to spot the diet frauds: someone, who may even be a qualified medical doctor, promising easy, fast weight loss by cutting out just one specific ingredient, or category of food. Like sugar, carrots, grapes, or carbohydrates. It just isn't that simple. These diets don't allow you to eat in restaurants and often require special foods."

# What About Counting Fat Grams? Is That Still the Best Way to Shed Pounds?

We don't want to advocate some kind of diet for weight loss, because diets just don't work. The potential for failure is too great. We know from experience that the best approach to weight management is a basic lifestyle change that involves increased exercise and decreased calorie intake. It's not an easy road, but it can be easier than many people think.

When Brigit first started being aware of weight gain and began to want to shed pounds, she counted the fat grams. Then she found out that fat grams that weren't the only important factor; it also involves total calorie intake. Even though it was a bit of an effort, she counted calories and fat grams for 3 weeks to see what her total intake was. Then she started gradually reducing her calorie intake, reducing fat grams as well. She realized that by only counting fat grams, she had avoided the more important issue of counting calories, and it seems she was not alone. She asked Mary her opinion.

**BB:** "Is there too much attention paid to counting fat grams in the diet and not enough paid to total calorie intake?"

**MD:** "It is important to limit fat from a calorie viewpoint, because fat provides a dense source of calories. A fried chicken breast, for example, may contain double the calories of a broiled one. Counting fat grams is just a part of counting total calories. So eating a lowfat diet is a smart first step. Next, pay attention to the total quantity of food you eat. Be aware that carbohydrates like pasta and bagels may be fat-free, but can lead to weight gain if they contribute to excess calories. Calories consist of protein, carbohydrates, *and* fat."

Pamela lost 50 pounds (22.5 kg) 12 years ago and has kept her weight within about 10 pounds (4.5 kg) of her goal for all that time. However, with the birth of her son and the lifestyle changes that followed, her eating habits deteriorated, her exercise routine went out the window, and the weight piled back on. Now it's back to counting calories, working off stored fat, and getting fit again. She asked **Rosie Schwartz**, **RD**, and author of *The Enlightened Eater* (Macmillan) for some advice.

**PS:** "Can we lose weight by following the Food Guide Rainbow?"

**RS:** "Usually, there needs to be more to it than that. The Food Guide is a good foundation but without further structure and a routine, you may not succeed in meeting your goals. When it comes to losing weight there is something many people don't understand: People think if they simply eat the right foods their body will find the right weight, and this is not true. Wherever your body is, regardless what weight a healthy body would be—it wants to stay at that weight. If you consume fewer calories than your body is accustomed to, it thinks you are starving it and your body doesn't want that. So, if you just follow the Food Guide without a plan of action, eating foods in the wrong amounts at the wrong times of day, your body may not permit you to lose weight.

"When you start a weight-loss plan, your mind is declaring war on your body. Losing weight is a war. To try to lose weight in a quick manner generally fails because your body will likely slow down your metabolism. You need a plan of subversive warfare. Lull your body into thinking you're nice and you're not trying to starve it, then trick it by decreasing overall calories in a way that is not obvious. If you follow the Rainbow and just eat what you want, when you want, your body may not go into fat-burning mode; you may be in storage mode. The Food Guide Rainbow is excellent for outlining your nutrient needs, but to lose you have to plan it so your calorie intake works with how your body burns fuel. Only in this way will you be able to steal fat stores from your body."

**PS:** "Do you need to consult your doctor or a dietitian so you can formulate a successful eating plan that will let you lose weight, or is this something you can do yourself?"

**RS:** "You can do it yourself with the right guidance, but you need valid information. Certainly, dietitians and physicians can be helpful. Does your doctor know about nutrition? Maybe, maybe not. Doctors can't be experts in every area, and that is why there are dietitians, who specialize in nutrition.

"It's important to avoid fad diets, starvation plans, and any extreme method of weight loss for several reasons. One thing to consider is that you may be able to get away with it once but then your body learns and you have to pay a penalty. Sure, you will lose 10 pounds (4.5 kg), but you will gain back 15 pounds (7 kg).

"Balance is important. Some of the recommendations of extremely high-protein diets are valid but some are not. Breakfast and lunch should always includes a protein food to help stabilize blood sugar levels so they don't fluctuate. Have more protein foods at breakfast and lunch, things like fish and lowfat cheese, and keep protein intake light later in the day.

"Eating more, early in the day, helps you to stick to your resolution to reduce calorie intake because you end up having consumed smaller portions overall.

"If you are eating often and your blood sugar levels are stable, then you will stay in touch with appetite regulation—if you don't know when you're satisfied, you nibble. Often this is due to not eating properly early in the day. Breakfast is still the most important meal of the day. It is vital that you eat lunch on time, too, or eat something every 3 or 4 hours. This boosts your metabolism and helps you to recognize when you are hungry. If you are doing things properly, most days you should be hungry at appropriate times and satisfied after eating. Then, out of the blue, you will end up with a day when you want to eat everything in sight. This means that your weight is dropping and, even though it may be hard to do, it is essential to stick to your routine on that day."

**PS:** "Is a lowfat diet important?"

**RS:** "It is important to be FAT SMART. Fat is an important element of a healthy diet, but it is equally important to moderate intake. I think striving for fat levels of 30 percent of calories is adequate for most people. Use the best kinds of fat to increase the palatability of your food. Extra virgin olive oil or sesame oil added at the end of cooking maximizes taste. Also, a really lowfat diet, especially if you have extra weight around your middle, won't give you the best cholesterol profile. People with that type of body shape tend to have higher levels of triglycerides and low levels of the "good" HDL cholesterol so they need to reduce levels of artery-clogging cholesterol and boost the beneficial HDL cholesterol to achieve a better overall cholesterol profile."

**PS:** "How much 'weight' do you give to the 'French Paradox' and the fantastic health claims of the Mediterranean diet?"

**RS:** "These are two separate things. I think the French Paradox isn't really a paradox at all. It is more of a time lag. The French traditionally had a diet that was low in fat and high in fruit, vegetables, and grains. The high-fat specialty foods we associate with French cooking were reserved for special occasions or eaten in small quantities. They have only been eating the high-fat diet that researchers now credit them with for over a decade. Heart disease is a progressive disease and I believe we will start seeing the results of this change in their diet. Another point to consider is that they may have a lower rate of heart disease but they have a higher rate of death from unknown causes. In North America, we are more likely to record that a death is due to heart disease so their figures may seem lower than they actually are. The French also have a higher incidence of death from things like cirrhosis of the liver, car accidents, and violent deaths—the types of things related to alcohol consumption. While moderate alcohol consumption can have health perks, you still can't wash your butter down with red wine and think you are looking after your heart health.

"The Mediterranean diet is something else. The typical Mediterranean diet has so many things going for it its hard to point to any one thing as the reason these people enjoy such good health. The diet is low in saturated fat and contains plenty of fresh fruits and vegetables, which are full of antioxidants. There is a focus on fibre and much less meat, and all this is combined with lots of physical activity. This diet has every nutritional principle going for it: high fibre, lower levels of artery-clogging fat, a plant-based diet, an emphasis on beans and legumes, and very little meat. One average North American serving of meat would be considered enough for a whole family. And they are eating more fat, but it's mostly good fats and people are so much more active. Here, we may go to the gym, but for the rest of the day we drive around looking for the closest parking spot. We need to exercise and be more active in every moment; then we will start seeing a positive change in our health."

**PS:** "There are figures that suggest Canadians are keeping their fat intake to 30 percent of our daily calories. Why, then, are we still overweight?"

**RS:** "My guess is that Canadians are not eating less fat, we're eating more calories. So the same amount of fat is a smaller percentage of our overall calorie intake. I suspect that people are not cutting down on their food consumption and they are not active enough. And in many cases people are reducing fat intake but burning fewer calories due to a sedentary lifestyle. Watching people in Amsterdam lining up for Flemish fries recently, I noticed that not one person was overweight. I also noticed that there was not one car in sight; everyone had walked or pedalled their bike to get to this spot. In North America, we don't even get out of our cars to get our fries—we just drive through, and the only effort we expend is raising one arm to pay."

## *Rosie's Ten Rule*

When you are going to eat something that isn't nutritious—and I say when not if because you will—take one bite. Then rate it on a scale of 1 to 10 as though you were judging a food contest. Only eat it if it's a 10. There are not many tens around and when you have the best you will feel satisfied. These are foods that have nothing to do with sound nutrition and they are fabulous. Allow yourself to eat well. Enjoy. And, remember, when you are eating the tens, there's no room for guilt.

Rosie Schwartz, RD, is a consulting dietitian with a practice in Toronto and is the author of *The Enlightened Eater* (Macmillan).

---

### The Least You Need to Know

➤ Health Canada is the most dependable expert for most of us to listen to. Just pay special attention to portion size on their Food Guide Rainbow. This is especially true for a small person.

➤ New studies on fat and weight loss may be released before the established medical community has had time to fully examine and interpret the results. Don't change your lifestyle based on a brand-new finding. Wait until it becomes part of conventional nutritional advice from respected, qualified sources.

➤ Fad diets are just a flash in the pan. If they work, it's usually because they are just lowfat, low-calorie diets that have been jazzed up to seem exciting.

➤ There is no easy way out, and experts who claim otherwise are cashing in on the dollars of North America's desperate weight-conscious millions. Lifestyle changes (including exercise) and long-term adjustments of eating habits are the only solutions to weight-loss problems.

# Chapter 5

# What's Next: Healthy Living in the New Millennium

---

### In This Chapter

➤ Putting the new regime to work, daily

➤ Lowering the fat in your favourite recipes

➤ Entertaining in the new regime

➤ Exercise and the metabolism

➤ Wine: The French Paradox

---

This book contains a lot of detailed information, advice, and hard—maybe even frightening—facts. Everything you need to do to cut down on fat in your diet is somewhere within these pages, but the decision to pursue this worthy goal is within you.

Only you can choose—or not—to put this information to work. We are at the beginning of a new millennium, a rare moment. We've all made a New Year's Resolution to beat all our previous ones. But to change your life, to follow a different path, takes more than just a book. It takes commitment, not just from you, but from the people around you.

If you live alone, it's easier in some ways, but it's also easier to slip because no one is there to see you. If you live as part of a family or with close friends, you'll need their support and—one hopes—their participation to succeed, unless you've got a will of steel. Nothing throws off a diet resolution like the arrival of a spouse, friend, or child with a cheesecake or a bag of chips.

**Tidbits!**

A healthy human body requires more than 40 different nutrients to survive—there is no single food that supplies them all. Single-ingredient diets are one of the worst of the diet fads (remember "I'm on a green grape and Welch's grape juice diet"?). You could easily end up with serious nutrient deficiencies, and most such diets tend to end with a bang, such as a carton or three of mocha madness ice cream.

To make this new regime work for you, you have to fit it in to every day of your life, whether you're entertaining, dining out, or reproducing mom's favourite dinner from the 1950s. And exercise must play a major role in your life. Mild, medium, or strenuous physical activity is a vital factor not only in reducing weight, but also in living a healthier, longer life.

We've explained our belief in the "balance system," whereby you *average* your weekly calorie and fat consumption in order to allow for some indulgence, as long as it's preceded or followed by some abstinence. It's not an effort-free diet; in fact, it's not a "diet" at all. This system is far less likely to lead to a feeling of abject failure and a reversion to past bad habits than a strict diet would. Rigorous diets that limit every day's calorie and fat consumption to a specific figure are too inflexible to succeed over the long term.

The key here is to pay attention—keep records for a while if necessary—but make sure you know your bad habits, good habits, and areas of possible failure. No one will do it for you. No magic bullet will make you a healthier, leaner person; the responsibility is on your shoulders, so go forth and change the world! (Or at least your waistline.)

# Diet Tips You Don't Want to Follow

The following list of diet tips came to Brigit in a wonderful self-published collection of family recipes put together by sisters Roz Roseberg and Shirley Hargrave for their far-flung, extended families. Once of Cleveland, Ohio, and now of points south and west, the sisters filled the little volume with common sense, family anecdotes, and everybody's favourite recipes (some still in grandmother's handwriting). It includes this tongue-in-cheek list of tips for family members feeling the need to cut down . . . Remember, motivation is within yourself; it can't come from anywhere else.

## *Diet Tips*

➤ If no one sees you eat it, it has no calories.

➤ If you drink a diet pop with a candy bar, they will cancel each other out.

➤ Calories don't count if you eat with someone and you both eat the same amount.

➤ If you fatten up everyone around you, you'll look thinner.

➤ Pieces of cookies contain no calories. The process of breaking causes calorie leakage.

➤ Late-night snacks have no calories. The refrigerator light is not strong enough for the calories to see their way into the calorie counter.

➤ Whatever you eat standing up over the kitchen sink has no calories.

# Adapting Old Recipes for the New Regime

You may have a wealth of family recipes or love to browse through cookbooks or food magazines looking for inspiration. As long as you apply the principles of this book, you're not limited to lowfat, low-calorie cookbooks and magazines forever.

## Be Sensible: Five-Cheese Pizza Can't Change

First of all, use common sense. If a recipe relies on several cheeses or a hunk of prime rib for success, it's probably not a good candidate for change. Save such dishes for a week when you've been extra good and kept your fat consumption below 20 percent all week long.

## Cutting the Fat

Next, check the ingredient list. If you've been keeping records and studying nutrition labels, you will have become familiar with the fat and calorie content of certain dangerous foods. For example, if a recipe starts out by saying "sauté an onion in 2 tablespoons (25 mL) of butter or oil" (as so many seem to do), choose a nonstick pan and cut the oil by at least $2/3$. And as long as the flavour won't be affected adversely, use olive oil instead of butter or vegetable oil.

If not (e.g., in Asian dishes where the flavour of olive oil would be inappropriate), use canola oil. You can sweat an onion in a covered pan over low heat with a little water or chicken stock and get a similar result with no oil at all. The key is the nonstick pan. You'll get to know your pans and after a while will be able to predict how much oil is necessary to sweat or sauté a certain amount of ingredients. Try to keep the total amount of oil in a recipe well below 1 teaspoon (5 mL) per person.

➤ Salad dressings are just fine with $1/2$ the oil replaced by chicken stock or fruit juice (white grape is our favourite). Add a teaspoon (5 mL) of mustard for a flavour punch-up, if appropriate to the recipe.

➤ Substitute lean cuts of meat (flank, sirloin) for fattier cuts, or substitute lean pork if possible. Trim visible fat either before or after cooking (afterwards will lead to juicier results). Remove the skin from poultry after cooking.

➤ If a recipe calls for ham or bacon, substitute lean ham, smoked turkey, or peameal bacon.

➤ Substitute lean dairy products for whole milk, etc. If it won't have an impact on the finished dish (hidden in a taco or quesadilla, for instance), use low- or even nonfat cheeses and always cut the quantity by $1/3$ or $1/2$. Avoid nonfat sour cream as it is unpleasantly Jello-like (probably because it is thickened with gelatin). Lowfat sour cream is fine. Lowfat yogurt is an even better substitute and is a reliable standby for the lowfat cook. The lowfat cook should always have a large tub of plain lowfat or nonfat yogurt in the fridge for morning smoothies and snacks and for thickening sauces.

➤ If possible, convert a frying recipe to baking, grilling, or even steaming. Add flavour with garnishes and condiments like soy or Worcestershire sauce.

➤ When making soups, stews, and braised dishes, skim all the fat off the surface of the liquid. To make this easier, refrigerate overnight and lift off the fat layer with a spoon, then reheat. If you don't have time to chill the dish, skim the fat off carefully with a large, flat spoon and then lightly drag a paper towel across the surface of the liquid to absorb the getaway fat globules. Remember, animal fat is saturated fat, and adding a little olive oil at the end for flavour and "mouth feel" is better than leaving the beef, pork, or poultry fat in the liquid.

➤ Last but not least, try to choose recipes that don't depend on fat for their character and flavour. Using nonfat cheese in your favourite lasagna will never be as satisfying as the original, but you can modify a favourite chicken recipe by removing the skin, changing the butter to olive oil, and cutting the oil quantity by $2/3$. The chicken dish will still taste like its old self. (And have you ever tried to grate nonfat cheese? It's like trying to grate a tire.)

### Watch Out!

Be aware that shrimp are very high in cholesterol (166 mg cholesterol for a 3-ounce/90-g serving). This is double the amount of cholesterol in lobster and nearly 4 times that of Alaskan king crab. Crayfish are also high, but not as high as shrimp. Substitute crab for shrimp in recipes, if possible, or if you need a firm consistency, consider using monkfish, an ugly white-fleshed fish that is often snapped up by restaurants because many people think it tastes even more like lobster than lobster! Insist that your market or fishmonger carry it, if possible. Three ounces (90 g) of monkfish contain 21 milligrams of cholesterol.

# Entertaining: Why Would Anyone Want to Come Over Now?

Most people don't even notice the substitution of lowfat ingredients and methods in their favourite foods. If they do, they'll probably be happy that they're having something healthy for dinner. Your friends should be supportive of your switch to a healthier lifestyle, and maybe they'll even follow your lead, taking it as a challenge to create exciting, lowfat meals the next time they invite *you* over.

## Make It Fun

Instead of serving macaroni and cheese or big hunks of steak at your next get-together, try adopting an ethnic theme to liven things up. If the idea doesn't make you gag, decorate the dining room, table, and yourself in line with the theme of the evening. Mediterranean, Middle Eastern, Asian, and Latin American cuisines offer lots of naturally lowfat recipe options. If the featured cuisine comes from a wine-producing country, ask guests to bring wine from the region.

## If They Don't Ask, You Don't Have to Tell

Make this a silent challenge. Create a menu from this book with lots of high-flavour, lowfat choices and don't mention to anyone that it will be a lowfat dinner. Choose from the menus below as a starting point, or create your own depending on taste, season, and availability of ingredients.

### Watch Out!

The summer menu here demonstrates the principles of averaging that are crucial to understanding the role of calories derived from fat and fat gram counting. It is virtually useless to calculate the percentage of calories from fat in any given *dish*: it's the whole menu that's important. A salad dressing or a main course might get up to 40 percent or even more of its calories from fat, but it's only when you place that dish in a balanced menu and average the total for the meal that the percentage number has any meaning.

### Summer Menu

Emerald Green Chilled Pea Soup
Roasted Snapper with Garlic Purée
Orzo with Spinach and Pine Nuts
Grilled Peaches with Ricotta-Honey and Balsamic Vinegar

Per portion, the whole menu stacks up like this:

Calories: 707; Protein: 61.2 g; Fat: 20 g (9.26 monounsaturated); Cholesterol: 85.8 mg; Calories from Protein: 34%; Calories from Carbohydrates: 40%; Calories from Fat: 25%

This menu is spot-on in terms of guidelines for daily calorie, carbohydrate, and fat consumption. It is also quite high in protein. Often, most of our fat calories are eaten at dinner, when the more protein- and fat-rich foods are normally consumed. Eating out at friends' homes or restaurants is usually an excuse for overindulgence, yet this menu is elegant, easy, and derives only 25 percent of the calories from fat (5 percent below guidelines, right where you want to be).

## Fall Menu

> Asparagus and Tofu with Sesame Dressing
> Roasted Eggplant and Goat Cheese Ravioli
> Baby Greens with Raspberry Vinaigrette
> Pears Poached in White Wine

Per portion, for 4:

Calories: 727; Protein: 21.3 g; Fat: 17.6 g (6.45 monounsaturated); Cholesterol: 21.4 mg; Calories from Protein: 12%; Calories from Carbohydrates: 48%; Calories from Fat: 22%

This vegetarian menu may seem low in protein, but is in line with what most nutritionists feel is an adequate protein intake for a main meal. It is also very low in fat and cholesterol. Vegetarians can supplement their protein intake with bean soups, legumes, nuts, and the occasional soy-protein supplement.

## Winter Menu

> Garbanzo Bean and Spinach Soup
> Pork Chops
> Baked Polenta with Not-Your-Own Tomato Sauce
> Cinnamon Applesauce

Per portion, for 4:

Calories: 688; Protein: 38.3 g; Fat: 20.8 g (7.59 monounsaturated); Cholesterol: 60.5 mg; Calories from Protein: 22%; Calories from Carbohydrates: 51%; Calories from Fat: 27%

This winter warmer is low in calories but still packs plenty of protein and carbs to get you through the cold, dark days. It's a little higher in fat than the other menus, but that'll keep you warm and is still below the 30 percent daily guideline. Skimp a little on lunch if you feel the need to drop your fat count for the day even lower.

## Spring Menu

> Cucumbers with Two-Salmon Filling
> King Crab with Kuta Beach Dippin' Sauce
> Sesame-Soy Snow Peas
> Pink Grapefruit Granita

Per portion, for 4:

Calories: 586; Protein: 42.3 g; Fat: 16 g (5.55 monounsaturated); Cholesterol: 129 mg; Calories from Protein: 29%; Calories from Carbohydrates: 47%; Calories from Fat: 24%

Getting ready for bathing-suit weather means a menu that's low in calories and low in fat, but packs a good carbohydrate punch to keep you going through your exercise regime.

# Umm, Do I Still Have to Exercise?

In a word, yes. A slow metabolism burns fat more slowly, and any excess calories that come into the body when there is no need for them will quickly be turned into fat. It's a simple equation: If you take in more calories than your body needs, you will gain weight. If you expend more energy than you take in, you will burn off excess fat.

Exercise plays an important role in weight control by increasing energy output and speeding up the metabolism, then drawing upon stored calories for extra fuel, thereby decreasing fat reserves. Recent studies show that not only does exercise increase metabolism during a workout, but it also causes your metabolism to stay increased for a period of time after exercising, allowing you to burn more calories over a longer period.

Aerobic exercise is the important factor when it comes to weight loss. If you want to do weight training to add definition and build up muscles, do so *along with* a program of aerobic exercise. Weight training without aerobic exercise will cause bulky muscles to build up, still covered with a layer of fat.

To erase the fat and let those finely honed muscles shine through, you've got to do adequate aerobic exercise. For definition without bulk in weight training, use lighter weights and do lots more repetitions. Weight training will add definition to muscles but will *not* burn off fat. Do be sure to stretch right after weight training, when the muscles are still warm. This will lengthen muscles instead of bulking them up.

To make a difference in your weight, the amount of aerobic exercise required depends on the amount and intensity of your physical activity, and on how many calories you consume. A medium-sized adult would have to walk more than 30 miles (50 km) to burn up 3,500 calories, the equivalent of 1 pound (500 g) of fat. But don't be scared! Though that may seem like a lot, you don't have to walk all that distance all at once.

Walking a mile (or about a kilometre and a half) each day for 30 days will achieve the same result, providing you don't increase your food intake to negate the effects of walking. Exercise tends to make you hungry, and if you're feeling virtuous about the 3 miles

## Watch Out!

Faster and harder is not better when it comes to aerobic exercise. If you increase your heart rate beyond 80 percent of normal, your muscles will make energy from carbohydrates, not from fat. This is called anaerobic exercise and also includes weight lifting and resistance training. Your stored fat will not be used or reduced. Brisk walking, rowing, swimming, and jump-roping are good ways to keep burning fat in aerobic mode. If you run, make sure you do so at a slow enough rate that you can maintain a conversation at the same time. If you're running so fast that you're breathless, you've entered the anaerobic mode and will burn carbohydrates, not fat.

### What's the Skinny?

Many a new diet-and-exercise convert has been disturbed by an increased reading on the bathroom scale a month or two after starting the new regime. It's because lean muscle mass weighs more per the same volume than fat. But it's better weight, and it should be firmer as well. Most well-muscled people are overweight by the standards of the classic "height/weight tables." Use a tape measure rather than a scale to keep track of your progress.

(5 km) you just ran on the treadmill, you may feel like rewarding yourself with a snack. Make it a handful of dried fruit or all your effort will be erased by the extra calorie intake.

The combination of exercise and diet offers the most flexible and effective approach to weight control. It's something you can depend on to make your heart healthier and your body leaner. There is no substitute for exercise in maintaining a balanced and healthy lifestyle.

## Can I Still Drink Wine?

There has been a lot of press in recent years about the "French paradox." Researchers coined this phrase when they found that although people in France consume more fat per capita by far than any other western civilization, they also have the lowest rate of heart disease. After exhaustive research around the world, a compound called resveratrol was discovered in red wine that can actually counteract the artery-damaging effects of a high-fat diet. Basically, the 2 glasses of red wine that a Parisian quaffs with a "steak frites" may counteract some of the effects of the beef fat (which no self-respecting French cook would dream of trimming off a steak) and the oil that was used to make the "frites" nice and crisp.

Further investigation of the French population revealed an increased rate of cirrhosis of the liver and of death by accident, rates that tend to mitigate the exciting effects of resveratrol. But many medical doctors admit that wine, particularly red wine, and only in moderation, is good for the heart. Studies vary, but 1 to 2 glasses a day for women and 2 to 3 glasses for men seem to be the upper limit. Anything above that and the less pleasant effects of alcohol come into play, such as liver damage, high blood pressure, stroke, and certain types of cancer. Not to mention clouded judgement and, in severe cases of alcoholism, malnutrition. Pure alcohol contains 7 calories per gram (about 196 calories per ounce), but chances are your consumption of pure alcohol will be fairly rare. More practically, wine and beer both stack up at about 118 calories per 4-ounce (125-mL) glass. Whatever your choice, it should be counted as part of the daily calorie intake.

The relaxing benefits of a glass of wine with dinner should also be considered. Stress reduction is important in our busy world, and if your calorie intake can take it, we highly recommend allowing yourself moderate consumption of wine. Wine has been consumed as a complement to meals for many centuries—far be it for us in our modern know-it-all way to consign it to the history books. Moderation is the key, as it is with all aspects of a healthy lifestyle.

### Tidbits!

The same heart-healthy compound found in red wine, resveratrol, also appears in peanuts. Red wine features about 160 mcg of resveratrol per fluid ounce (30 mL), while peanuts contain only about 73 mcg per ounce or 30 mL (that's about a handful of peanuts). Unfortunately, 1 ounce (30 mL) of shelled peanuts with their skins also has about 14 grams of fat, meaning that to get the same resveratrol as 1 glass of red wine you'd have to eat 2 ounces (60 mL) of peanuts and 28 grams of fat. We know which one we'd choose, but for teetotallers this is a great choice. Resveratrol is also found in nonalcoholic grape juice, particularly that made from the muscadine grape.

## The Least You Need to Know

➤ There is no magic bullet for weight control and healthy living, but there are a lot of facts at your fingertips to help you along.

➤ You will not be condemned to using lowfat cookbooks and magazines forever—just learn to convert appropriate recipes to lowfat by using your common sense and a little extra effort.

➤ Entertaining is no excuse to revert to bad habits. There are plenty of menus to choose from that are naturally low in fat, and we've suggested an elegant choice for each season of the year. Make it a challenge and see how many people complain.

➤ Aerobic exercise must be a part of any concerted program of weight loss. It is the only way to speed up the metabolism and keep the fat burner going longer—weight training can add definition to lean muscle mass but will not burn off fat by itself.

➤ Wine *in moderation*, particularly red wine, is good for you. This is accepted and confirmed by most of the medical and nutrition community. Besides being good for the heart and a cholesterol-fighter, it relaxes stressed bodies and makes a wonderful complement to your good home cooking, as it's done for millennia.

# Part 2
# Fat-Free Is NOT Flavour-Free

# Chapter 6

FLAVO-METER

# Enhancing Flavour Without Adding Fat

You may think that the only food that really *satisfies,* really tastes *good,* is fatty food. The prospect of a pile of asparagus without butter leaves you bored, a sandwich without cheese makes you frantic, salad without a creamy dressing gives you the willies. You've forgotten there's a long list of good things that are *not* bad for you. If you reacquaint yourselves with them, stock your pantry with them, and remember them every time you start to cook—you'll have plenty of excitement on your plate and a pretty exciting lack of fat on your body, too! Can you imagine how awful it would be if you couldn't eat garlic? Say, for instance, it was unhealthy, or so expensive you could only serve it once or twice a year—now *that* would be deprivation!

Much of the flavour of food is contained in the fat. Fat acts as a flavour "vehicle" in sauces like a traditional Bolognese or in a beef stew, for instance. This is why you, as a new lowfat cook, must understand how, when, and how much to enhance flavour with the use of herbs, spices, vinegars, citrus juices, spice pastes, and other nonfat condiments. Simply by adding a spoonful of mustard to a quick sauté, you've added excitement.

## The Fat-Free Flavour Enhancers

Spices, herbs, some root vegetables (like garlic, onions, and ginger), vinegars, mustard, flavour pastes (like miso, curry, chile), and condiments like Vietnamese fish sauce—the list is long. These are all the things you can use to give your food a burst of flavour without adding fat. Some flavoured oils can be used in moderation, since most of them are monounsaturated fats like olive or canola oils that have been infused with flavours such as hot pepper, herbs, lemons, or even truffles.

Learn the options, taste each one carefully to be sure you do not overwhelm the food you are flavouring, and make these versatile ingredients part of your everyday dining routine.

## Vinegar and the Role of Acid in Cooking

Vinegar has so many uses in the household that it's hard to imagine living without it. From cooking to window-cleaning, it's an integral part of our daily lives. Hats off to whoever first realized that a batch of soured wine had turned into a wonderful product in its own right!

A dash of vinegar is the secret ingredient in many wonderful ethnic dishes, like a classic Ragu Bolognese, for instance. A spoonful of red wine vinegar lifts the flavour, making it less muddy and heavy, and adding a nice complexity. Chefs call this "layering" flavour. We know a little goes a long way and adds a welcome tang to a dish that might otherwise be a bit low-key.

One vinegar that was little known in this country 15 years ago is balsamic. Balsamic vinegar can be a great boon to the lowfat cook because it is lower in acidity than wine vinegars. This means that you need less oil in a dressing to balance the tartness of the vinegar (because it isn't as tart!). Try drizzling a teaspoon (5 mL) of balsamic vinegar over simply steamed vegetables and a mound of rice—you've "layered" the flavours and pepped the dish up a notch or two without affecting calories or fat!

Lemon juice serves a similar function, adding a bright, fresh note to heavy or dull foods. It is the most popular "condiment" in the world. Other citrus juices are also useful, say, for instance, lime juice in a fresh salsa, or orange juice as a light and simple sauce for baked chicken breasts. Combine acids like vinegar and citrus juices with herbs and spices for all-out flavour enhancement.

## Herbs

Fresh and dried herbs have been part of cooking almost since we first applied flame to protein and gnawed bones together around a communal fire. When hunters took down a large animal, it often had to last the group for some time. After a day or two without benefit of refrigeration, the meat tended to get a little "ripe." Surrounded by vegetation, some bright cook had the idea of using strongly scented plants to disguise the taste and aroma of none-too-fresh meat, and thus herbs became an integral part of cooking. It wasn't long before the flavour of the herbs themselves became desirable, and their use has persisted long after humans learned to preserve their food. Herbs also have a rich history of medicinal use (in China, cilantro is said to cure indigestion, flatulence, migraines, and arthritis—not necessarily in that order). Many of the drugs we depend on today are derived from herbs that were used for centuries in their natural form.

Herbs are available either fresh or dried, and each one has its benefits. Some herbs, like oregano and thyme, are fine in dried form, in fact, many good cooks believe oregano is *better* dried than fresh. Others, like basil, parsley, and chervil, are virtually tasteless when dried and should only be used fresh. If a recipe calls for basil, do your best to get it fresh; otherwise substitute fresh parsley. In between is a whole range of herbs that can be used dried but will be better fresh: rosemary, sage, dill, tarragon, marjoram, and chives. If you use dried herbs, be sure they are not so old they've turned to sawdust! Take a whiff—you should smell something pungent; otherwise it's time to replace. Be sure to store dried herbs away from heat and light (the traditional herb rack over the stove is the *worst* place you can store them), and crumble the herbs between your fingers first before adding them to a dish; it helps to activate the flavour of the essential oils.

Markets are carrying an increasing variety of fresh herbs these days, and you can experiment with different combinations as garnishes for fish, poultry, starches, and vegetables. Following are a few suggestions to get you started:

### What's the Skinny?

If you are unclear about the difference between herbs and spices because they both come in little jars at the supermarket, here's the deal: herbs are green, spices are some other colour, usually red, yellow, or brown. To add a little detail, herbs are usually used for their leaves, spices for their seeds or roots. Basil, parsley, oregano, thyme, sage, rosemary, chives, cilantro, and dill are herbs; pepper, cumin, ground coriander (seed), turmeric, curry, chile powder, cinnamon, nutmeg, allspice, and mace are spices.

## Table 6.1: Fresh Herb Combinations

**Herb: Arugula**
Taste: pungent, peppery bite
Best with: salads, egg dishes, sautés
How to Use: whole or shredded leaves (fresh only)
Combine with: basil, watercress, dill, mint, sage

**Herb: Basil**
Taste: sweet, warm, clove-like flavour
Best with: tomatoes, cheese (especially goat and mozzarella)
How to Use: whole or shredded leaves (fresh only)

Combine with: bay, garlic, marjoram, oregano, thyme (cooked dishes); chives, dill, garlic, mint, parsley (raw dishes)

---

**Herb: Chervil**

Taste: slight anise flavour

Best with: salads, egg dishes, soups, salads

How to Use: chopped or whole leaves (fresh only); cook briefly, if at all

Combine with: dill, sorrel

---

**Herb: Chives**

Taste: delicate, onion-like flavour

Best with: potatoes, vegetables, eggs, fish, soups, salads, sauces

How to Use: snipped fresh stems or freeze-dried; cook only briefly

Combine with: basil, chervil, cilantro, dill, marjoram, oregano, parsley, sorrel, tarragon, thyme

---

**Herb: Cilantro (Coriander)**

Taste: distinctive, minty-hot flavour

Best with: best friends: avocados and hot peppers; also chicken, ceviche, tomatoes, sauces

How to Use: snipped or chopped leaves (fresh only); add at end, do not cook

Combine with: chives, garlic, marjoram, oregano, parsley

---

**Herb: Dill**

Taste: refreshing, slightly sweet, hint of caraway

Best with: seafood, potatoes, cucumbers, eggs, chicken, salads, carrots, tomatoes, salads, breads

How to Use: chop fresh leaves or use dried

Combine with: basil, bay, chervil, chives, garlic, mint, parsley, sorrel, tarragon, watercress

---

**Herb: Garlic**

Taste: sweet, pungent, stronger than onion; adds intensity to food

Best with: meat, fish, lamb, salads, dressings, pasta sauces, vegetables, cheese dishes, bread

How to Use: chop cloves, roast whole cloves; blanch to tame bite if desired

Combine with: goes well with most herbs but beware when using with chives and mint

---

**Herb: Marjoram**

Taste: sweet, mild, flavour

Best with: meat or vegetable; poultry, game, fish, pizza, stuffings, cheese & egg dishes

How to Use: whole or chopped fresh leaves or dried, crumbled

Combine with: basil, bay, chives, cilantro, garlic, oregano, mint, sage, parsley, rosemary, thyme

---

**Herb: Mint**

Taste: cool, refreshing flavour

Best with: peas, lamb, green or fruit salads, fish, poultry, cucumbers, iced drinks

How to Use: whole sprigs, chopped leaves (fresh only)

Combine with: use carefully with other herbs; basil, parsley, tarragon, and watercress are OK

---

**Herb: Oregano**

Taste: robust, pungent flavour, similar to marjoram but stronger

Best with: tomatoes, lamb, pork, beef, chicken, dressings, bean soups, seafood, all vegetables

How to Use: dried and crumbled, or chopped fresh leaves

Combine with: basil, bay, chives, cilantro, garlic, marjoram, mint, parsley, thyme

---

**Herb: Parsley**

Taste: faint celery-like flavour; Italian or flat-leaf is stronger

Best with: virtually all foods, enhances both flavour and appearance

How to Use: snipped or chopped leaves (fresh is preferable)

Combine with: combines well with all herbs

---

**Herb: Rosemary**

Taste: piquant, pine-like flavour

Best with: lamb, poultry, pork, grilled meats and vegetables, marinades, breads

How to Use: use sprigs or strip leaves from stem and chop; or use dried and crumbled

Combine with: bay, garlic, sage, marjoram, oregano, parsley, thyme

---

**Herb: Sage**

Taste: aromatic, woodsy flavour

Best with: main flavour in sausage and bread stuffings; game, vegetables

How to Use: whole sprigs, chopped leaves, or use dried and crumbled

Combine with: use with other robust herbs such as bay, garlic, thyme, marjoram, oregano, rosemary, parsley

---

**Herb: Sorrel**

Taste: spinach-like greens with a sour, lemony tang

Best with: excellent in soups, green salads, sauces, or as garnish

How to Use: whole or shredded leaves (fresh only), add during last minute of cooking

Combine with: OK with basil, chives, dill, garlic, parsley, tarragon

---

**Herb: Tarragon**

Taste: piquant, mild, licorice flavour

Best with: seafood, poultry, marinades, dressings

How to Use: sprigs or chopped leaves or dried and crumbled

Combine with: great with basil, bay, chervil, garlic, parsley, dill, mint, sorrel, thyme

---

**Herb: Thyme**

Taste: spicy, slightly sweet flavour

Best with: chicken, vegetables, marinades, soups, stews

How to Use: use sprigs, or strip leaves and use whole; or use dried, crumbled

Combine with: basil, bay, chives, garlic, marjoram, oregano, parsley, tarragon, rosemary, sage

---

# Adding a Little Spice to Your Life

Certain countries use spices like a virtual orchestra of flavours, enhancing taste, adding excitement, and changing the basic nature of a dish with the flick of a spoon. Mexico, Central America, the Middle East, and India—these cultures use spices in a way we are only beginning to understand, and most of these cuisines are low in fat.

The concept of adding spice to food was born to cover up the "off" flavours that occurred in the days before refrigeration, but each culture evolved its own spices from the plants that grew locally. The combinations that resulted were unique to each area, and when refrigeration came along to preserve foods, people found they didn't want to go without the flavours they had come to love. And thus were individual cooking styles, or "national cuisines" born.

**Toothsome Tips**

"Gremolata" is one of the most popular garnishes in Italian cooking and is a good last-minute choice for the lowfat cook. Just combine 2 parts finely chopped parsley (preferably the flat-leaf variety, which has more flavour) and 1 part each of finely minced garlic and lemon zest. This makes a good topping for grilled, roasted, or steamed foods (see Steaming, page 85), and should be added 1 or 2 minutes before the food is finished cooking to soften the bite of the garlic.

Before you begin exploring your spice cupboard to add excitement to your lowfat cooking repertoire, there's an important chore to be done: Throw Everything Away. Ground spices last about 18 months in a cool, dark, dry place; leaf spices like dill and oregano last about 1 year. Unfortunately, the trend has been to install spice racks right over the stove, in the hottest, brightest position possible, and then ignore them. It won't be difficult to convince you of this point—just unscrew one of the caps and smell the unidentifiable substance inside. Can't tell what it is? Might be sawdust? Can't remember when you bought it? Throw it all out. And throw out the rack, too. Or move it to the garage and use it to store tools.

## Purchasing Spices

Restocking your entire spice shelf may seem like an expensive proposition, and if you buy spices at the supermarket, it certainly can be. Since spices last such a short time, it is wise to buy them in small quantities, but supermarket prices can be completely unreasonable, unless they sell in bulk. If you're buying from a bulk bin, give the spices a whiff and don't be shy to question the staff about freshness. Buy from local markets if you are lucky enough to have them. If you have any friends with a dust-covered spice rack (we suspect you do), form a spice-buying club and use recycled glass jars as you divvy up the goods. And store your new purchases in a dark cupboard.

## Spice Rubs

Making your own spice blends and rubs is a worthy endeavour for the lowfat cook. Particularly if you enjoy grilling, the spice-rub approach is an invaluable way to add flavour to meat, poultry, fish, and vegetables that are about to hit the hot grill. Leaving the food to "marinate" in the spice rub will make the taste stronger but is not necessary. Spice rubs are widely available in stores, and they are made from every spice and in every flavour imaginable. It has become quite a business for chefs to package their own condiments and spice rubs. These are handy things to have in the pantry cupboard, but tend to be quite expensive and will last only 6 to 12 months. For pennies (after your initial investment in spices—see Stocking a Lowfat Pantry, Chapter 7), you can make your own spice blends and vary the ingredients to suit your personal taste. Your rubs will have more flavour, since they are fresher (spices begin to lose flavour soon after they are ground). Here are a few to start you off. Note: don't forget to label your spice blends and rubs!

## Medium-Hot Grilling Rub

1 teaspoon (5 mL) black peppercorns
1 teaspoon (5 mL) celery seeds
$1/2$ teaspoon (2 mL) cayenne pepper
$1/2$ teaspoon (2 mL) dried thyme
$1/2$ teaspoon (2 mL) dried marjoram

2 teaspoons (10 mL) paprika
1 tablespoon (15 mL) mustard powder
$1/2$ teaspoon (2 mL) salt
1 tablespoon (15 mL) soft brown sugar

Crush the peppercorns and celery seeds in a mortar and pestle or spice grinder. Mix all the ingredients and store in a clean, dry glass jar, tightly covered, for 3 to 4 months.

## Fish-Grilling Rub 1

*(for delicate fish like flounder, halibut, sea bass)*

1 teaspoon (5 mL) black peppercorns
2 teaspoons (10 mL) fennel seeds
$1/2$ teaspoon (2 mL) coriander seeds

1 clove garlic, finely minced
1 teaspoon (5 mL) grated lemon zest
1 teaspoon (5 mL) dried thyme

Grind the peppercorns, fennel seeds, and coriander seeds in a mortar and pestle or spice grinder. Mix with the garlic, lemon zest, and thyme. Use within 1 day.

## Fish-Grilling Rub 2

*(for stronger fish like swordfish, salmon, and tuna)*

2 tablespoons (25 mL) juniper berries
1 teaspoon (5 mL) black peppercorns
6 allspice berries

3 cloves
3 bay leaves
$1/2$ teaspoon (2 mL) salt

Grind the juniper berries, peppercorns, allspice berries, cloves, and bay leaves in a mortar and pestle or spice grinder. Transfer to a clean, dry glass jar and mix in the salt. Cover tightly and store in a cool, dark place for 3 to 4 months.

# Can You Say Soy?

Soy products may sound boring, but reading about what good things they can do for your body may change your mind. Recent studies show that soy can lower "bad" or LDL cholesterol by 10 to 12 percent, while slightly increasing "good" HDL cholesterol. That's not all. Studies also show that soy can protect against certain types of cancer, like prostate, colon, endometrial, and breast cancer. In Asian populations, where people often consume a mere 7 to 8 grams of soy protein per day, the rates for these cancers are substantially lower. But this may also correlate with the fact that most Asians eat a diet that's low in fat and high in fibre. Perhaps this is why people of Asian origin are so rarely overweight (sumo wrestlers excepted).

Soy is also surfacing as a preventive against osteoporosis and some of the less pleasant side effects of menopause. In studies, post-menopausal women who consumed 40 grams of soy protein daily experienced an increased mineral content and bone density.

The recommended quantity for health-enhancing benefits is currently 20 to 40 grams of soy protein per day, which may be difficult to achieve if you've made a point of avoiding tofu all your life. There are other sources of soy protein besides tofu, and it's worth giving some of them a chance. We're all familiar with soy sauce, but it's impossible to consume soy sauce in any quantity that's likely to be beneficial to your general health without shooting your salt consumption and probably your blood pressure right off the scale.

Give tofu a try—it has a pleasant texture and a flavour that is so subtle that whatever flavourings you decide to add will change the whole character of the dish. Brigit once spent a month in a Buddhist monastery on an island near Hong Kong, where three meals a day were tofu disguised as chicken, pork, and fish. Every one of them was delicious.

## Miso

Since we're in the flavour-enhancing chapter, we'll touch on miso first. Miso is a fermented soybean paste, and just in case you're getting ready to turn the page let us tell you a secret—it's very, very tasty. Miso has long been the property of vegans and other holistic dieters, but now it's sneaking into fancy restaurants, mainstream cookbooks, and just about any kitchen that wants to de-emphasize fat-heavy flavour enhancers like butter, cream, and bacon. In Japan, there are myriad misos to choose from, but here in Canada there are two basic types that you are likely to see. White, or mellow, miso is pale yellow and relatively mild. It tends to be more acceptable to the western palate. Red, or Hatcho, miso, is darker and saltier, and much more pungent. It should be used with restraint.

Miso is a good source of essential amino acids and some vitamins and minerals, and it is also low in calories and fat. Centuries of Japanese folklore and recent scientific studies indicate that the daily use of miso may lower cholesterol, alkalinize the blood, cancel the effects of some carcinogens, counteract the effects of radiation exposure, and neutralize the effects of smoking and environmental pollution. If it could balance your cheque-book, you'd marry it. Miso certainly deserves a chance in your culinary repertoire.

Like yogurt, unpasteurized miso is also full of lactic-acid bacteria and enzymes that aid in digestion and food assimilation. Note: don't boil miso, or some of the beneficial bacteria will be destroyed. Add it at the end of cooking time.

# Tofu

For the lowfat cook with an open mind, tofu is a godsend. We can choose from firm or silken tofu, depending on the dish, and both these products are increasingly available in mainstream supermarkets, not just in Asian or health food stores.

Firm tofu can accompany vegetables (and plenty of spices) inside a variety of wrappings where you might once have used meat, for example, tortillas, omelettes, ravioli, pita bread, and fajitas. It works well in clear soups if the broth is flavourful (add a few sliced mushrooms and some fresh herbs for colour and texture). And firm tofu can be stir-fried, if you're careful. Since you are using the tofu as a fairly central ingredient in most cases, do make up for its lack of flavour by upping the garlic, soy sauce, spice, onion, or other flavour component in the dish. Once you try firm tofu in a well-seasoned dish, we think you'll give it a chance on your table, especially when you realize that $1/2$ cup (125 mL) of tofu contains 20 grams of soy protein! Note that Chinese tofu tends to be sweeter and firmer than Japanese tofu.

**Tidbits**

According to ancient Japanese mythology, miso was a gift from the gods. An integral part of a traditional Japanese diet, it has evolved along with other foods in that diet to find its place in the modern kitchen. Not only is miso closely associated with the Zen Buddhist grain-centred vegetarian diet, but it is also linked with such foods as rice vinegar, sake, and mirin (sweet rice wine), which were often used with miso for balance. Like many ancient foods, we can use and enjoy miso as part of a modern, lowfat, and health-enhancing diet.

Soft, or silken, tofu is good for dressings and even baking, and as a fat replacement. You can substitute soft tofu for ricotta in lasagna and other pasta dishes, as long as you taste for seasoning and consider increasing the amount of garlic and onions in the dish. Soft tofu can be stirred together with a little miso for a dip, or substituted for sour cream or mayonnaise in dairy-based salad dressings. You can replace half the cream cheese in a cheesecake recipe with soft tofu (again, increase the amount of spices and sugar slightly).

Think of tofu as an artist's canvas—a healthy ingredient that must have some additional flavours "painted" onto it, just as we do with potatoes, pasta, rice, and boneless chicken breasts. You'll learn to incorporate this versatile food into your cooking.

## Soy Milk

Soy milk is not just for the lactose-intolerant! It's great in smoothies, as a stand-in for milk in puddings and other desserts, and especially in cream-style soups. One cup (250 mL) of soy milk contains 6.6 grams of soy protein and slightly less fat than the same amount of 2 percent lowfat milk (4.6 g).

Brigit's favourite use for soy milk is in mashed potatoes: use lots of garlic, salt, and pepper, and use the soy milk in place of the milk, butter, and cream—or all three. Stir in a little Parmesan at the end for a flavour booster.

### Watch Out!

A recent study by McGill University indicates that Canadians, particularly women, are not eating enough protein. According to the Food Guide, 100 grams of tofu is the equivalent of one of the recommended 2 to 3 servings per day. Although protein is relatively low in calories, they can still add up. If you consume more protein than your body requires, your metabolism will store it as fat. Also, your kidney will have to work harder to process the protein byproducts.

## The Least You Need to Know

➤ Much of the flavour of food is carried in the fat, so when you subtract fat it is imperative that you add flavour. Learning to use vinegars, herbs, spices, and condiments will allow you to turn a blank canvas into a riot of colour and flavour.

➤ Small amounts of vinegar, lemon, and citrus juices will elevate the flavour in a dish to a completely new level—learn from the professional chefs!

➤ Fresh herbs can make the difference between bland and beautiful; careful use of pungent spices can take a dish from India to Mexico to Morocco—just make sure the spices are reasonably fresh, because they don't last long.

# Chapter 7

# Stocking a Lowfat Pantry

---

### In This Chapter

➤ Spices: Grind your own for top-level flavour

➤ Olive oil: The star of your kitchen

➤ Vinegars and mustards equal easy flavour

➤ Chicken broth is your friend

➤ Starting your own global pantry

---

What's a pantry? Well, in some long-ago, far-off time it was an actual room off the kitchen that was stocked with everything from summer's best tomatoes to dad's chutney to a few gamy pheasants hanging from the beams. Today, most people are lucky to have a decent-sized cupboard to serve as their "pantry." Modern house- and apartment-builders seem to believe a pantry and a linen closet are relics of the past, whereas most of us now have much more "stuff" to put in them than our grandparents did.

No matter where you put it, your pantry is the most important space in your home if you have decided to adopt a lowfat lifestyle. We won't say "diet," because to us that word connotes a deprivation-style regime that's engraved in stone and is just waiting to be broken.

Consider the contents of a typical shopping bag: a chicken, a cucumber, green beans, some rice, oranges, lemons, and onions. If your pantry contained only salt and pepper, dinner might be a bit boring. Now imagine opening the cupboard to find soy sauce, sesame seeds, pickled ginger, dill weed, garlic, slivered almonds, wine vinegar, and extra virgin olive oil. Suddenly, the prospects for dinner are looking up. Now, the menu can start with a crisp, sliced cucumber salad garnished with pickled ginger and sesame seeds, dressed with a soy-laced dressing. Follow with braised lemon chicken, green beans tossed with almonds and olive oil, and dilled rice.

We are fortunate to live in a time when all the exotic ingredients of the world are either in the local supermarket or available by mail within a few days. Most of these non- or semi-perishable flavourings don't even require refrigeration to be good for weeks, months, and sometimes even years. Once you've got them, they'll be there, ready to use, until you use them up. Any initial expense can be averaged over the months and the many meals that are enhanced by the contents of your versatile, globe-trotting, lowfat pantry.

# Where Do I Start?

Stocking a pantry all at once could be quite expensive, depending on which cuisine you are after. A well-stocked pantry lets you enjoy your favourite foods, like Italian or Indian, and be in complete control of what goes into the dish. You can reduce the oil, choose baking rather than deep-frying, use nonstick pans, and trim all the fat from leaner cuts of meat. So you'll still enjoy your favourite flavours without worrying about what the chef was up to back in the kitchen, and how it might affect your waistline or cholesterol count. Note that fat carries a lot of flavour, so many restaurant chefs add fat rather than other, more expensive or time-consuming routes to flavour. Unfortunately, customers are none the wiser.

The categories of nonperishable pantry items follow below. Pick and choose among them, and start with at least the basic selections. As your repertoire increases, purchase a few more goodies based on your favourite ethnic foods and methods of cooking. The next time you come home with a shopping bag containing a few, inexpensive but impeccably fresh items, you'll know that the world is virtually your oyster.

### Toothsome Tips

If your pantry includes good Italian canned tomatoes, dried pasta, coarse bread crumbs, olive oil, and canned anchovies, you can whip up a steaming dish of spicy pasta without even a trip to the store. Pasta just loves to be combined with the great, flavourful items that make up the Italian pantry. Add a few more things, like olives, capers, sun-dried tomatoes, dried mushrooms, and a good wine vinegar, and your recipe repertoire will become exponentially larger.

# Getting to Grips with the Spice Rack

The first step is to examine your spice cupboard and throw away anything that you can't remember buying, or any spices that do not smell of anything specific besides sawdust. Most dried herbs last only 6 to 12 months, as long as they are stored in a cool, dry place (please, please, not a rack above the stove—the hottest, brightest place in the kitchen!). Ground spices last longer, about 18 months, and whole spices last up to 2 years. Discover the herbs and spices you use regularly and buy them in larger quantities. Otherwise, you'll be paying up to 10 times more for a tiny glass jar in the supermarket. While you're at it, experiment with a few spices you haven't used before. Make it a habit to replace tired herbs and spices every 6 months and gradually increase your repertory.

### Watch Out!

From a flavour standpoint, preground black pepper is one of the worst products you can use in your kitchen. Peppercorns come with a tough, hard exterior shell, which is where the flavour resides. Once ground, it will lose its pungency within weeks. Never, ever use packaged ground black pepper. The goal of the lowfat cook is to add flavour without fat, and that means adding lots of good, fresh flavour to foods—not stale, sawdust-like preground spices that may have been ground months, or even years, in the past.

## The Basics

*Basic Dried Herbs and Spices*: bay leaves, whole black peppercorns, ground white pepper, cayenne pepper, mustard powder, dill weed, oregano, thyme, sage, marjoram, tarragon, celery salt, chile powder, curry powder, red chile flakes, paprika, cinnamon (ground and sticks), ground coriander, ground cumin, cloves, fennel seeds, whole nutmegs (use with grater), poppy seeds, ground allspice, sesame seeds, vanilla beans, ground ginger, wasabi powder.

*Taking It Up a Notch*: white peppercorns, saffron threads, dill seeds, celery seeds, mustard seeds, ground turmeric, ground cardamom and fenugreek seeds (for Indian cuisine), star anise, juniper berries, ground mace, pink peppercorns, Sichuan peppercorns, black sesame seeds, togarashi pepper (Japanese pepper), wasabi paste, ground chipotle (a Mexican pepper) powder, hot and mild curry powders.

## Grinding Your Own

Many of the popular spice blends, like Chinese five-spice and curry, are much more pungent and deeply flavoured if the individual ingredients are mixed and ground at home. Use either a good, heavy mortar and pestle or an electric coffee grinder reserved solely for spice grinding. (To clean the spice grinder before the next batch of spices goes in, grind half a piece of white bread and discard.) More spice-blending information can be found in Chapter 6.

## Chinese Five Spice

1 tablespoon (15 mL) star anise

1 tablespoon (15 mL) Sichuan peppercorns

$1/2$ tablespoon (7 mL) cinnamon

1 tablespoon (15 mL) fennel seeds

$1/2$ tablespoon (7 mL) cloves

Blend to a powder in a mortar and pestle or an electric spice grinder. Place in a clean, dry glass jar, cover tightly, and keep in a cool, dark place for 3 to 4 months.

## Basic (Medium-Hot) Curry Powder

*Ask 10 Indian cooks to make up their favourite curry powder from scratch and you're likely to get 10 different blends. This is a basic recipe—vary the heat and balance to suit your own tastes.*

6 small dried red chiles

1 ounce (30 mL) coriander seeds

2 teaspoons (10 mL) cumin seeds

$1/2$ teaspoon (2 mL) mustard seeds

1 teaspoon (5 mL) black peppercorns

1 teaspoon (5 mL) fenugreek seeds

$1/2$ teaspoon (2 mL) ground ginger

1 tablespoon (15 mL) ground turmeric

Blend to a powder in a mortar and pestle or an electric spice grinder. Place in a clean, dry glass jar, cover tightly, and keep in a cool, dark place for 3 to 4 months.

## Garam Masala

2 cinnamon sticks, broken into pieces

3 bay leaves, crumbled

$1^1/_2$ ounces (45 mL) cumin seeds

1 ounce (30 mL) coriander seeds

$^3/_4$ ounce (20 mL) green cardamom seeds

$^3/_4$ ounce (20 mL) black peppercorns

$^1/_2$ ounce (15 mL) cloves

$^1/_2$ ounce (15 mL) ground mace

In a small, nonstick pan, dry-roast all ingredients except the mace: over medium heat, shake the pan and stir to prevent scorching until the spices darken and smell very pungent. Let cool, then grind with the mace in a spice grinder. Place in a clean, dry glass jar and cover tightly. Keep in a cool, dark place for 3 to 4 months.

# Olive Oil: Building Block of Healthy Cooking

We all need at least some fat in our diet to maintain a healthy, strong body and to keep our skin and hair supple and shiny. Many of us also crave fat, because it gives our food a rich "mouth feel," that silky coating on the roof of our mouth that tells us we're having something really good. This reaction may be left over from the days when getting enough animal fat meant the difference between life and death, but the craving is still with many of us. By far the best choice among fats is olive oil, which is high in monounsaturated fat. Monounsaturated fat has been shown actually to increase our "good" HDL cholesterol and lower our "bad" LDL cholesterol. All oils and animal fats have the same amount of fat grams (14 g) per tablespoon or 15 millilitres, but olive oil has no cholesterol at all. Butter has 33 milligrams of cholesterol per tablespoon (15 mL).

Science aside, if you can train yourself to cook with a limited amount of olive oil instead of butter or margarine, you'll be doing your body a big favour. You still need to limit your intake, but it's hands-down the best choice. You may want to have two different kinds of olive oil on hand: for cooking use a "light" pure olive oil; as a condiment and for salad dressings where the delicate taste won't be destroyed, use the more expensive extra virgin olive oil. This oil is made from the first cold pressing of the olives and is full of deep, fruity, sunny flavour.

## Tidbits!

Garam masala is the principal spice blend of northern Indian cooking, while curry is more popular in the south. Garam masala is usually milder than curry powder, and there are literally hundreds of different blends. A good cook is often known in the local countryside for the quality of his or her garam or curry blend. Garam masala can be used in pilafs and meat dishes and substituted for curry powder in any recipe.

### Tidbits!

Olive oil is one of the world's oldest foods. There is evidence of olives being pressed somewhere in the eastern Mediterranean as long as 6,000 years ago. Olive oil features prominently in the Bible, and it was used as a lamp oil in the Mediterranean for centuries. Spain produces 45 percent of the world's olive oil, but only a few brands are top quality. Italy produces 25 percent, and many of the greenest, fruitiest oils come from Italy. Greece makes 20 percent and some of the Greek oils are very good. California has recently improved the quality of its oil to the point where connoisseurs have noticed, but it's quite expensive.

# Other Oils and Vinegars

There are times when cooking oil must have no flavour at all, for instance in Mexican or Asian dishes or when substituting oil for butter in baked goods. In this case, choose the almost tasteless canola oil, which is lower in saturated fat than olive oil but doesn't contain as much of the "good" monounsaturated fat. You may want to invest in some hazelnut oil, which, like olive oil, is also high in monounsaturated fat, or walnut oil, which is mostly polyunsaturated (like corn oil or margarine). For the lowfat cook these nut oils should be used only as a condiment, to be drizzled sparingly over steamed vegetables or grilled fish (hazelnut is the better choice). Luckily, a little goes a long way, especially on warm food, which amplifies the flavour. Be sure to refrigerate nut oils, or they'll quickly go rancid. Rancid oil will smell "off" and slightly musty. Smell your oil when you first purchase it and then every few weeks or months afterwards—you'll soon come to recognize the smell of rancid oil.

When buying vinegar, be aware of the total acidity, which is always featured on the label. When you are making salad dressing, a higher acidity vinegar will require more oil to balance

### Toothsome Tips

Vegetable oil cooking spray has been available for some time, and it is an important resident of the lowfat pantry. A 1-second spray generally dispenses about $1/4$ teaspoon (1 mL) oil, and it's the best way to get a very light film on a nonstick pan or baking sheet. However, most of the popular brands contain not only propellant but also alcohol. A recent introduction is the non-aerosol stainless steel pump bottle, which dispenses oil at the same rate. If you use a lot of canola oil, keep 2 separate bottles.

the flavour (but you can always substitute chicken broth for half the oil). Balsamic contains less acidity than wine vinegars, and has a pleasing sweetness that makes it useful as a condiment on its own, without any oil. Rice vinegar is also quite low in acidity, making it ideal for the lowfat kitchen. Some Chinese vinegars are as low as 2 percent acidity.

## Basic Vinegars

White and red wine, rice, cider, balsamic, tarragon

## The Vinegar Adventure Club

Sherry, rosemary, Chardonnay, Merlot, pear, Champagne, raspberry, passion fruit, etc.

### Watch Out!

Vinegars containing a low level of acidity are desirable for salad-making because less oil is required to balance their tartness. But don't try to use a low-acid vinegar like balsamic or rice vinegar for pickling—low acidity equals low preservation qualities. Food meant to be quietly pickling could start to ferment!

# Capers and Anchovies

These are two basic Mediterranean flavourings that should be part of your first pantry-stocking purchase. Both are available in several different forms, and they must both be rinsed well and patted dry before being added to a dish. Salt-packed capers and anchovies are the best, but may be hard to find. If you do find them, one thing you won't need to worry about is using them up. Both will last virtually indefinitely when refrigerated in nonmetal containers. Brine-packed capers are easiest to find, and these are perfectly fine (don't forget to rinse before using). Anchovies are often packed in oil—discard the oil, rinse the anchovies and pat them dry with paper towels before using. Don't be tempted to save the oil for salad dressings—it's the lowest quality olive oil approved for food use.

Capers can be scattered on a salad, strewn over a grilled or poached chicken breast, or chopped and stirred into lowfat yogurt for a quick sauce. And the best news of all: they're fat-free. Anchovies do have a little fat, but surprisingly little! Five anchovies feature only 1.9 grams of fat—and when you rinse them most of that is discarded. Any fat that is left over is the heart-healthy Omega-3 fatty acid, making anchovies a great source of rich and complex flavour for the lowfat cook.

Many people will turn their noses up at the mention of anchovies, but slip one or two (finely minced) into some mashed potatoes and they'll never know—all that's noticeable is a super-intense flavour. That's why Brigit likes to refer to anchovies as "rustic salt." Note: If you decide to add anchovies to a recipe that doesn't call for them, decrease or eliminate the salt—you usually don't need both.

71

# Mustard

The millionaire son of Mr. Coleman (of Coleman's mustard fame) once quipped that he got rich on what people left behind on the plate. Sure, everyone takes more mustard than they need at a barbecue—but teach yourself to use mustard as a flavouring paste rather than a condiment. In the lowfat kitchen, mustard serves many purposes. When added to lowfat salad dressings, it helps to form an emulsion with less oil needed. When stirred into a simple pan sauce, it adds zing without fat. You can even coat a whole skinless chicken in Dijon mustard and roast it as usual (mustard loses much of its potency when cooked, so it won't be too strong).

Today, you can choose from flavoured mustards in dizzying profusion: herbs, citrus, garlic, peppercorns, horseradish, and even chocolate are used to flavour mustard. Two of my favourites are honey-Dijon and dill-Dijon. The Dijon-style mustards and their derivatives are much milder than typical ballpark-style hot mustards. When following a recipe, don't try to substitute one for another!

When stocking your pantry, we suggest buying the largest size jar available of Dijon mustard—you'll be using lots of it. For the more eclectic mustards, buy them in small quantities a few at a time (they can be expensive) and experiment to find the ones you like.

### Toothsome Tips

When trying different flavoured mustards, do this little experiment: make the recipe for Chicken Scallops with Dijon Sauce on page 272, using plain Dijon; a week or so later, try the same recipe using horseradish mustard. It's a flavour revelation (but still tasty)!

# Chicken Broth: A Resource You Can Depend On

Lowfat canned chicken broth is a slightly pricey but integral part of the lowfat pantry. Powdered stocks, bouillon cubes, and concentrates just don't measure up, so invest in either cans or the convenient new cartons (keep open cartons in the fridge for up to 14 days). Following are a few ways to use chicken broth:

➤ Use it to replace the butter in your favourite mashed potato recipe.

➤ When a recipe says to start by sautéing onions in oil, place them instead in a covered nonstick skillet over low heat with a tablespoon (15 mL) of chicken broth. Sweat until tender and voilà, no oil!

➤ Reduce prepared broth by $2/3$ of its volume to thicken and strengthen flavour, then add chicken breasts and cook until the chicken is golden brown and the broth is just a syrupy glaze.

➤ See the recipe for Double-Chicken Broth on page 128 to intensify the flavour in dishes calling for just a little broth, for salad dressings, mashed potatoes, etc.

➤ Substitute prepared or Double-Chicken Broth for half the oil in your favourite salad dressing (using reduced broth will give more body to the dressing).

# Lowfat Diary Products

We are seriously opposed to using most of the available nonfat dairy products. There are plenty of dishes that don't need lots of dairy anyway. Why bother to doctor up traditionally high-fat dishes, trying desperately to make them taste acceptable? You will always be comparing the new version to the real thing, and chances are it will come up wanting.

Lowfat yogurt is very good, as are lowfat cottage cheese and cream cheese, because they still taste great. We prefer to avoid nonfat sour cream and nonfat cheeses completely.

### Toothsome Tips

If a recipe calls for sour cream and you want a lowfat alternative without the unpleasant texture of nonfat sour cream, try this: blend $1/2$ cup (125 mL) nonfat yogurt, $1/2$ cup (125 mL) lowfat cottage cheese, and 2 teaspoons (10 mL) lemon juice in a blender until smooth.

Most of these have a texture that is too glossy and rubbery to be appetizing (probably because gelatin is used to thicken them). The one exception is lowfat mayonnaise, which has both a pleasant texture and flavour. For garnishing, nonfat sour cream is only just marginally acceptable; lowfat is much better.

# The Global Pantry

Having the world in your cupboard is a comforting feeling. Choose your region, or sample them all. Start with a few things, then increase the selection as your cooking expertise, sense of adventure, and your wallet allow.

## The Mediterranean Pantry

Canned plum tomatoes, tomato paste, artichoke hearts in brine, roasted red peppers, capers, anchovies or anchovy paste, olives in brine, Dijon mustard, canned tuna in brine, bread crumbs, dried mushrooms, pasta, polenta, arborio (risotto) rice, dried white beans, green lentils, sun-dried tomatoes (dry-packed), tapenade (black or green olive paste), giardiniera (pickled Italian vegetables), vine leaves packed in brine, clams and mussels in brine

**Watch Out!**

No matter how often we have reminded ourselves (or been told) not to shop on an empty stomach, it's amazing how quickly one forgets. If you shop while hungry, you tend to buy things that you wouldn't even consider after a nice lunch. Remember, if you buy it, you'll eat it. If you have family members who aren't watching fat intake, encourage them to satisfy their cravings outside the home, so you won't be tempted. Remind them that their support is much appreciated.

## The Latin American Pantry

Canned beans, dried black beans, canned jalapeños and chipotles, assorted dried chiles, long-grain rice, fideo (angel hair) noodles, chile sauce, salsa (hot, medium, and mild)

## The American Pantry

Dried cherries and cranberries, relishes, hot mustard, sweet mustard, fat-free croutons, bottled fruit salsas

## The Middle Eastern Pantry

Chutneys, dhal mixes, bulgur wheat, couscous, brown lentils, brown rice, curry paste

## The Asian Pantry

Long-grain rice, low-sodium soy sauce, sesame oil, rice vinegar, mirin (sweet cooking wine), fish sauce, oyster sauce, hoisin sauce, plum sauce, chile and garlic paste, black bean sauce, cellophane noodles, seaweed, kimchee (Korean pickled cabbage), miso paste, wasabi powder or paste

# The Semi-Perishable Pantry

Keep your fridge stocked with lemons, oranges, limes, fresh ginger, scallions, chiles, celery, carrots, and parsley. Onions, potatoes, garlic, and shallots can be kept in a basket or, if you won't use them up quickly, in a covered but ventilated crock (they'll keep longer this way). These are all important ingredients for rounding out and complementing the contents of your nonperishable pantry.

---

### The Least You Need to Know

➤ The Bad News: Chances are that most, if not all, of your spice cupboard needs to be replaced.

➤ Olive oil and canola oil should become the only fats you use in cooking. Learning to use olive oil as a condiment makes its great flavour go a long, long way.

➤ Capers, anchovies, and mustard are nonperishable standbys that add Mediterranean flavour with no hassle and virtually no fat.

➤ Use chicken broth instead of butter in mashed potatoes, to "sauté" vegetables, to cut the oil in salad dressings, and to add flavour to soups, sauces, and marinades.

➤ Stocking a pantry can open up a whole new world of lowfat and nonfat cooking, but it can be expensive. Start slowly, make lists of priorities, and don't try to build Rome in a day!

---

# Chapter 8

# Dining Out Means Making Smart Choices

---

## In This Chapter

➤ Some lowfat foods you may already love

➤ Ok, then learn to love the lowfat things

➤ Ask for what you want! You're the customer!

➤ Stick to restaurants that offer viable choices

---

The world is full of food, much to our great joy and sometimes, our frustration. Food makes us happy: we eat it with friends and family in a convivial atmosphere; it gives us a sense of fulfillment. But because it helps us celebrate and cheers us when we're down, sometimes it brings guilt, which isn't good for us at all.

The key to reducing fat intake is to find a balance between some of the high-fat foods you love and the lowfat foods that must make up most of your diet if you really want to succeed. The secret—which tends to get lost in the constant lowfat media hype we are subjected to—is that there are plenty of lowfat foods that are pretty lovable, too.

Many people just abandon their lowfat eating regime when they dine out, but this is entirely unnecessary and can have a discouraging impact on your resolve. Whether eating out or cooking at home, there is a wealth of lowfat choices. Your first step to dining out lowfat style could be as simple as ordering sliced fresh tomatoes with some garlic and balsamic vinegar—easy on the olive oil, please.

When we refer to lowfat dishes we don't mean three-cheese lasagna made with lowfat cheese and lowfat ricotta, nor do we mean meat-loaf made with soy cakes. What we're talking about are the foods that don't need to change to be part of a healthy diet,

## Watch Out!

Restaurant chefs don't have anyone looking over their shoulders telling them to lighten up, so they don't. Adding flavour without fat takes time, thought, effort, and expense, as we saw in Chapter 5. Most restaurants take the easy way out. Some good French restaurants spend many hours simmering and skimming stocks to get the maximum flavour without the need for butter or cream, but they are rare and often somewhat pricey. The best route when dining out is to order the simple things, without sauce, and to choose the dishes that don't require much fat, if any, in order to taste good, such as sushi, pork fajitas, or fruit sorbet.

because they are already low in fat without any alteration. Can you imagine if pungent garlic, juicy tomatoes, or ripe peaches were bad for you? Life would not be worth living. Take a new look at some familiar—and some possibly unfamiliar—dishes that are naturally good for you.

# Don't Forget Portion Size!

Portion size is critical in the crusade to reduce fat. A look at the Food Guide Rainbow can alert you to the discrepancies in portion size that make it so hard to follow and understand nutritional guidelines. For instance, 1 serving of bread = 1 slice, but in many restaurants a sandwich would contain 2 double-thick slices of bread, which equals 4 servings. Restaurants seem to be increasing the normal portion size every year, so that 1 order of pasta can be as much as 4 servings of grains. Be aware of this, and fight back by ordering half portions or splitting things with a friend.

Never be afraid to ask for what you want in a restaurant. The staff should be happy to grant any reasonable requests. Of course, if the broccoli soup is made with cream they can hardly take out the cream, but they can certainly bring the salad dressing on the side, provide half or children's portions, and grill poultry and meat with little or oil. Ask for the starch accompaniment to a main dish to be cut in half (i.e., half the rice, potato, or pasta). If a waiter quibbles about providing half servings of pasta, particularly when it's only offered as a main course, have the rest wrapped up and take it home for tomorrow's lunch or dinner. Just remember that tomorrow doesn't mean 2 minutes after midnight.

# Asian Restaurants

The Japanese have the lowest incidence of obesity of any country in the world, and this is likely due to their national cuisine. Fish, rice, and vegetables (with little if any oil) form the backbone of the local diet. In Japanese cooking, condiments are more likely to be soy sauce or vinegar than oil or butter, and when you visit a Japanese restaurant, you'll never have to tell the chef to "hold the oil," because there isn't any (except in tempura, which can soak up a lot of fat if not perfectly done).

If you like sushi and have a good sushi restaurant in your area, this is likely to be your best choice for lowfat dining out. There is more to Japanese food than sushi, however, and many restaurants feature yakitori and kushiyaki (skewer-grilled foods). The best choices for skewered dishes are fish, vegetables, and chicken. Japanese soup counters have been taking many parts of the country by storm: stick to the thinner soba noodles and choose toppings like spinach and chicken rather than pork or eggs.

Thai food is another naturally lowfat Asian cuisine—the use of fresh herbs and the emphasis on freshly prepared, clean, and healthy foods make Thai a good choice for dining out. Again, choose chicken, fish, and vegetables rather than beef or lamb, and avoid any deep-fried foods such as spring rolls and tempura. Cucumber salads are good options at Japanese, Thai, and Korean restaurants. Try the Korean specialty kimchee (pickled cabbage in pepper sauce), but start out with a mild variety since it can be very spicy.

**Tidbits!**

Not all carbohydrates are created equal. Potatoes pack 4 to 5 times as many calories as lettuce, so order half a baked potato or half the usual portion of rice and extra vegetables if a dinner comes with both. If you opt for the salad, get the dressing on the side and use only a teaspoon (5 mL) or so. Do not, as my father always said, fill up on bread! Even without the butter it's adding a lot of extra calories to your meal. (There's nothing wrong with eating unbuttered bread with a small meal, as long as it fits into your calorie count for the day.)

Chinese food usually features a much larger ratio of vegetables to proteins such as beef, chicken, pork, and fish. Calorie-rich carbohydrates come in the form of rice, and can be kept to a minimum. The problem is that many authentic Chinese restaurants tend to oil-blanch meat, making it taste great but sending the fat count into the stratosphere. Beef with broccoli, chicken with snow peas, and other such combinations are viable as long as the ratio of vegetables to protein remains high. Ask for the meat simply sautéed, rather than oil-blanched, and you can avoid that little pitfall. Sauces appear thick, but are thickened with cornstarch rather than butter or cream and are usually nothing more than flavourful stock combined with ginger, garlic, soy sauce, and often black bean or plum sauce. Steamed dishes, like chicken with snow peas, are always a great choice in Chinese establishments.

Indian restaurants are a great place to start learning how to use spices judiciously to liven up lowfat food. Not by choice but because of economic need, Indian cooks have learned to prepare food without much fat. Their spicy food makes such good use of flavour that you won't miss the fat for a minute. Tandoori chicken, cucumber raita, lentil dhal, pork kebobs, and vegetable curry are all good choices.

## Watch Out!

With any generalizations there are bound to be exceptions, and you'll find several in this chapter. For instance, avoid tempura when dining in a Japanese restaurant, and watch out for excess cheese in Mexican establishments. Mexican chefs don't use cheese anywhere near as much as their "Norte-americano" counterparts. In Indian restaurants, avoid deep-fried items like samosa and pakora, and watch out for dishes containing a lot of ghee (clarified butter, with fat grams still intact). If in doubt about the method of preparation, ask!

# Latin American Restaurants

When we think of dining out at a Mexican restaurant, cheese is often the first thing that comes to mind. This doesn't represent true Mexican cooking at all. Ceviche is an excellent choice, as long as you trust the quality of the kitchen (or, see the recipe on page 254 to reproduce it at home). Order whole fish roasted or grilled with lime juice, chiles, and cilantro. Or try these other healthy options: chicken or fish fajitas, tortilla soup, vegetable burritos without the cheese, and chicken or fish tacos with shredded lettuce and salsa fresca. Vegetarian bean dishes are always good, but don't combine beans with meat or poultry because the calorie count will go through the roof. As always, keep portion size in mind. Even if a dish is low in fat, excessive calorie intake will still cause weight gain.

# Mediterranean and Middle Eastern Food

Cooking Mediterranean-style at home is a quick and delicious route to good health, but Italian restaurants tend to load up on olive oil and cheese behind the scenes. Unfortunately, the chef is long gone by the time your waistline and cholesterol levels show the damage. But there are options: choose minestrone soup, vegetarian pizza with half the usual cheese, focaccia with simple toppings, grilled vegetables, pasta with fresh tomato sauce. If it's on the menu, order a fish soup like cioppino, but pass on the garlic or red pepper mayonnaise that sometimes comes with it. Salads are only a good choice if they don't contain cheese or meat and you ask for the dressing on the side. Use a scant teaspoon (15 mL) or two of the dressing and ignore the rest. In better Italian restaurants you should be able to order a little plate containing some minced garlic and balsamic vinegar. Add a teaspoon (15 mL) or two of olive oil from the cruet on the table and use as a sauce for chicken or fish, which you've correctly ordered *sans* its usual sauce.

In Middle Eastern establishments, choose hummus (recipe, page 193), tzatziki (recipe, page 194), and baba ghanoush (eggplant spread). Stuffed grape leaves (dolmas or dolmades) usually contain grains, dried fruits, and nuts (see recipe, page 275), but check to make sure they don't feature sausage or fatty cuts of pork. Always go for grilled foods rather than the baked dishes, which often arrive drenched in heavy sauces. Chutneys and sambals make a good substitute for high-fat sauces. They are usually fat-free, though do contain a lot of sugar. Never be afraid to request a fish or chicken dish without the sauce—good restaurants are there to serve you. For dessert, choose biscotti and fruit sorbet.

You can make dining out almost as healthy as eating at home.

# The Melting Pot

Many naturally lowfat dishes from eclectic world cuisines don't fall easily into any of the above categories. The Scandinavian marinated salmon called gravlax is one (see the recipe on page 151). Shrimp, crab, or lobster cocktails are always good choices if you feel the need for a first course (in which case, skip dessert). Northern European countries make some lovely open-faced sandwiches with pickled fish, sliced mild onions, and capers. Jerk chicken is a Jamaican specialty that is now being adapted to shrimp, fish, and pork. Ask for fish grilled or sautéed with minimal oil, then ask for a lemon and some chopped parsley to add excitement, just as you might do at home.

Spanish cuisine has elevated pork cookery to an art and doesn't use dairy products anyway, so ask for lean cuts of pork (see Chapter 25) to be cooked with minimal oil and select a tomato-based sauce.

---

### The Least You Need to Know

➤ You're the boss in all but the fast-food establishment, which is usually off limits anyway. Order half portions, naked grilled fish—whatever you need to make dining out a viable option.

➤ Most fat in restaurant food is hidden in heavy sauces and complicated dishes—stick to the basics and you'll be able to see exactly what's on the plate, not wonder what *might* be there.

➤ Asian, Latin American (once you learn to avoid the inauthentic tendency to overuse the cheese), Mediterranean, Middle Eastern, and Indian cuisines offer a wealth of choices for lowfat dining. Just remember that portion control is everything and don't hesitate to wrap it up or leave it on the table if you are exceeding the average recommended portion.

---

# Part 3
# Lowfat-Friendly Cooking Methods Explained

# Chapter 9

VEGGIE SAUNA

# Simply Steaming: Naked Vegetables and Feel-Good Fish

## In This Chapter

➤ The science of steaming

➤ Gearing up to steam

➤ Good candidates for steaming

➤ Build flavour with garnishes, drizzles, and sprinkles

Steaming is the gentlest way to cook, so it is perfect for delicate foods like fish, shellfish, and vegetables with a high water content, like squash, peas, and even potatoes. Brigit was surprised to learn that steaming turned out to be one of the best nonfat ways to cook a boneless, skinless chicken breast. The result is succulent and juicy, not dry at all. This method does not overwhelm the food's intrinsic flavour, letting the character of your ingredients be the stars of the show.

Because steaming requires no added fat, it can be the lowest-fat cooking technique. You need to choose the right foods, trim them to sizes that will cook evenly and in a relatively short time, and refrain from overcooking. Adding aromatic vegetables and herbs to the steaming water not only perfumes the food being cooked, but also gives you a delicate broth to serve over the food. Adding salt to the steaming water is crucial.

The heat generated by steaming in a covered pan is hotter than boiling water, so food will cook more quickly than if boiled. The true bonus of steaming is, of course, the retention of vitamins that would otherwise be poured down the drain with the boiling water.

Though it is low in fat, nutritious, gentle, and simple, steamed food can be dull if it is not finished or garnished with something tangy and delicious. Garnishing options depend on your average fat and calorie count for the day. They range from the no-fat (slivered herbs, a bit of soy sauce, or chopped parsley and lemon zest) to the little-fat ($1/2$ tablespoon/2 mL of butter will do wonders for a plate of steamed green beans, and adds only 51 calories and $5^1/2$ grams of fat to your daily total).

# Why Choose Steam?

Steam is the right cooking method to choose when your ingredient is delicate (whitefish, sole, bluefish, perch, oysters, etc.) or has a high water content (zucchini, summer squash, peas, spinach), but there are other reasons to choose steam, particularly for the lowfat cook. If you are serving salmon fillets, for instance, steaming will de-emphasize the fatty, oily nature of the fish (even though the oil in salmon— Omega-3 fatty acid—is very good for you). When cooking new potatoes for a salad, you want the potato chunks to be firm, not crumbly or mealy, and steaming is much better than boiling for keeping control of the potato's consistency. This is also true for firm vegetables like winter squash, turnips, rutabaga, and beets. The key to successful steaming is to cover the pan and check often—you'd be amazed how quickly small cubes of even the firmest vegetables can cook with this method. Brussels sprouts are good candidates for steaming, too—remember to cut a shallow cross in the base of each to help them cook evenly.

# What Kind of Equipment Do I Need?

If you have a large saucepan, a heatproof cup, and a plate, you can steam. Simply place the cup, rim side down, in the bottom of the saucepan, fill the pan with water to just below the base of the cup, and place a plate on top of the cup, right side up. Place your food to be cooked on the plate, cover the pan and bring the water to a low simmer. Voilà! You're steaming!

If you will be doing a lot of steaming, the common collapsible steamer baskets are ideal, though they only hold a limited quantity of food. These baskets are great for vegetables like zucchini and peas. Just be sure not to accidentally dump all the vegetables into the pan when you lift out the steamer at the end of the cooking time. Those steamers can be a little awkward.

Many cookware manufacturers make steamer inserts designed to be used with their standard range of saucepans. These have the advantage of being easy to lift out (they have a handle), and they allow the pan to be completely covered while in use. We don't recommend using a strainer basket or a metal colander for steaming because the lid of the pan will likely not fit tightly. This would cause the intense steam atmosphere to be lost and cooking to be uneven. If your colander fits completely inside your pan with the lid closed, then it's all right, as long as it's metal.

# Getting Ready to Steam

Assemble the equipment you plan to use based on the information above, and choose one or two ingredients that will take well to steaming (recipes follow). For nonfatty fish like snapper or whitefish, lightly oil the steamer basket or plate—oil spray is ideal for this. Fill the saucepan with water to just below the bottom of the steamer insert (not touching!). Cover the pan and set over high heat. As soon as steam begins to escape, add your ingredients, reduce the heat to low to keep the liquid simmering, not boiling, and begin timing based on the guidelines below or your own experience. Steam until the food is only just tender—vegetables should still have a little bite, and fish should be opaque all the way to the centre.

## Watch Out!

Steaming is a gentle cooking method, ideal for delicate vegetables, fish, and poultry breasts. An easy, quick, and healthful option for the lowfat cook, it allows the natural, clean flavour of the ingredient to shine. Steaming, however, is actually a hotter cooking method than boiling, and ingredients can overcook quickly, leaving a mushy, unidentifiable mess. Keep a log taped inside one of your kitchen cabinets and make a record of the perfect timing for some of your favourite steamed foods. With a little experimentation you can set the timer and ignore the steamer while you attend to other cooking chores. Then when the timer goes off (after, say, 5 minutes for thick-sliced zucchini), you'll be rewarded with perfectly cooked, bright green vegetables.

# What Can I Steam?

Fish and vegetables are ideal candidates for steaming. Generally, meat is not as good steamed; the result is grey and unappetizing. Boneless, skinless chicken breasts can be steamed, and it helps them cook evenly if they have been lightly pounded to a uniform thickness. This chicken method is great for those individuals who have virtually no calories or fat grams to spare in their daily quota, and it's actually quite delicious. Salt, pepper, lemon juice, and parsley rounds out the dish to give a thoroughly virtuous

### Toothsome Tips

When steaming, the liquid in the pan is a good source of flavour that won't add calories or fat to the finished dish. At the very least, add a teaspoon (5 mL) of salt per pint of water. For more flavour, add a little wine, vermouth, fruit juice, stock, or even beer to the steaming water, depending on what you are cooking (white cabbage does well with a little beer in the steaming water, for instance). This is a good time to add fresh herbs and aromatic vegetables, too, particularly if you plan to serve the steaming liquid as a brothy sauce over the cooked food (strain first to remove the flavouring agents). You can add whole, not ground, spices, but only in moderation. The foods that we usually steam are delicate in flavour—anything more than a pinch or two of spice could overwhelm their delicate flavour.

protein punch with less than 4 grams of fat for a 3½-ounce (105 g) serving. Most cookbooks gloss over the technique of steaming anything other than a few simple fish dishes, but this is the ideal cooking method for lowfat cooking, so make it a standard in your kitchen.

## Naked Vegetables

With vegetables, adding spices, herbs, wine, or other aromatics to the steaming water really isn't necessary, since you don't want to cover the good, honest flavour of the vegetables themselves. One exception is the artichoke, which definitely benefits from the addition of a tablespoon (15 mL) of vermouth, vinegar, or lemon juice to the steaming water. For longer cooking times, be sure to check and replenish the water below the steamer so that it does not boil away!

Do always stir in 1 teaspoon (5 mL) of salt for each pint of steaming water when steaming any vegetables, as this does wonders for bringing out their flavour.

## Some Vegetable Steaming Guidelines

Artichokes: 30 to 40 minutes, bottom side up

Asparagus, pencil thin: 4 to 5 minutes; medium: 6 to 7 minutes; thick: 7 to 10 minutes

Beets, small: 25 to 30 minutes; medium: 35 to 40 minutes; large: 55 to 60 minutes

Broccoli, Broccoli Rabe, Cauliflower, and Chinese Broccoli (separated into florets, broccoli stalks peeled): 3 to 5 minutes

Carrots, sliced or matchsticks: 7 to 10 minutes; whole baby, or halved: 16 to 20 minutes

Eggplant, whole: 20 to 30 minutes

Green Beans: small filet beans (haricots verts), single layer: 5 to 7 minutes; string beans, single layer: 8 to 12 minutes (add 3 to 5 minutes when beans are more than one layer deep)

Green or Savoy Cabbage, cored and cut into 6 wedges: 12 to 15 minutes; shredded: 5 to 7 minutes

Leeks, white part only, whole: 10 to 25 minutes; white part, halved: 6 to 8 minutes; slices: 3 to 5 minutes

Parsnips, Turnips, and Rutabaga, $1/2$-inch (1-cm) cubes: 5 to 6 minutes

Peas, fresh: 5 to 10 minutes (if more than a single layer, stir once halfway through)

**Tidbits!**

Turnips and rutabaga tend to get short shrift in the modern kitchen—for no good reason. With a wonderful earthy flavour and smooth, nonstringy texture, these two vegetables go well together or when added to potatoes. When steaming, lift the lid for a moment after 2 minutes to release the slightly sulphurous compounds—you'll never smell them again. For an exotic, colourful mash, steam turnips or rutabagas, or both, until completely tender, then stir into an equal quantity of mashed potatoes.

Potatoes, whole, small: 15 to 20 minutes; whole, medium: 30 to 35 minutes; whole, large: 35 to 45 minutes; $1/4$-inch (5-mm) slices, in one layer: 10 to 15 minutes

Red Cabbage, cored and cut into 6 wedges: 15 to 17 minutes; shredded: 8 to 10 minutes

Snow Peas: 2 to 5 minutes

Spinach, leaves only, well washed: 2 to 3 minutes

Sweet Potatoes and Yams, whole: 30 to 45 minutes; halves: 15 to 20 minutes; 1- to 2-inch (2.5- to 5-cm) cubes: 13 to 18 minutes

Swiss Chard and Bok Choy, whole leaves: 8 minutes; stem pieces: 8 to 10 minutes

Winter Squashes and Pumpkin, 1-inch (2.5-cm) cubes: 12 to 15 minutes; small squash halves: 15 to 20 minutes; larger pieces: 25 to 30 minutes

Zucchini, Summer Squash, Patty Pan, $1/2$-inch (1-cm) cubes and $1/4$-inch (5-mm) slices: 4 to 6 minutes

# Feel-Good Fish

Shellfish such as clams, mussels, lobsters, and crab are so flavourful in themselves that they barely need any additional flavouring in the steaming liquid, though a little wine or vermouth and a sprig of dill could never hurt. The best bonus with this method is that the liquid under the steamer basket becomes a fish stock that you can use for a light sauce or freeze for future steaming and poaching projects, and for making marvellous rice pilaf or even risotto—don't throw it away!

All shellfish must be thoroughly scrubbed with a firm brush before steaming, and, in the case of mussels, beards removed. Wash the seafood using several changes of water until it's clear, just as you would for spinach or other dirty greens. This not only keeps the broth clean and clear, but also prevents you from biting into a gorgeous piece of fish only to find grit between your teeth—one of the least pleasant food experiences.

Flat and round fish like sole, sea bass, whitefish, bluefish, perch, cod, and halibut are more delicate in flavour than shellfish and will definitely benefit from wine and aromatics like fresh herbs and spices added to the steaming water. Some sliced garlic in the water is also nice, as are sliced mild onions, peppercorns, and red pepper flakes.

# Fish That Can Be Steamed

Fish come in all shapes and sizes, and often have different names depending on which river or ocean they're pulled from. Below is a list of fish suitable for steaming—choose those available in your area.

| | | |
|---|---|---|
| Arctic Char | Halibut | Sea Trout |
| Bass | John Dory | Shark |
| Catfish | Mahi Mahi | Skate |
| Chub | Monkfish | Snapper |
| Clams (hard and soft-shell) | Mullet | Sole |
| | Mussels | Sucker (Carp) |
| Cod | Ocean Catfish | Tilapia |
| Corbina | Orange Roughy | Tilefish (Grouper) |
| Croaker | Perch | Trout |
| Cusk | Pike | Turbot |
| Dab (Sole) | Pollock | Walleye (Pickerel) |
| Flounder | Porgy | Whitefish |
| Fluke | Ray | Whiting |
| Grayling | Rockfish (B.C. Snapper) | Wolf Fish |
| Grouper | Sablefish (Sturgeon) | |
| Haddock | Salmon | |
| Hake | Sea Bass | |

Steaming Times:

Blue Crabs (live): 15 to 20 minutes, until bright pink

Lobster, Dungeness Crab, King Crab Legs: $1^1/_2$ pounds (750 g): 15 minutes, until bright red; 2 pounds (1 kg): 20 minutes; 2 $^1/_2$ pounds (1.25 kg): 25 minutes

Mussels, Clams, and Oysters: steam until the shells gape open slightly, 5 to 10 minutes, then remove immediately and pry open the shells, saving the liquor inside the shells for the broth. Any shellfish that have not opened after 10 minutes must be discarded.

Scallops, side muscle removed: 3 to 5 minutes, depending on size (don't overcook!)

Shrimp, legs and heads pulled off, deveined through the back of the shell if the vein is dark and visible: steam 3 to 5 minutes, until the shrimps turn pink and opaque all the way through

Soft-Shell Clams, well rinsed: steam 5 to 10 minutes. Any shellfish that have not opened after 10 minutes must be discarded.

Whole Fish, Fish Steaks, and Fillets: 5 to 8 minutes per pound (500 g), or 9 to 10 minutes per inch (2.5 cm) of thickness

## Creating a Sauce from the Steaming Liquid

Fish doesn't take long to steam, so it doesn't require much liquid underneath the steamer. The liquid absorbs flavour from the fish as well as vice versa, and can easily be served as a light broth over the finished fish. Add aromatic vegetables, like diced carrots and scallions or sliced mushrooms, and fresh herbs, such as a sprig of thyme or basil. A few peppercorns and a bay leaf will add to the flavour but must be fished out before serving. Just transfer the fish from the steamer to a warm bowl and spoon a few spoonfuls of the broth on top.

# Garnishing as a Gift

Steaming is a simple, elegant art. Flavour and nutrients are the important factors here, not fancy cooking techniques. When you are cooking simply and honestly, however, you still want to be pleased by what you see on the plate. Visual impressions of food are important, and although we may garnish mostly for the taste, a tasteful garnish can do wonders for ringing that abdominal dinner bell. Imagine a perfectly cooked, juicy, steamed sea bass steak on a white plate. Fine. Now imagine the same dish with a few flakes of red pepper, some slivered fresh basil, and a sprinkle of fresh lemon zest. Point taken?

Garnishes need not be fatty, such as a dollop of sour cream in the middle of a bowl of chile. A garnish should excite the eyes and imply that you're getting a little extra gift on the plate. When you wrap up a birthday present, the ribbon is the garnish. If you curl your ribbons and add little gold grapes underneath the bow, you are a natural-born garnisher. Create some simple masterpieces in your kitchen.

### Toothsome Tips

Herbs are perfect for garnishing, but only the soft-stemmed herbs like parsley, mint, basil, dill, and chives will do. Garnishing, by definition, takes place after the cooking process is over, and woody-stemmed herbs like thyme, rosemary, and sage are too tough to use as garnish. They should be used for flavour when there is still some cooking time left to soften them up. You can add whole sprigs of woody-stemmed herbs during the steaming process, either in the steamer basket or in the liquid below. Then discard them before serving—the flavour will linger.

## Colour, Colour, Colour

Of course, the flavour of the garnish should match the dish, but there is something "zen" about colour-coordinating garnishes. Here are a few starter ideas:

Red: diced red pepper or canned pimiento; red chile flakes; paprika, diced tomato

Green: finely chopped soft-stemmed herbs; diced pickles or gherkins; grated lime zest; diced green pepper; minced green olives; wasabi (spicy Japanese mustard paste)

Yellow: grated lemon or grapefruit zest; diced yellow pepper

Orange: grated orange zest; diced orange pepper

White and Pink: diced or grated radish; Japanese pickled ginger; cooked baby shrimp

## Treat Olive Oil and Butter as Garnish

Let's take an example: If you sautéed several tuna steaks you might use up to 2 table-spoons (25 mL) of oil or butter in the pan. Instead, consider steaming the fish and dolloping on a teaspoon (5 mL) or two of extra virgin olive oil just before serving. The richness will be there in the "mouth feel" (that first luxurious bite that coats the roof of your mouth and tells your brain cells you're eating something rich), but the fat grams will be minimal.

Change the way you look at olive oil and butter and you'll benefit from their flavour much more, since most of their flavour but none of the fat is lost during the cooking process, anyway. The exception is "browned butter, " i.e., butter which is melted by itself in a pan and allowed to turn nut-brown before being rapidly whisked off the heat. It tastes more buttery than uncooked butter, and will extend the rich flavour of butter all throughout a dish with only a few small spoonfuls. The key is to view these flavour-adding fats as garnish, not as a cooking medium or integral ingredient.

## Herbs and Spices

Use a gentle hand when adding herbs and spices to steamed food. The flavours are clean, bright, and honest—you want to complement the natural flavour of the food, not conflict with it or cover it. The hard or woody herbs, like rosemary, thyme, and sage are not normally appropriate for steaming. Instead, choose the soft-stemmed herbs like parsley, chives, dill, fennel greens, basil, and chervil. Chop and scatter the herbs after the food is steamed, just before serving. Even with steamed fish or poultry, you should still stick with the soft-stemmed herbs.

A piece of simply steamed salmon would shine if drizzled with $1/2$ teaspoon (2 mL) of soy sauce and a few chives, for instance. Or try $1/2$ teaspoon (2 mL) of extra virgin olive oil (this is where you'll really appreciate its superiority to pure olive oil), some diced tomato, and a few twists of freshly ground black pepper on a steamed chicken breast. Think about the flavours that are traditionally paired with your ingredient (carrots and dill, for instance) and garnish accordingly, always with a light hand.

### What's the Skinny?

Overwhelmed by olive oil choices? Perplexed by price differences? You're not alone. Extra virgin olive oil costs more because it is made from the first cold pressing of olives, and because of that it tastes fruitier and fresher than oils pressed later from the olives using heat to extract every bit of fat. It is absolutely marvellous for garnishing, i.e., using as a condiment, but is wasted if used for cooking. If you cook with olive oil, use a pure oil from one of the big producers. Italian extra virgin oils tend to be greener and fruitier, with a little peppery bite thrown in. Greece and Spain both make very good extra virgin oils. California is just starting to produce good oils. Buy in small quantities, store in a cool, dark place, and use within 3 to 4 months or the oil will go rancid.

### What's the Skinny?

All fats and oils have the same number of calories and fat grams per tablespoon (15 mL), i.e., 14 (that's 3.2 fat grams per teaspoon/ 5 mL). However, olive oil has only 1.9 grams of that nasty saturated fat and zero grams of cholesterol! In comparison, canola oil has only 1 gram of saturated fat but is lower in the beneficial monounsaturated fat. Butter has 33 grams of cholesterol. Too much like science class? Just remember that, especially when it's not cooked, a little olive oil or butter can go a long way in the flavour department. It's worth noting that whipped butter has fewer fat and cholesterol grams than solid butter, and it looks prettier, too!

## Versatile Vinegar

The adage "a little goes a long way" is always appropriate when it comes to vinegar. Half a teaspoon (2 mL) of wine vinegar or balsamic vinegar drizzled over steamed zucchini or carrots will quickly elevate the flavour, but don't add much more than that or all you'll taste is the vinegar. Think of vinegar as a strong condiment, rather than as an ingredient, and investigate some of the flavoured vinegars on the market. There are many, and in a simple application like this you'll actually taste the flavouring, which sometimes doesn't come through when it's used in a vinaigrette with garlic, mustard, and other flavours.

Brigit recently discovered pear vinegar, which pairs (sorry) very well with steamed poultry, squash, and asparagus. Sherry vinegar is a true wonder, but it might overwhelm delicate fish or vegetables, so use it with poultry and strongly flavoured vegetables like spinach. If a combination sounds right to you, try it and see.

## Salsas, Chutneys, Relishes

We are spoiled for choice when it comes to bottled condiments. Supermarkets carry a vast array, gourmet stores have even more, and if you venture into the world of mail order, well, the world's your oyster. Most condiments are low in fat and keep for some time in the refrigerator after opening, so it's easy to have them on hand. The keeping-factor of

### Toothsome Tips

You can make a quick, colourful topping for steamed vegetables, fish, and poultry that's decidedly Mediterranean in flavour. Halve and seed one or two plum tomatoes and cut them into 1/4-inch (1-cm) dice. Add four large leaves of fresh basil, slivered, a teaspoon (5 mL) of olive oil, and a generous pinch of both salt and pepper. Toss together and finish off with 1/2 teaspoon (2 mL) of balsamic vinegar.

condiments depends on either the sugar or the vinegar content, both of which retard spoiling. With salsas and chutneys, it's usually the sugar; with relishes, it's the vinegar. There is even Tequila Salsa, which sounds festive and would make a lovely topping for steamed chicken. If you are a fan of hot sauce, you'll already have some favourites, but remember, use a light touch or you won't know what's underneath. Check out your local market, or range further afield.

Pesto is a condiment, but it's one that doesn't keep very long because the chopped basil will darken when it's exposed to air. To counteract this, manufacturers load up commercial pesto with oil to keep the air from touching the basil or with citric acid to retard spoilage, which affects the flavour (badly). Pesto is also relatively high in fat, so it may not be an option, but again, a little goes a long way. Ideally, you should make your own pesto, but there are some good perishable products available in the chilled section of good markets. We don't recommend the glass jar-style pesto that's designed to last for months, but if you want to try it, look for one with a nutritional label and check it for fat content, and the list of ingredients for preservatives—it will probably change your mind.

## What's the Skinny?

From the Middle East to the Mediterranean, there is one condiment that is vastly more popular than any other. It is used on everything from steamed vegetables to roast suckling pig, and from the poorest outdoor cooking fire in Greece to the haute restaurant kitchens of France. Is it expensive? No. Is it hard to find? No. Actually it grows on trees. It's the lemon. Catch an octopus off a little beach on a Greek island and throw it on the fire, but first make sure you have a lemon. Grill a porterhouse from your local butcher, but first make sure you have a lemon. If you eat fatty food, lemon juice cuts the fat and lightens the flavour. If you eat lowfat food, lemon juice adds excitement and complexity. Make lemons a permanent item on your shopping list. Don't get caught at home without one.

## The Least You Need to Know

➤ Steaming is quick, hot, and intense. Use a timer and keep records for guaranteed and consistent success.

➤ Choose delicate foods for steaming. Don't try to steam red meat, and remove the skin from fish and poultry after they're cooked. Cut vegetables into evenly sized pieces.

➤ Garnishing creatively is the key to keeping steamed foods from being bland and boring. Learn to use vegetables, herbs, lemons, and purchased condiments, always with restraint.

# Chapter 10

# Grilling: The Oldest and Newest Cooking Method

---

**In This Chapter**

➤ Equipment: An embarrassment of options

➤ Indirect and direct heat: Two choices for different results

➤ The nuts and bolts of grilling

➤ All the stars of the grilling stage

---

Long before there were covered kettle grills, natural hardwood charcoal, or even the now seemingly ancient hibachi, there were campfires. It didn't take long for that first person who discovered fire to figure out that fire applied to meat made it more palatable, and more digestible.

Grilling is essentially a method of cooking fresh, raw ingredients over a bed of hot coals, or—lacking an outdoor fire source—cooking directly on the surface of very hot, well-seasoned cast iron. Grilling requires little or no fat but unlike poaching or steaming imparts an exciting and unique, smoky flavour to the lowfat menu.

## What Kind of Equipment Do I Need?

Browse through a few cooking magazines and, if your town has one, an outdoor cooking specialty store. You'll probably be overwhelmed by the choices available and go home scratching your head. However, all the bells, whistles, and comic aprons can't disguise the fact that grilling is a simple process that, in our opinion, should take place over hardwood or standard charcoal briquettes, preferably in a grill with a cover.

## Open Grills

Open grills present several problems for efficient grilling, but they are inexpensive and there is probably one lurking in 95 percent of the garages in this country. On an open grill you are more likely to have flare-ups, so stick to poultry breasts, fish, and vegetables without marinades—these are less likely to cause a fire than fattier cuts or those doused in an oil-based marinade. Always keep a spray bottle of water on hand to douse fires quickly, no matter what you're grilling. You can improvise a cover for an open grill with a large cooking pot lid or a tent of heavy-duty aluminum foil, thereby approximating the effect of indirect heat, but don't expect perfect results.

## The Covered Kettle Grill

The covered kettle grill was designed with a meticulous eye to the problems of grilling: the need to raise and lower the grilling surface to change the amount of heat reaching the food, the problem of flare-ups, and the inability to maintain an even heat. Covered kettle grills are designed to be used with the lid on, and reading up on the use of the strategically placed vents will make you an expert griller in less time than it takes to light a fire. You can choose direct or indirect heat, and you are well served by the growing number of books about grilling that specifically address the use of kettle grills.

Covered kettles use solid fuel rather than gas, though the most recent and truly wonderful innovation for the kettle grill is a gas igniter, eliminating the need to struggle with the often messy and sometimes intensely frustrating process of lighting your charcoal.

### Toothsome Tips

News Flash: Smoking Can Be Beneficial to Your Health!

Using hardwood chunks (for charcoal grills) or chips (for gas grills) is a tasty option for all grilling except, unfortunately, indoor grilling. Tossing a few chunks of well-soaked wood on a grill fire is a completely fat-free way to add a smoky flavour to foods, including meat, fish, fowl, and vegetables (smoked tomatoes make a very special salad). Use only oak, mesquite, alder, hickory, cherry, or pecan, and avoid soft woods like pine, or pressure-treated woods, which can be impregnated with harmful chemicals. Remember: wood, not lumber. Soak the wood chunks or chips for at least 30 minutes and then place them in direct contact with the hot coals. For a gas grill, place the soaked chips in an old metal or disposable pie plate and place directly on the lava rocks. More is not better in the case of smoke-cooking food; subtlety is the key.

When choosing fuel for your kettle grill, be informed. Read the labels on your charcoal and avoid those that are made with petroleum products (most of them). Try to find natural hardwood charcoal or mesquite charcoal and please, please, don't use lighter fluid to start your fire, unless you want your food to have that piquant aroma of gasoline. Better to use the cylindrical metal starters that use only newspaper and work very well.

## The Gas Grill

Gas grills have come a long way since the first inefficient products came on the market, but take our advice and hire someone to put it together for you. Unless you are an engineer, the process of assembling one of today's high-tech gas units could easily reduce you to a quivering mass of jelly. Not only will you be unable to grill, but you'll also be unable to face your family and neighbours in the ignominy of defeat (just look at the list of parts to get an idea of what you are up against).

Many grilling purists believe that food cooked over a gas grill does not gain the same level of smoky flavour as food cooked over a true bed of coals. This is something you must decide for yourself. If you already have a gas grill,

### What's the Skinny?

For outdoor grilling, there are two main methods of cooking: direct heat and indirect heat. Each is perfectly suited to certain ingredients. Direct heat is great for tender cuts of meat, steaks, chops, poultry pieces, fish steaks, sliced and whole vegetables, and kebabs. Indirect heat is the only option for larger cuts of meat and whole poultry that you would normally roast in the oven, like leg of lamb, whole chickens and turkey, loin of pork, and whole fish. Depending on your equipment, you will be able to choose the correct method for whatever you wish to grill.

then use it with pleasure, but invite yourself to the home of a friend who uses charcoal to taste the difference. Of course, the ideal solution is to have both: a gas grill for busy weeknights when you don't have time to wait 30 to 40 minutes for the coals to burn down, and a charcoal grill for leisurely weekend afternoon barbecuing. In some cases, small pieces of food that are on the grill for only a very brief time will not pick up the smoky flavour anyway, so gas is a fine choice.

If you are using a gas grill, the option of indirect cooking is still available as long as you have three or more burners on separate controls. This allows you to turn off the centre burner and place the drip pan over it, leaving the side burners on, and put the grilling candidate in the centre over the drip pan.

## Tidbits!

It's imperative that the fire reach the correct heat level before you place the food above it—too hot and the food will burn, too cool and it will poach, yielding a dry, grey, unappetizing result. Luckily, there is a time-honoured method of determining this. Place your hand palm side down 1 inch (2.5 cm) above the cooking surface. If you can hold your hand there for only 1 or 2 seconds, the fire is too hot, about 400°F to 450°F (200°C to 230°C). If you can hold your hand in position for 4 seconds, the fire is medium hot, or about 350°F to 375°F (180°C to 190°C), good for most grilling. At 5 seconds, the coals are too cold for most meat and poultry, about 300°F to 325°F (150°C to 165°C), but would still be fine for grilling vegetables.

## Indoor Grills

Fancy, expensive countertop grills are available, allow you to bring your grilling indoors for the winter, and let apartment dwellers dabble in grilling—provided they have their very own exhaust fan/air extraction arrangement. However, these items must be built in and require special wiring and clearances, as do the exhaust fans and air extractors. Unless you are considering a multi-thousand dollar kitchen remodel, this may not be a viable option. But never fear, there is an alternative that is better, easier, and ridiculously less expensive.

Cast iron is one of the best cooking surfaces available. Many people have cast-iron skillets that have been handed down through generations, with an interior that has been carefully tended to provide a fool-proof, last-forever, all-natural nonstick cooking surface. What is relatively new, however, is the ridged cast-iron stovetop griddle pan, a long name for an ingenious piece of equipment. The ridged griddle pan can easily be heated to the very hot temperatures required for searing food—one of the most important requirements of grilling. The heat under the pan can quickly be reduced after searing to provide the gentle heat necessary to finish the cooking process. Best of all, the ridged griddle pan leaves those wonderful, charred grill marks that make grilled food look so rustic and delicious.

Seasoning a new cast iron is imperative, and is the same for any new product as it would be for an old, rusted pan discovered in the garage (just be sure to scrub off all the rust with steel wool before you begin). To season a new ridged, cast-iron griddle pan, first scrub it vigorously with a mild detergent and rinse it thoroughly. Note that in principle this is the last time you will apply soap to the pan, though some cooks use a drop or two of mild soap on their pans occasionally. Dry the pan thoroughly and brush all surfaces generously with a flavourless vegetable oil like canola. Place the pan in a 350°F (180°C) oven for 2 hours. Again wipe the pan with vegetable oil and return it to the oven, this time reducing the temperature to 200°F (100°C). After 2 more hours, wipe the pan again and return it to the oven. Repeat this a third time, for a total of 6 hours at 200°F (100°C). Your pan is now seasoned, but will always require special care. After cooking in your griddle pan, you will need to rinse it immediately in very hot water, using a scrub brush but, in general, no soap. Rub the cooking surface with a tiny bit of oil on a corner of paper towel. Dry the pan for at least 30 minutes in a turned-off gas oven (if you have a pilot light), or in an electric oven set on the lowest temperature. The pan will not be harmed if it is left in the warm oven for a longer time.

If you have Helpful Friends lurking about the kitchen and one of them scrubs out your pan with soap or (horrors), scouring powder, don't despair. Just repeat the original seasoning process and assign that friend to other cleanup chores in the future.

# Indirect Grilling

Indirect grilling takes place at medium heat, whereas direct grilling involves much higher heat. This method is good for larger cuts of meat that, if cooked over direct heat, would char on the outside before the inside was cooked through. Use indirect grilling for whole poultry, and larger cuts of beef, pork or lamb that you would normally roast in your oven (leg of lamb, loin of pork, etc., all well trimmed of fat). Indirect heat is also good for whole fish, which would char outside, be raw inside, and probably fall apart anyway if cooked over direct heat.

**Tidbits!**

Owners and lovers of cast iron know that the superb cooking surface of these great pots and pans is not an accident but a result of careful nurturing, often by several generations of the same family. People will tell you that a good cooking surface on cast iron takes years to achieve, but that's part of your own history with the pan and, besides, it's still plenty good in its first year or two of use. Seasoning not only prevents the food from sticking, but also prevents the pan from rusting. It is an ongoing process, though the first seasoning is the only one that requires any time at all.

**Toothsome Tips**

Throughout this book we have advocated the use of nonstick cookware, because it is without a doubt the lowfat cook's best tool. When using a nonstick surface, you can cut the oil required for a sauté by 66 percent, i.e., if a recipe calls for 1 tablespoon (15 mL) of oil in the pan, you can reduce it to 1 teaspoon (5 mL) or even less without fear of scorching. Well-seasoned cast iron is the original nonstick cookware and, unlike modern nonstick surfaces, it cannot be nicked by metal utensils and will not wear out, ever. Another benefit is its cost: approximately $1/4$ that of good, heavy nonstick cookware.

For indirect grilling, the fire is spread to either side of the fire pit, while the food is placed on a grill above the fire, in the centre so that it is *not* directly above the heat. A drip pan is placed underneath the food, between the divided coals, and it catches the dripping juices that would otherwise cause flare-ups. The grill is always covered during indirect grilling, and the vents are adjusted to maintain an even heat (read the literature that came with your grill for advice about using the vents). There is no need to turn the food, as the design of the grill causes the heat to circulate around the food, just like in a convection oven. This means that food will cook more quickly than it would in a regular oven, but you can use regular roasting recipe times as a guideline if you shave the time by 20 to 25 percent.

### Watch Out!

Salt is a versatile condiment that does wonders in bringing out the flavour of any food, especially grilled food. Recent studies show salt is not as bad for high blood pressure as originally thought (but don't get cocky, soon there will be another study contradicting that one). We all need salt in our diets—especially if we are getting a lot of exercise in hot weather—so don't be afraid to use it, but salting food before grilling can cause the exterior to dry out too much. A good rule of thumb is to salt the cooked side only, i.e., when one side is done and you turn the food over (for instance, a tuna steak), salt the cooked side. When the steak is done and you transfer it to a plate or platter, you can salt the side that was cooked second. Pepper can be applied with impunity before, during, and after grilling—it will not dry out the food.

## Indirect Grilling on a Charcoal Grill

Prepare a fire as usual and, after 20 minutes or so, when the coals are covered with a fine grey ash, rake them apart into two even piles on either side of the kettle. Place the drip pan in the centre and put the grilling rack in place above the fire. If you want to sear the food first, start it on the part of the grill that is directly over the fire (this would be appropriate with smaller cuts), then move the food to the centre and finish cooking with the grill covered. For larger cuts, you may need to add more briquettes to keep the fire at a constant temperature over several hours. Consult the directions that came with your grill, but for kettle grills the guideline is 8 standard-sized briquettes on each side, every hour.

## Indirect Grilling on a Gas Grill

Preheat the grill with all burners on high for about 10 minutes. Turn off the centre burner and position the drip pan over it. Place the food on the grill rack over the drip pan and close the lid of the grill. Regulate the heat inside by adjusting the flame on the two outside burners, keeping the heat at medium for recipes that specify a heat of 350°F to 400°F (180°C to 200°C). For recipes calling for temperatures of 300°F to 325°F (150°C to 165°C), keep the burner controls on low. It is not necessary to use the high heat setting for indirect grilling after the initial preheating process. Do not turn the centre burner on.

# Direct Grilling

This is the method most people had to use for centuries until our creative grill manufacturers invented the covered grill. It is still a superb cooking method for searing foods that are small or are low in fat (which might dry out in prolonged indirect heat). Direct grilling requires the use of no special equipment (though a few things will make life easier). All you need is a container in which to build a fire, or some other high heat source such as gas or even electricity (for indoor grilling), and a surface over the heat on which to place the food to be grilled. Things to grill over direct heat include fish and meat steaks and kebabs, sliced vegetables and vegetable kebabs, fish fillets, chops (remove the fat after cooking), and ground turkey burgers. Most foods are seared at high heat first, after which they are moved a little further from the heat source to allow the heat to penetrate gently and evenly toward the centre. Some items will not need to be moved further from the heat and can be cooked over high heat throughout their short cooking time.

Searing is a term that is overused in cooking literature, and recent studies show that high-heat searing does nothing to preserve the juiciness of food. However, it sure makes a nice crisp outside crust and some attractive grill marks that tell us we're having something cooked by the oldest method.

### What's the Skinny?

You may have thought that embarking on a lowfat diet meant no more huge hunks of steak. You're right. But it doesn't mean no more steak. Portion control is everything in lowfat cooking, so keep your portion to $3^1/_2$ ounces (105 g) (about the size of a pack of cards), and trim away all visible fat after the steak is cooked. Refer to the fat-count table for commonly grilled meats on page 109, and, remember, it's the average of fat grams that's important. We think a steak is worth a few days of penance, either before if you're really a saint, or afterward, like most of us.

## *Direct Grilling on a Charcoal Grill*

Start your fire as usual. After 30 to 45 minutes, the coals should be covered in a fine, light grey film of ash. Spread the coals out in one layer, thus providing an even heat source. Place the grill rack into position above the coals and let it heat up for 4 to 5 minutes. You are now ready to grill, but don't delay. The coals will only last about 20 to 25 minutes before they begin to lose heat. This should be enough time for most direct heat cooking, otherwise you will have to add more coals. If you are using a kettle grill, close the lid. This will prevent flare-ups but still keep the heat at a high enough temperature to accomplish the task. Food will cook more quickly in a covered kettle grill than on an open grill because the heat surrounds the food, cooking from all sides (but you still have to flip the food halfway through).

### Tidbits!

Hardwood and mesquite charcoal both sell for quite a bit more than charcoal briquettes. Are they worth it? Mostly, yes. Hardwood and mesquite burn faster and hotter than briquettes, so you'll need to add more to the fire to keep it burning, but that high heat really makes a difference with most foods, particularly when you are direct-heat grilling. For longer grilling over indirect heat, briquettes are fine, but they won't add the smoky flavour of real wood.

## Direct Grilling on a Gas Grill

Light the grill and turn all burners to high heat. Close the lid and preheat the grill for about 10 minutes. When you are ready to cook, decide if you want to leave the controls at high, or turn them down to medium or low. This depends on the food you are cooking. A general guideline is to start steaks and chops at high heat and turn down to medium after the initial 2-minute searing. Start and keep poultry at medium heat; fish and vegetables should be cooked over a lower heat. Keep the lid closed during cooking except for basting, flipping, or checking the food.

## Grilling Safety Tips

Grills get very hot and are often in use amidst large groups of people, sometimes in a cramped space, and often accompanied by alcoholic beverages, which have been known to cloud judgement. Use common sense and keep in mind the following guidelines:

➤ For goodness sake, don't try to use any grill designed for outdoor use inside a house. Toxic fumes can accumulate and cause serious injury or even death. This happens more often than you think.

➤ If it is extremely windy, it's probably not a good day to grill. Burning embers that fly through the air can play havoc with your or your neighbours' shingle roof.

➤ Don't leave small children and pets unattended near a hot grill. Children can easily be burned while investigating, and pets can often figure out an ingenious method for transferring the food on the grill to the ground next to it.

➤ Use tongs, spatulas, and forks with nice, long heatproof handles, preferably those designed for use with grills. A pair of sturdy oven mitts should be close at hand.

➤ Do not wear clothing with loose, flowing sleeves while grilling, for obvious reasons. Conversely, grilling in a bathing suit can be dangerous, too.

➤ If you must use lighter fluid, never, ever use it on hot or even warm coals. After using it, securely cap and store the lighter fluid at a good distance from the hot grill.

➤ Don't empty the ashes until they are completely cold, and never attempt to move a hot barbecue.

➤ Remember to turn off the valve after use.

➤ Never add "self-starting" briquettes while the food is cooking. These are impregnated with lighter fluid and will give that "essence of high octane" flavour to any food being cooked at the time.

# What Can I Grill?

Grilling over direct heat is suitable for most tender cuts of meat and for poultry, fish and vegetables. For larger cuts and those with little fat, choose indirect heat. When grilling meat, poultry, and fish it is beneficial to leave most of the fat and skin on during the grilling, then remove it afterward. This helps keep the food moist during the intense cooking process. Remove and discard the fat and skin after cooking (no nibbling)—the food will be juicier and tastier, but no higher in fat, as a result.

### What's the Skinny?

Some books and grill-meisters swear by basting, others swear at you if you do it. It really depends on the grilling subject. Delicate foods like poultry, fish, and vegetables benefit from a little basting—you can use your marinade or some stock mixed with a little fruit juice. Long-cooking authentic Southern BBQ-style meats are "mopped" with a basting sauce for many hours. Steaks and chops under 2 inches (5 cm) thick should not be basted or you defeat the searing process and end up with meat that has a "poached" texture. (Back! Back! all you enraged experts!)

### Watch Out!

Vegetables and tofu taste absolutely wonderful grilled. In fact, it's the cooking method of choice for eggplant and zucchini in Brigit's household. But vegetables have no fat of their own and will quickly scorch and burn if not sprayed or brushed with at least a light film of oil before grilling. A little goes a long way, so don't worry about fat grams, just flavour. Mix some olive oil with a little minced garlic, some dried oregano, salt, and pepper. Brush each slice of vegetable or tofu just before it goes on the grill, and again when you flip them over.

## Table 10.1: Foods Suitable for Direct and Indirect Grilling

| Food | Direct | Indirect |
|---|---|---|
| **Beef (visible fat removed after cooking):** | | |
| sirloin, T-bone, porterhouse, strip, rib-eye | X | |
| filet | | X |
| flank and skirt | X | |
| prime rib | | X |
| lean hamburgers | X | |
| short ribs | X | |
| brisket (marinate) | | X |
| **Pork (visible fat removed after cooking):** | | |
| sausage | | X |
| chops | X | |
| whole rolled or bone-in loin | | X |
| tenderloin, medallions | X | |
| tenderloin, whole | | X |
| **Lamb:** | | |
| neck and loin chops | X | |
| leg steaks | X | |
| whole or butterflied leg or saddle | | X |
| **Poultry (all skin removed after cooking):** | | |
| chicken pieces | X | X |
| turkey breast | | X |
| whole game hens | | X |
| duck | | X |
| **Fish (skin and visible fat removed after cooking):** | | |
| lobster | X | |
| shrimp | X | |
| clams | X | |
| oysters | X | |
| mussels | X | |
| whole fish | | X |
| fish steaks, skin on | X | |
| fish fillets | X | X |
| fish skewers | X | |

| Food | Direct | Indirect |
|---|---|---|
| **Vegetables:** | | |
| zucchini, $^1/_2$-inch (1-cm) slices | X | |
| eggplant, $^1/_2$-inch (1-cm) slices | X | |
| whole bell peppers, stemmed and seeded | | X |
| firm tofu, drained | X | |
| corn, silk removed and husk tied back in place | | X |
| small potatoes, in foil packet | X | |

**Toothsome Tips**

The "Touch Test" is how the experts judge when meat is cooked: To get started, first judge the temperature or doneness by eye, then familiarize yourself with how the food feels at certain stages of doneness. With your index finger, press down hard on the surface: rare meat will be soft and yielding, medium-rare meat will be slightly springy, well-done meat will be quite firm. Get to know these feelings and the next time you won't need to cut into the meat or use a thermometer to judge when it's done.

# When Is It Done?

One of the biggest dangers when grilling, especially lowfat grilling, is overcooking the food. Surely there's nothing more disappointing than overcooked food, for your family, or, worse, for a larger gathering. You've been to a barbecue where the host overcooked the meat; there's a palpable but unspoken sense of dismay, of embarrassment among the guests. Conversation ceases briefly, while all search for something encouraging to say—or for more A-1 sauce. If you are the host in question, you want to shrink into the stucco and disappear. There is no remedy, only the assurance that it never happens again.

With a practiced eye and a good dependable timer, you can take the guesswork out of grilling, but for serious grillers there's nothing like the instant-read thermometer, particularly when cooking larger cuts over indirect heat.

Wrangling over the correct internal cooked temperature of meat and fowl is a major food issue, right up there with discussing the perfect potato gratin with a French chef. In the old days, when trichinosis was rampant in the pork population, we were advised to cook pork to an internal temperature of 180°F (82°C). To today's tastes that seems like sawdust. The Canadian Pork Council now recommends 160°F (71°C), thank goodness, and many esteemed and widely published grilling experts claim that 145°F (63°C) is fine. Trichinosis is now absent from 90 percent of the pork population, because pigs no longer root in garbage. Be sure to take the thermometer reading toward the centre of the cut but not touching any bones, which will throw off the reading. All cuts of meat and fowl continue cooking after they have been removed from the heat; the larger cuts continue cooking longer. So be sure to take the meat off the heat when it is a few degrees below optimum. If you don't trust your thermometer, make a little cut near the bone with a small, sharp knife and look at the meat yourself, remembering that it will cook a little more during the required resting period. Do try to avoid this method as you get more confident, because it wastes precious juices.

## Table 10.2: Interior Temperatures for Cooked Foods

Since the rise of food-borne bacteria like *E. coli* and campylobacter, health officials recommend cooking all meats well done, even though it is less than ideal from the point of view of taste and texture. Certainly, it is necessary when cooking for anyone whose immune system is compromised, for the very young, the elderly, and for pregnant women.

**Beef:**

Health Canada recommends an internal temperature of 145°F (63°C) for roast beef and 160°F (71°C) for ground meat or smaller cuts.

rare: 115°F to 120°F (46°C to 48°C)

medium-rare: 130°F to 135°F (54°C to 57°C)

medium: 140F° to 145°F (60°C to 63°C)

medium-well: 150F° to 155°F (65°C to 68°C)

well-done: 160F° to 170°F (71°C to 77°C)

**Lamb:**

rare: 140°F (60°C)

**Pork:**

done: 160°F (71°C)

**Poultry:**

Health Canada recommends an internal temperature of 180°F to 185°F (82°C to 85°C) in the thickest part of the bird.

breast: 150°F (65°C)

thigh: 165°F (74°C)

# It's Not Tired, So Why Does It Need to Rest?

Almost any good grilling or roasting recipe will specify a resting period for meat and fowl, anywhere from 5 minutes for thin cuts like steaks and chops to 20 minutes for a turkey or a prime rib. This resting time allows the juices to penetrate slowly back toward the centre of the meat so they are not lost to the cutting board when you carve. You can tent the food with aluminum foil while it's resting to prevent it from cooling off too much, and in fact this is highly advisable when you remove skin from poultry and fish, as it might tend to dry out while it rests.

# Meat: Choosing the Right Cuts for a Lowfat Meal

Fish, poultry, and vegetables don't present much of a problem for the lowfat cook, but meat is another story. Flank steak is, of course, one of the all-time great lowfat cuts for grilling, and because of its dense texture it does not dry out. Compare the recommended portion of $3^1/_2$ ounces (105 g) of cooked flank steak (10.1 fat g) with an equal-size portion of beef short ribs (18.1 fat g). Use the chart below to plan your fat intake for the day and remember to average it over the day or a few days. If you choose the cuts carefully, pork can be a good alternative to red meat. After all, pork producers are trying hard to gain a name as "The Other White Meat," and if you consider a $3^1/_2$-ounce (105-g) portion of pork tenderloin at 4.8 fat grams, you can see that they may be onto something.

## Table 10.3: Fat Content of Commonly Grilled Meats (all visible fat trimmed after cooking)

| Meat ($3^1/_2$ ounces/105 g) | Fat Grams |
| --- | --- |
| **Beef:** | |
| brisket | 12.8 |
| flank | 10.1 |
| lean ground beef | 18.5 |
| extra-lean ground beef | 16.3 |
| rib-eye | 11.7 |
| beef shortribs | 18.1 |
| porterhouse | 11.5 |
| T-bone | 10.1 |
| filet | 11.2 |
| sirloin | 8.0 |
| **Lamb:** | |
| blade steaks | 19.9 |
| leg and leg steaks | 9.2 |

| Meat (3$^1$/$_2$ ounces/105 g) | Fat Grams |
| --- | --- |
| loin chop | 9.7 |
| rib chop | 12.9 |
| **Pork:** | |
| centre cut loin chops | 8.1 |
| blade loin chops | 13.9 |
| rib chops | 10.1 |
| whole loin | 9.6 |
| sirloin chops | 6.7 |
| spareribs | 21.5 |
| tenderloin (whole and medallions) | 4.8 |

## Grilled Asparagus with Lemon Dressing

Serves 4

*If you place the asparagus perpendicular to the grill bars, they're less likely to fall through. This dish is spectacular with grilled fish. Peeling the bottom of the stalks means lots less waste, even cooking, and a nicer appearance.*

1$^1$/$_4$ pounds (625 g) large asparagus
Vegetable cooking spray
$^1$/$_2$ teaspoon (2 mL) salt
$^1$/$_2$ teaspoon (1 mL) freshly ground black pepper
3 tablespoons (40 mL) fresh lemon juice

1 medium shallot or 3 scallions (white and light green parts), minced
1 tablespoon (15 mL) lowfat chicken broth
1 tablespoon (15 mL) extra virgin olive oil
2 tablespoons (25 mL) finely chopped fresh parsley leaves

1. Snap off the woody ends of the asparagus (most spears will break about an inch (2.5 cm) or so from the bottom). With a vegetable peeler, peel the bottom 2 inches (5 cm) of the stalk.

2. Meanwhile, prepare a charcoal fire for medium-high heat grilling or heat a gas grill. If you're cooking indoors, heat a ridged cast-iron griddle pan over medium heat until it's very hot.

3. Place the asparagus spears in one layer on a work surface and spray them lightly with the vegetable spray. Roll over half a turn and spray again. Season well with the salt and pepper. Grill until tender and browned in spots, turning once or twice, 8 to 10 minutes total.

4. Mix together the lemon juice and shallots, then stir in the chicken broth and olive oil. The mixture will be quite tart. Stir in the parsley and spoon over the asparagus. Serve hot or at room temperature.

**Nutrition:**

Calories: 70.4

Protein: 3.5 g

Carbohydrates: 8.49 g

Fibre: 3.17 g

Total Fat: 3.76 g

 Sat: .547 g

 Mono: 2.52 g

 Poly: .439 g

Cholesterol: .078 mg

Vitamin A: 92.6 mg RE

Vitamin B6: .21 mg

Vitamin B12: 0 mcg

Vitamin C: 26.9 mg

Calcium: 35.8 mg

Iron: 1.47 mg

Potassium: 430 mg

Sodium: 287 mg

Zinc: .702 mg

## The Least You Need to Know

➤ The ideal equipment for grilling is a covered kettle grill, but you can make gas grills work almost as well. Open grills are fine for direct-heat grilling.

➤ Indoor cooks can take advantage of cast-iron stovetop griddles, which are capable of achieving the high heat necessary for grilling but tend to smoke a little, so open a window.

➤ The two main types of grilling are direct (cooking the food right above a high heat source), which is good for smaller, more tender cuts, and indirect (cooking the food near but not directly over a medium heat source), which is good for larger cuts, whole poultry, and whole fish.

➤ The lowfat cook has many options when grilling, but a small amount of fat is always necessary to prevent drying out the food. For this reason, skin and visible fat are removed after grilling, and vegetables to be grilled must first be basted with a small amount of oil.

# Chapter 11

# Redolent Roasting: From Pork to Parsnips, This Is Wintertime Food

---

### In This Chapter

➤ Help! My kitchen has an oven!

➤ Make your oven work for you

➤ A tomato for all seasons

➤ A complete vegetable-roasting guide

➤ Simple roast chicken

---

Ovens are often seen as the least exciting piece of equipment in the kitchen, overlooked, dull, just *there*. Now that we have the microwave we don't use our oven to reheat leftovers, and frozen dinners are quicker in the microwave, too. Sure, you need your oven for turkey at Thanksgiving and later that week for your famous Turkey Tetrazzini, but how often do you use it the rest of the year? We're cutting down on red meat these days, anyway. If you're a baker, maybe you make cookies, but on a lowfat diet that kind of thing is somewhat, well, indulgent, isn't it?

You are simply not giving your oven a chance. Your new ridged cast-iron griddle pan may be sexier, your food processor may be more high-tech, and your microwave may be a life-saver you can't imagine going without—but can a ridged griddle pan make sweet and succulent roasted carrots? Can your food processor turn out juicy roasted tomatoes for pasta, omelettes, and pizza? And have you *ever* seen your microwave turn anything a deep, golden brown?

Roasting in your oven is a joyous art, by no means just for meat and poultry. It takes no advance preparation like marinating and requires minimal chopping and attention during the short cooking time. Best of all, most ingredients require little added oil or fat (sometimes none) to become crisp-on-the-outside, tender-on-the-inside, healthy, and delicious food.

# What Is Roasting, Anyway? And What's a Pot Roast?

The term comes from the original method of roasting first used around an open fire: spit-roasting. Those same ancestors (or maybe their grandchildren) who, in the last chapter, learned that food tasted better grilled over an open flame than it did raw later realized that for larger pieces of meat (they weren't into cooking their vegetables back then), a more tender result could be obtained by turning the meat slowly on a spit in front of a fire. That way, the heat penetrated equally from all sides, instead of burning the side facing the fire, leaving the other side raw and the centre uncooked.

A pot roast is not actually roasted, it's braised, and we'll touch on it in the braising chapter. Pot roast is notoriously difficult to do well and the Italians have a much better version called Beef in Barolo.

# What's the Difference Between Roasting and Baking?

The difference is largely a matter of usage (when has anyone ever "baked" a prime rib or "roasted" a cherry pie?). Inside an oven, hot air circulates around the food, bathing it in penetrating heat from all sides, just like what happened in front of an open fire on a spit, only less messy and with no elbow grease. In roasting, the food is almost always uncovered, unless certain parts are in danger of overcooking, in which case they may be covered with foil (like poultry feet or wing tips, and fish tails).

When roasting anything other than large cuts of meat, it's important to spread the food evenly in one layer in the pan, without the pieces touching one other. This is the only way to insure optimum browning and crisping. Overcrowded or layered foods produce steam, which can cause the food to poach instead of roast, giving a pale, limp, and insipid result.

There's another cooking method that takes place in an oven: braising. Braising is defined by the liquid that is added to the food while it cooks—it is a slow, gentle method suitable for tough cuts of meat and some of the firmer vegetables and fish. For a full explanation of this method, see Chapter 12. During roasting, you may baste the food occasionally to keep it from drying out, but only a small amount of liquid or oil is used. The pan should be almost dry to promote the lovely browning and crisping that is characteristic of roasted food.

# So, Now What Kind of Equipment Do I Need to Buy?

Presumably, you already have an oven, so you're about 95 percent of the way there already. One item you'll want to find is a heavy-duty roasting pan. A thin aluminum pan just won't do, because the metal won't pick up enough heat to brown the food. Glass baking dishes will do, but won't provide the same results. One exception: when roasting delicate foods like tomatoes, eggplant, onions, mushrooms, finned fish, and fruits, glass or ceramic baking dishes are fine. But for meat, poultry, and firm vegetables like potatoes, carrots (roasted carrots are one of the world's all-time greatest flavours), winter squash, and parsnips you'll obtain far superior results with heavy cast-aluminum, copper, or thick stainless roasting pans. If in doubt, choose the largest size you can afford, because the cardinal rule for successful roasting is Don't Crowd the Pan!

# What Can I Roast?

Most people are familiar with roasting meat and poultry, and it's certainly a great method that produces succulent results. But for the lowfat cook, what's more important are the delectable results you can get when roasting vegetables and fish. Smaller than the usual cuts of meat, fish and vegetables don't take long to cook and so can be real time-savers in the kitchen. Roasting them leaves you and your stove top free to produce another dish or two, or you can just relax while the oven does all the work. Vegetables do benefit from being turned now and then, however.

Be sure to use really fresh ingredients when roasting, because they're not disguised in any way: what you see is what you get. A tough, dried-out potato will not improve after roasting, so faced with such a choice it's probably better to boil and mash it. Roasting uses high heat, so it can easily dry out and toughen an ingredient that is not at its best.

### What's the Skinny?

Convection ovens are touted as the next must-have piece of kitchen equipment, and some of the enthusiasm is justified. These ovens contain a fan that circulates the heat evenly within the entire area of the oven. If you've ever had the cookies on the bottom shelf burn before the cookies on the top shelf were done, you'll know why this item was invented. Sure, you can move the cookies back and forth, but wouldn't it be easier just to close the oven and set the timer? Convection ovens cook faster than normal ovens by about 20 percent, so if you have one and you didn't read the instructions you may be overcooking your food. Do you really need one? No, but they do make a super-crisp roasted potato, and Brigit loves hers.

# How Long Does it Take?

Because we generally roast at high heat, the cooking time is very important in roasting. Fish and vegetables do vary in size, so I've given only general guidelines. Use the tip of a sharp knife to test the food when it gets close to the end of the estimated cooking time. When vegetables are tender and fish is opaque—they're done. Be sure to follow all the universal points listed below.

# A Guide to Successful Vegetable Roasting

➤ Some smaller or tougher vegetables should be blanched first before roasting, to stop them from scorching. Simply plunge the trimmed vegetable into salted boiling water and cook until not quite tender, then drain and pat dry with paper towels.

➤ Give vegetables a light film of oil before roasting. Use an olive oil spray or toss thoroughly in a bowl with a small amount of oil, again preferably olive.

➤ All vegetables should be generously seasoned with salt and pepper before roasting.

➤ Shake the pan halfway through the roasting time to redistribute the vegetables and encourage them to brown evenly, or if large, turn them over so the other side touches the hot pan, making a crisp, golden crust.

➤ When adding minced garlic to roasting vegetables, add it only during the last 2 or 3 minutes of cooking time, otherwise it will scorch and produce an acrid, unpleasant smell.

➤ If vegetables seem dry after cooking, drizzle with a little vinegar, stock, soy sauce, or lemon, orange, or other fruit juice.

## Table 11.1: Vegetable Roasting Times and Temperatures

| Food and special preparation | Heat | Minutes |
|---|---|---|
| Asparagus (blanch first for 4 minutes and dry, film with oil) | 450°F (230°C) | 10 |
| Green Beans (blanch first for 3 minutes and dry, film with oil) | 450°F (230°C) | 8 |
| Bell Peppers (core, seed, and quarter lengthwise, oil the pan only) | 450°F (230°C) | 15 |
| Beets (trim tops, film with oil) | 450°F (230°C) | 15–30 |
| Broccoli (peel stems, halve lengthwise so no part is wider than about 2 inches/5 cm; film with oil) | 450°F (230°C) | 15 |
| Brussels Sprouts (Blanch first for 5 minutes and dry, halve, film with oil, roast cut side down) | 375°F (190°C) | 20 |
| Cauliflower (cut into large florets, film with oil, add 2 tbsp/30 mL water to pan) | 400°F (200°C) | 25 |
| Corn (fresh kernels; add to pan with other vegetables like broccoli or peppers for last 5 minutes cooking time) | | |
| Eggplant (whole, pricked; drain and peel) | 400°F (200°C) | 60 |
| Eggplant (1/2-inch/1-cm slices; film with oil; turn over halfway) | 450°F (230°C) | 20 |
| Fennel (blanch first for 10 minutes, slice lengthwise through core 1/4-inch/5-mm thick, film very lightly with oil) | 400°F (200°C) | 30 |
| Green Cabbage (quarter, core, and cut into 1/2-inch/1-cm strips; drizzle with a small amount of oil and toss) | 500°F (260°C) | 15 |
| Onions (medium, root ends trimmed but skins left on; halve and remove skin to serve) | 375°F (190°C) | 75–90 |
| Parsnips (peel and cut into 1/2-inch/1-cm cubes, film lightly with oil) | 375°F (190°C) | 30–40 |
| Boiling-Style Potatoes (golf-ball sized, peeled or unpeeled; film with oil, turn over halfway, add chopped rosemary and garlic for last 5 minutes) | 450°F (230°C) | 40 |
| Baking-Style Potatoes (1/2-inch/1-cm slices in single layer, peeled or unpeeled; film with oil, turn halfway through) | 450°F (230°C) | 25 |
| Shallots (small, peeled and trimmed; film with oil) | 450°F (230°C) | 20 |
| Winter Squash (1 1/2 pounds/750 grams, pricked; trim base flat, halve and discard seeds, film cut surface with oil) | 450°F (230°C) | 40–45 |
| Zucchini (cut in 2-inch/5-cm chunks, lightly film with oil) | 450°F (230°C) | 20 |

# Roasted Garlic: An Indispensable Ingredient in the Lowfat Kitchen

Roasted garlic is less a vegetable than a seasoning, especially in the lowfat kitchen. The uses are endless, the fat is minimal, and the flavour is spectacular, so it's worth making a double or even triple batch. To keep roasted garlic, press the pulp out of the skins into a bowl and mash to a purée with a fork. Transfer to a small jar and shake to level the top. Film the top very lightly with olive oil to retard spoilage by stopping oxygen from getting to the purée. Refrigerate and, when ready to use, discard the oil. If you don't use it all, film again with fresh oil. It will stay good for up to 1 week. You can use roasted garlic:

➤ to thicken lowfat or nonfat sauces and salad dressings

➤ as a spread on crackers or bread

➤ stirred into hot soup for added flavour and body

➤ as a filling for stuffed mushrooms, and topping for homemade pizza (page 199)

## Roasted Garlic

1. Choose 4 large, firm heads of garlic that have not sprouted (sprouted garlic is difficult to digest and is past its prime).

2. Preheat the oven to 325°F (165°C). With a sharp knife, cut off the top $1/3$ of each head horizontally, exposing a cross-section of most of the cloves. Pull away the excess papery skin but don't peel the head completely.

3. Place in a medium baking dish and pour in enough lowfat chicken stock to come $1/3$ of the way up the heads. Drizzle evenly with 1 tablespoon (15 mL) olive oil and 1 tablespoon (15 mL) more of the stock. Season with salt and pepper.

4. Cover with foil and roast for about 1 hour, or until the pulp is softened. Squeeze the heads with the side of a large knife to extract the garlic pulp. Mash to a smooth purée if desired, and serve warm or cool.

**Nutrition:**

| | |
|---|---|
| Calories: 121 | Vitamin A: .025 mg RE |
| Protein: 3.64 g | Vitamin B6: .634 mg |
| Carbohydrates: 17 g | Vitamin B12: 0 mcg |
| Fibre: 1.1 g | Vitamin C: 15.9 mg |
| Total Fat: 5.13 g | Calcium: 92.9 mg |
| Sat: .878 g | Iron: .918 mg |
| Mono: 3.05 g | Potassium: 217 mg |
| Poly: .786 g | Sodium: 517 mg |
| Cholesterol: 1.88 mg | Zinc: .6 mg |

## What's So Special About Roasted Carrots?

There's something so rich and luscious about roasted carrots—they're almost like a dessert. Root vegetables like carrots, onions, and parsnips have more natural sugar than other vegetables, and when roasted at high heat these sugars caramelize into a sweet, golden crust on the outside.

Carrots take longer to roast than most vegetables because they are so dense and firm, so the heat must be turned down to avoid burning the outside before the centre is tender. Whole carrots can be roasted as follows: for 3 ounces (90 g) carrots, toss them with a little olive oil to film lightly, and season with salt only.

Roast in a baking dish in a single layer at 450°F (230°C) for 10 minutes, then reduce heat to 350°F (180°C) and roast for 50 minutes more, tossing halfway through and seasoning with pepper 10 minutes before they're done.

We prefer to roast chunks of carrot, however, since there is more exterior surface that's exposed to the heat. This means more of that delicious caramelized crust. Roast as for whole carrots, reducing the cooking time by 10 to 15 minutes. If you have a sprig of fresh thyme, throw it into the pan with the carrots and discard afterwards. Try drizzling the carrots with $^1/_2$ teaspoon (10 mL) of Pernod or other anise-flavoured liqueur just before serving.

### Watch Out!

Many vegetables can be roasted whole, such as eggplant, winter squash, onions, potatoes, parsnips, and carrots. It's a quick and convenient cooking method, but be careful! Vegetables with an outer skin, like eggplant and squash, must be pricked in several places, or the buildup of steam inside may cause the vegetable to explode. Other vegetables that are roasted whole (like onions and potatoes) generally need some kind of protective liquid or oil coating to keep them from drying out, though only the thinnest film is required. Vegetable or olive oil sprays are excellent for this purpose, since one spray is equal to less than $^1/_4$ teaspoon (1 mL) of oil.

## A Tomato for All Seasons

Use your oven to work for you while you're doing chores, taking a nap, or trying on outfits for tonight's party. These tomatoes are a great basic, and can be used as a topping for toasted bread, cooked rice, or pasta, or even cottage cheese for a lowfat lunch. You can make them into a sauce, add them to a salad, or even purée them into a salad dressing. No one will believe you made them yourself!

**119**

## Oven-Roasted Tomatoes

8 portions

1¹/₂ pounds (750 g) plum tomatoes, stem ends removed, halved, and seeds scraped out
Olive oil spray

¹/₄ teaspoon (1 mL) salt
¹/₄ teaspoon (1 mL) freshly ground black pepper

1. Preheat the oven to 200°F (93°C). Spray a baking sheet with a light film of olive oil and lay the tomatoes on it in a single layer, cut side up.

2. Sprinkle them with half the salt and pepper, then turn cut side down. Spray the tops of the tomatoes very lightly and sprinkle with the remaining salt and pepper.

3. Roast for 4 hours, regulating the heat, if necessary, so that it doesn't get so hot that the tomatoes burn. The tomatoes are done when they are shrunken, dehydrated, and shrivelled on top but still quite juicy underneath. Cool on the baking sheet and wrap with plastic wrap until needed.

### Nutrition:

Calories: 46

Protein: 1.46 g

Carbohydrates: 8 g

Fibre: 1.78 g

Total Fat: 1.69 g
  Sat: .230 g
  Mono: .916 g
  Poly: .325 g

Cholesterol: 0 mg

Vitamin A: 106 mg RE

Vitamin B6: .136 mg

Vitamin B12: 0 mcg

Vitamin C: 32.5 mg

Calcium: 9.17 mg

Iron: .809 mg

Potassium: 380 mg

Sodium: 149 mg

Zinc: .156 mg

### Toothsome Tips

Here's an easy, nonfat sauce for roasted fish, poultry, or vegetables: mix 1 teaspoon (5 mL) powdered mustard with 1 teaspoon (5 mL) water until smooth, and let sit for 10 minutes. Thoroughly whisk in 1 tablespoon (15 mL) Japanese white miso paste. Stir in 2 tablespoons (30 mL) minced scallion, 1 tablespoon (15 mL) each of fresh lemon juice and rice vinegar, and 2 teaspoons (10 mL) soy sauce. Use on roasted whitefish, skinless chicken pieces, roasted carrots, eggplant, and winter squash.

# What About Roasting Fish?

Yes, roasting is a superb choice for whole fish. It's relatively foolproof and smellproof—no one will know you're cooking fish until you bring it to the table. Timing is easy: just use the universal fish-cooking rule of 10 minutes per inch (2.5 cm) of thickness. Unlike vegetables, fish skin has its own oil so it will not dry out during roasting and there's no need to film with oil before roasting. And you don't lose precious nutrients into the cooking liquid as you do in poaching.

## Whole Firm-Fleshed Fish

Make sure the fish is scaled and gutted, and rinse the inside under cool running water to get rid of any blood left behind. Season inside and out with salt and pepper and inside the fish place some thinly sliced lemon, fresh ginger, or scallions and a few sprigs of thyme, parsley, or marjoram. Place the fish on a flat surface and measure its thickest point with a ruler.

Make a shallow slash in the skin in two or three places, then place in a pan large enough so the fish can lie flat (often easier if the fish lies at a diagonal). If you can fit more than one fish flat in the pan, go ahead—the cooking time is based on the thickness rather than the weight of the fish.

Roast at 400°F (200°C) for 10 minutes per inch (2.5 cm) of thickness (say, 25 minutes for a 2$\frac{1}{2}$-inch/6-cm thick fish). This method will work for any firm, white-fleshed, fresh, or salt-water fish except bluefish and mackerel, which will take slightly less time due to their delicate flesh.

**Toothsome Tips**

When roasting fish you can add any number of aromatic vegetables, herbs, spices, and Asian condiments to the inside of the fish, all fat-free. Whatever is inside will perfume the fish subtly and then be discarded before eating. Try one or two of the following, mixing and matching according to flavours and season: sliced orange, lemon, or lime; peeled and sliced ginger or garlic; Thai fish sauce, soy sauce, rice vinegar, or mirin; sprigs of fresh parsley, thyme, chervil, mint, marjoram, or basil; sliced scallions or lemongrass; bay leaves; sliced olives.

## Whole Soft-Fleshed Fish

For bluefish, mackerel, and other soft fish, use the same basic method as above but reduce the cooking time by about 20 percent. Check the flesh near the bone by probing

**121**

### Tidbits!

Cooking chicken in separate pieces is popular because it's almost impossible to get chicken breast and thighs done at the same time while they're still attached to the same bird. This is because chicken breast is done and begins to dry out anywhere from 5 to 15 minutes before the thighs are safely cooked through. An evenly roasted chicken is an eternal quest for many people. We may not have the definitive answer, but there are some steps you can take to help, according to food-science guru Harold McGee:

1. Don't truss the chicken; leaving the legs splayed out encourages them to cook more quickly.

2. Place the chicken in the oven with the legs toward the rear, which stays hotter and thus cooks the legs more quickly.

3. Invest in a good meat thermometer.

4. Remove the chicken as soon as the thigh meat near the bone reaches 165°F (74°C) (don't touch the bone with the thermometer as it'll throw off the reading).

Note: Health Canada recommends an internal temperature of 180°F to 185°F (82°C to 85°C) for poultry.

with a small, sharp knife: if it looks opaque it's done. Don't overcook these fish or they can be mushy and bland. Use acid flavourings like lemon juice and vinegar to balance the slight oiliness and stronger flavours of soft-fleshed fish.

# What About Poultry?

Roast chicken, roast turkey, duck, goose—yes, they are delicious, but sadly they don't roast well without their skin, which is full of fat. If you are going to roast poultry, use your favourite recipe without any added fat in the form of basting, and for goodness sake leave the skin on during the cooking time. Let the bird rest for 5 minutes, then remove and discard the skin. This will keep the flesh much juicier than roasting the poor naked thing without its skin, which many lowfat cookbooks recommend. We just don't agree, because the skin acts as a protective layer to stop the meat from drying out during cooking.

Be sure to rinse the bird with cool water and pat dry, and place on a roasting rack to keep the bird from resting in the rendered fat, which you will discard.

Roast poultry at 350°F (180°C) in a preheated oven and allow 20 minutes per pound (500 g) for unstuffed birds that are at room temperature before they go in the oven.

To render out even more fat, you can roast at 450°F (230°C), but it's a smoky process so be sure to crack open the window or you'll be explaining the smoke to the patient firefighter knocking at the door in response to your smoke alarm (this has happened to Brigit). Here's a recipe for high-heat roast chicken for those of you who can't live without a roast chicken every once in awhile.

## Easy Roast Chicken

Serves 5

3-pound (1.5 kg) roasting chicken
2 lemons, halved
2 tablespoons (30 mL) chopped parsley
1 teaspoon (5 mL) dried oregano, crumbled
$1/4$ teaspoon (1 mL) salt
$1/2$ teaspoon (2 mL) freshly ground black pepper
1 clove garlic, finely chopped

1. Preheat the oven to 450°F (230°C). Rinse the chicken under cool running water inside and out, and pat dry with paper towels. Place the chicken on a rack in a roasting pan and place two lemon halves inside the cavity. Place the other two halves in the pan. Combine 1 tablespoon (5 mL) of the parsley, the oregano, salt, pepper, and garlic, and push this mixture up under the skin covering the breasts.

2. Place the pan in the hot oven with the legs toward the rear (they'll cook faster). Roast for 45 to 50 minutes, or until the juices from the thigh run clear and the internal temperature is 170°F (77°C).

3. Let the chicken sit, loosely tented with foil, for 5 minutes, then remove the skin and squeeze the lemon from the roasting pan all over the chicken. Sprinkle with the remaining parsley. Carve, and serve.

**Nutrition:**

Calories: 335

Protein: 58.7 g

Carbohydrates: 2.96 g

Fibre: .989 g

Total Fat: 8.55 g
  Sat: 2.16 g
  Mono: 2.46 g
  Poly: 2.07 g

Cholesterol: 190 mg

Vitamin A: 52 mg RE

Vitamin B6: 1.19 mg

Vitamin B12: 1 mcg

Vitamin C: 20.7 mg

Calcium: 49.6 mg

Iron: 2.82 mg

Potassium: 668 mg

Sodium: 317 mg

Zinc: 4.26 mg

## The Least You Need to Know

➤ Roasting is one of the simplest ways to cook. It requires little advance preparation or attention during cooking.

➤ Roasted foods need little extra fat to become crisp-on-the-outside, tender-on-the-inside, healthy, and delicious food.

➤ Roasting is for more than meat and poultry. You can get delectable results from roasting vegetables and fish.

➤ Roasted garlic is an indispensable ingredient in the lowfat kitchen.

# Chapter 12

# The Beauties of Braising: A Long, Slow, and Tender Method

**In This Chapter**

➤ If it happens in the oven, why isn't it "roasting"?

➤ Trimming and skimming: The lowfat solution

➤ Cheaper means better

➤ Using stock to add flavour

To braise food, you must cook it for a long time at a low heat, always with some liquid in the pan, and always covered. It's a method that has long been used for tough, fatty cuts of meat, and it's a great way to coax rich, succulent flavour and juices out of a less expensive ingredient. The fat in the meat keeps it moist during the long cooking time, and the tough sinews melt down into a lovely, gelatinous natural gravy.

In fact, the mysterious pot roast is actually a braised dish. Meat or fowl is often browned in a pan first before it's added to the braising liquid, and this extra step insures not only extra flavour but an attractive, golden colour as well.

Braised dishes traditionally taste better after a day in the refrigerator, because the flavours "marry" during the overnight rest. Another benefit of spending the night in the fridge is that all the pesky fat that kept the meat moist while it was cooking will conveniently rise to the top and form a white, waxy layer, and every bit of it can be removed. This means braising can be a naturally lowfat method of cooking meat (as long as you trim carefully, then chill and skim off all the fat).

You can braise chicken, of course. In general, the larger, older birds that might be tough if roasted are used for braising. A young chicken is prone to fall apart if braised, but the extra bone mass of an older bird provides lots of lovely gelatin to give body to the

### Tidbits!

Roasting and braising are usually used for very different ingredients: roasting for tender, prime meats, fowl, fish, and vegetables; braising for tougher, more muscular cuts of meat and birds. The exception to the rule is some of the firm vegetables, like fennel and celery, which can be roasted (but only if blanched in boiling water first) *or* braised. During braising, no vitamins are lost to the water, and a flavourful liquid like stock or wine enhances the natural flavours of the vegetable. It's a good choice for vegetables that are slightly over the hill, since their appearance will be wilted anyway, and masked with braising liquid.

juices. There are also some firm vegetables that take extremely well to this gentle method of cooking. Even certain large pieces of fish can be braised, like a big piece of centre-cut tuna—though this may not be to our contemporary taste. We once heard braising referred to as "a shortcut to getting a dish and a sauce at the same time."

# What's the Difference Between Roasting and Braising?

Braising is a completely different cooking method from roasting, and that's why it's used for such different types of ingredients. Roasting takes place quickly at a high oven temperature (usually 350° to 450°F/180°C to 230°C), in a dry, open pan. Braising takes place at a much lower temperature, usually around 325°F (165°C), in a closed pan with some liquid, and for a much longer time. If you're in a hurry, you're likely to want to roast, but don't forget you'll need prime, tender ingredients, which are usually more expensive. Braising is the perfect choice if you have more time and less cash—plus there is the benefit of an instant lowfat sauce.

## Can I Braise on the Stove Top?

Braising over a burner is fine, provided you have two essential pieces of equipment. Otherwise you will be unable to keep the heat low enough, the braising liquid will boil away, and your food will scorch or toughen. For stovetop braising you'll need:

1. Either a burner that can be turned down to the barest flicker of heat, or a "heat-cheater" or "flame-tamer" pad that can be placed over the burner to defeat some of its intense heat.

2. A heavy pot with a tight cover, made from either enamel-covered cast iron (this is what Le Creuset et al. are made from) or tin-lined copper. Bare cast iron is not suitable because the liquid you use may have a touch of acidity (wine, fruit juice), and over a long period in contact with unlined cast iron this can produce a chemical reaction that creates an "off" flavour. To make sure the cover is tight-fitting and no steam escapes, you can line the lid with aluminum foil.

# What Can I Braise?

Beef: tough, sinewy cuts from the active part of the animal; leg, shoulder, or neck, i.e., top or bottom round, eye of round, brisket (flat cut), chuck, stuffed flank

Lamb: shanks, shoulder

Pork: shoulder (butt is best)

Poultry: roasting chickens; duck; turkey legs and thighs; larger, more mature chickens; guinea hens, pheasant, and other game birds

Vegetables: Belgian endive, broccoli, cabbage, carrots, celery, fennel, turnips, rutabaga

# Browning First for More Flavour

Meat and poultry are often browned first before they go into braising mode, but vegetables are not. In fact, one of the best braised dishes we know is a head of fennel, which is braised in stock with the usual aromatics (bay leaves; a few slices of onion, carrot, and celery; and parsley) until almost tender, *then* browned very briefly on a hot grill. For the lowfat cook, browning should take place with a teaspoon (5 mL) of oil, if any, in a nonstick pan. Otherwise, too much oil will be added to the final dish, and braising loses its usefulness as a lowfat cooking method.

**Tidbits!**

The French (who of course have elevated every aspect of cooking to the level of intense craftsmanship) use a substance called *repére* to seal lids onto pans during a long braise. This is simply a paste made from some flour and just enough water to produce a gluey substance that will remind home handy-persons of wallpaper paste (try $3/4$ cup/175 mL flour to $1/3$ cup/75 mL water). This is rolled into a long snakelike tube and pressed around the rim of the pan just before it goes into the oven. The lid is pressed firmly down onto the paste, forming an airtight seal (if your pan lid has a small vent-hole in it, you'll need to plug that as well). This method produces incredibly tender results, so try it if you dare but be prepared to use substantial strength to break the paste at the end of the cooking time!

# Choice of Braising Liquid Can Make or Break the Dish

If you're in a rush and you have some aromatic vegetables like carrots, onions, celery, and garlic, you can add a few slices of each to lightly salted water and use that as the braising liquid, removing the aromatics at the end. See the recipe for Double-Strength Chicken Broth on the next page and simply add the same quantities of vegetables and spices to salted water, then braise away. But the flavour will be vastly enhanced if you choose a highly flavoured stock, red or white wine, or a mixture of both.

## Watch Out!

When the lowfat cook braises meat, it is absolutely essential that all visible exterior fat be trimmed away. There is enough fat inside to keep the dish moist, and that will be skimmed away after it's been chilled and risen to the top. For instance, a 3¹/₂-ounce (105-g) portion of braised brisket with all the exterior fat trimmed off carries only 6.2 grams of fat. If you leave ¹/₄ inch (¹/₂ cm) of the fat on before cooking and neglect to chill and skim off the fat after cooking, you're looking at a whopping 28¹/₂ grams of fat. (Yikes!) This is the same principle that makes poultry skin a complete no-no for lowfat cooking. It only takes a moment, but it makes a world of difference.

The alcohol in wine will have evaporated long before the dish is ready, and the calories in wine are hardly a factor. And don't feel you must use expensive wine for cooking. Certainly, the dish will be better if you use a decent wine rather than some boxed swill you wouldn't dream of drinking. The French (who love to braise) recommend using the same wine in the pot that you plan to drink at the table, which is reasonable as long as you aren't having an Haut Brion '66. There are some fantastic low-priced wines around right now that would be suitable for both pot and glass.

Stock is another matter. We are fortunate enough to have some excellent fresh, frozen, and canned stocks available, and lowfat, low-sodium chicken broth is a life-saver to the lowfat cook. For a braise, though, you might want to double the strength of the broth, because this is one place it really matters. If you have a big stock pot, double this recipe and freeze the resulting stock in containers (1 pint or 500 mL is a good size)—you'll have a flavour-packed, fat-free resource for the future.

## Double-Strength Chicken Broth

Yield: 5¹/₄ cups (1.3 L)

2 (28-ounce/796-mL) cans lowfat, low-sodium chicken broth
1 carrot, peeled and very coarsely chopped
1 rib celery, with tops, very coarsely chopped
1 small yellow onion, quartered

2 cloves garlic, no need to peel
5 black peppercorns
1 bay leaf
Sprigs of fresh thyme and parsley

1. In a large saucepan, combine all the ingredients and bring to a simmer. Partially cover and simmer very gently for 20 minutes.

2. Remove the lid, increase the heat and bring the stock to a boil. Boil the stock until the volume has reduced by about 25 percent (use a wooden spoon handle to help you estimate).

3. Cool almost to room temperature and strain into a large bowl, pressing down hard on all the vegetables to extract all their liquid and flavour. Discard the vegetables and use the stock or freeze in portions.

Note: Nutritional values below are per cup (250 mL).

**Nutrition:**

Calories: 69.2

Protein: 1.80 g

Carbohydrates: 3.96 g

Fibre: .985 g

Total Fat: 5.27 g
  Sat: 1.30 g
  Mono: 1.93 g
  Poly: 1.31 g

Cholesterol: 6.4 mg

Vitamin A: 389 mg RE

Vitamin B6: .057 mg

Vitamin B12: 0 mcg

Vitamin C: 3.38 mg

Calcium: 18.9 mg

Iron: .266 mg

Potassium: 131 mg

Sodium: 1291 mg

Zinc: .098 mg

# Gee, Isn't This Just Stewing?

No. Stewing is usually meant for small pieces of food, and there is generally much more liquid involved. Of course in a process as "fuzzy" as cooking, there will be some crossover, so if you are a person who requires firm definitions, you're out of luck. For instance, fish stews like bouillabaisse are made on top of the stove; chili con carne, and the *real* chile (beans only) are stews.

As you can see, there's a lot of leeway in names and definitions. For our purposes, braising is the slow cooking of large pieces of food in a small quantity of flavoured liquid. Ratatouille could be defined as a vegetable stew or a vegetable braise, and a lowfat version follows.

# The Importance of Skimming

Braising is only a lowfat option if you "trim and skim," i.e., trim the exterior fat from meat before cooking, then after cooking skim off the fat that has cooked out into the braising liquid. The easiest way to do this is rather time-consuming, but there's a big flavour bonus.

1. Cool the dish to room temperature after the recommended cooking time, then cover and refrigerate, in the original cooking pot if desired.

2. After 3 or 4 hours or overnight, spoon off the fat that will have risen to the surface. (This is from the marbling, or hidden fat inside the meat, which would have been impossible to remove before cooking.) Reheat the dish in a low oven and serve.

Of course, if you are a victim of that national affliction, the "No-Time Syndrome," there is another option, but it's a little more work and there's more washing up to do.

1. When the dish has cooled slightly, transfer the cooked food to a plate with a slotted spoon, leaving all the juices behind.

2. Pour all the juices into a measuring cup or a fat-separator (you should have one—see Equipment on page 160). Let the liquid sit for about 10 minutes, then use a large flat spoon to remove all the fat that has risen to the top.

3. Wipe the original cooking pan with a paper towel to remove the fat that will have filmed the inside, then return the cooked food and the skimmed braising liquid to the original pan, cover, and reheat in a low oven.

# Can I Adapt Recipes from Non-Lowfat Cookbooks?

If you or someone in your family likes to cook, you've probably got some wonderful cookbooks around the house. Just because you've decided to change to a lowfat lifestyle doesn't mean you can't continue to enjoy a classic recipe, or a new find from a "normal" cookbook. Just follow these pointers and don't be afraid to make notes in the cookbook to remind you of the changes you've made. That way, the next time you can be sure to get the same results and not fall back into a high-fat cooking mode!

➤ If the recipe calls for browning in a pan first before braising, use a nonstick pan and don't add more than $1/2$ teaspoon (2 mL) of oil for each serving (i.e., for a dish that serves four, not more than 2 teaspoons/10 mL of oil). That's plenty. Most braising recipes were written for use in conventional pans, and with nonstick only $1/3$ or less of the original amount of oil is required.

➤ Trim all the visible exterior fat from meat, separating it along the lines of the muscle tissue to expose hidden pockets of fat. Remove the skin from poultry.

➤ Use either the "chill and skim" option or the "separate and skim" option as detailed above, making sure to remove all the fat. If the juices from a poultry braise have turned to jelly in the fridge overnight, just scrape the spoon along the top to remove all the white fat. If you have not chilled the dish, it's a good idea to drag a paper towel quickly across just the top surface of the braising liquid to remove the droplets of fat the spoon couldn't get.

## Ratatouille

Serves 4

*Here's a stovetop braise that involves a fair amount of chopping. Choose this flavourful, classic Mediterranean dish on a day when you have an extra helper or two in the kitchen.*

1 small eggplant, cut in $1/4$-inch (5-mm) dice (about 1 pound/500 g)

2 teaspoons (10 mL) kosher salt

2 teaspoons (10 mL) olive oil

$1/2$ medium yellow onion, finely chopped

$1/2$ green bell pepper, cored, seeded, and chopped

$1/2$ red bell pepper, cored, seeded, and chopped

$1/2$ small hot chile (or to taste), cored, seeded, and minced

2 cloves garlic, minced

2 teaspoons (10 mL) dried oregano, crumbled

1 bay leaf

1 small zucchini, chopped

3 plum tomatoes, seeded and chopped

$1/4$ cup (50 mL) plain, bottled tomato sauce or purée

$1/4$ cup (50 mL) lowfat chicken or vegetable broth

1 tablespoon (15 mL) chopped fresh basil

1. Salt the eggplant as described on the next page, rinse, drain, pat dry, and set aside.

2. In a large nonstick saucepan, heat the oil over medium heat and add the onion, peppers, chile, garlic, and oregano. Cook, stirring occasionally, for about 5 minutes, or until softened. Add the bay leaf, eggplant, zucchini, tomatoes, tomato sauce, and broth.

3. Cover the pan and reduce the heat to low. Simmer for about 15 minutes. The vegetables should all be quite tender. Remove from the heat and let stand for 10 minutes, and remove the bay leaf. Serve warm or at room temperature, topped with the chopped basil.

**Nutrition:**

Calories: 69.5

Protein: 2.65 g

Carbohydrates: 10.7 g

Fibre: 3.29 g

Total Fat: 2.65 g
 Sat: .365 g
 Mono: 1.70 g
 Poly: .343 g

Cholesterol: 0 mg

Vitamin A: 156 mg RE

Vitamin B6: .208 mg

Vitamin B12: .017 mcg

Vitamin C: 45 mg

Calcium: 32.7 mg

Iron: 1.03 mg

Potassium: 427 mg

Sodium: 142 mg

Zinc: .3 mg

## Toothsome Tips

You may have read recipes that call for eggplant to be salted before it is cooked, and others that don't even mention the salting. For today's busy cook the process seems to have gotten lost in the rush, but there's a reason why the lowfat cook should consider it. Salting watery vegetables like eggplant and cucumber before they are fried means they absorb $^2/_3$ less oil during the cooking process. If you have a favourite eggplant parmigiana recipe that you thought would have to be retired, try salting and see the difference. To salt: cut the eggplant into the desired shape, spread on a double thickness of paper towels, and salt generously. Cover with another double layer of paper towels and weight down gently. After 30 minutes, rinse, drain, and pat dry. Proceed with the recipe as directed.

## Braised Turkey Legs with Lemon

Serves 4

*Use a vegetable peeler to remove the lemon zest from the lemon before you juice it, trying not to take any of the bitter white pith along with it. If you can remove it in 1 or 2 long spiral strips it will be easier to fish out at the end. If you chill the dish overnight, the braising liquid will turn to jelly from all the gelatin in the bones—don't worry, as soon as you heat it, it will liquefy. Although this recipe looks long, it's actually quite simple, and easy to work into and around your schedule.*

2 turkey drumsticks (about $1^3/_4$ pounds/ 825 g)

2 teaspoons (10 mL) kosher salt

$^1/_2$ teaspoon (2 mL) freshly ground black pepper

1 teaspoon (5 mL) dried thyme, crumbled

1 teaspoon (5 mL) olive oil

3 large red onions, sliced $^1/_2$ inch (1 cm) thick

Zest of 1 lemon, in several strips

$1^1/_2$ (20 mL) tablespoons fresh lemon juice

2 cups (500 mL) lowfat chicken broth, preferably the Double-Chicken Broth (page 128)

1 14-ounce (398-mL) can peeled plum tomatoes, drained

1. Trim the excess skin from the turkey legs, leaving the skin on (you'll remove it after cooking). Place the legs on a large plate. Mix together the salt, pepper, and thyme and rub into both sides of each leg. Cover and let stand for 1 hour at room temperature.

2. Preheat the oven to 325°F (165°C). Heat a large nonstick or cast-iron skillet over medium-low heat. Cook the turkey legs gently skin side down for about 20 minutes. Transfer the legs to a clean plate.

3. Wipe out the pan and add the olive oil. Cover the pan and cook the onions in the oil over medium-low heat for about 10 minutes, shaking occasionally and turning them over halfway through, until quite soft.

4. Transfer the onions to a heavy, covered casserole and place the turkey legs on top. Add the lemon zest and juice, chicken broth, and tomatoes and cover. Braise in the oven undisturbed for about $1^1/2$ hours, until fork-tender.

Choose one of the methods below to remove the fat:

1. Overnight: Cool to room temperature, discard the skin, and chill overnight, then remove the fat from the surface of the liquid with a spoon, remove the lemon zest, and reheat the dish in a low oven. Flake the meat from the bones and divide the meat, vegetables, and broth among four bowls.

2. Quick Skim: Transfer the vegetables and turkey to a platter and discard the turkey skin and lemon zest. Keep warm in a low oven, covered with foil. Pour the braising liquid into a measuring cup or fat-separator and let stand 10 minutes. Spoon off the fat from the top of the liquid. Flake the meat from the bones and divide the meat, vegetables, and broth among four bowls.

**Nutrition:**

Calories: 438

Protein: 53.7 g

Carbohydrates: 20.9 g

Fibre: 4.3 g

Total Fat: 14.9 g
  Sat: 4.70 g
  Mono: 3.93 g
  Poly: 4.29 g

Cholesterol: 136 mg

Vitamin A: 62.3 mg RE

Vitamin B6: .872 mg

Vitamin B12: .682 mcg

Vitamin C: 29.6 mg

Calcium: 123 mg

Iron: 5.77 mg

Potassium: 1072 mg

Sodium: 1535 mg

Zinc: 7.98 mg

### The Least You Need to Know

➤ Braising is a long, slow method of moist cooking in a covered pan with some liquid. It is suitable for the tougher cuts of meat, older fowl, and firm vegetables.

➤ The lowfat cook should choose braising only if you're willing to trim and skim fat, since the tougher cuts of meat tend to be fattier. If you pursue the rigorous removal of fat, you'll be rewarded with lowfat dishes that have the rich flavour and gelatinous juices that come from long, moist cooking of sinews and muscle tissues.

➤ Using wine and flavourful broths as the braising liquid in a dish can transform the mundane to the sublime. Take a little extra time to punch up the flavour of canned stock, and don't dream of using bouillon cubes.

# Chapter 13

# Bag It! Wrapping in Paper for Succulent Results

## In This Chapter

➤ Creating a mini–oven in a bag

➤ Locking in juices and flavour

➤ The "aroma explosion"

In classical French cooking, to prepare something *en papillote* is to bake it inside a packet of parchment paper. Silly as it may sound, sealing food inside a packet seals in a lot more than just the main ingredient. It seals in flavour and moisture, too. Suddenly there isn't any need for added fat to achieve quick and succulent results from a few small and simple ingredients.

When a paper packet is placed in a hot oven, the cooking action causes the packet to puff up, and hot air circulates over the ingredients inside. The food actually steams, but since there is no way for juices to escape, all the flavour and nutrients stay inside. When you tear into your individual packet at the table, the aroma bursts forth and envelops you in a heady, steamy cloud (it's a great conversation-starter at a dinner party). This is an excellent way to keep small pieces of fish moist, and no sauce is needed because whatever flavouring liquids you've added will cook together in the steamy packets to create a nice, light "jus."

## What Kind of Equipment Do I Need?

Not much. An oven, a baking sheet, and something to wrap the food in. It's best to use parchment paper, which is available in any good supermarket or kitchen equipment store. You can use aluminum foil in a pinch, but it won't puff up as much and thus cooks in a slightly less efficient manner. For large, whole fish, oven-roasting bags, which are widely sold, are ideal. If you are grilling something else, use foil and place the packet right on the hot grill. It'll cook in about the same time as in the oven.

## What Is This Cooking Technique Really Called?

Well, the French term is *en papillote*, or "in parchment paper." But this is not a fancy, expensive, or time-consuming effort. In fact, once you have some parchment it's one of the quickest and easiest methods for small, delicate ingredients. The packets are baked in an oven, at a relatively high temperature, so we call it "paper-baking."

## What Can I "Paper–Bake?"

Using parchment paper, this method is ideal for fillets of fish, small whole fish under 1 pound (500 g), boneless, skinless chicken breasts, and tender vegetables that don't require much cooking. Or you can finish partially cooked foods in a packet so that the flavours will meld together in the steamy and moist environment. Using oven-roasting bags enables you to cook a larger fish, like a 4-pound (9-kg) sea bass, but you may discover that the fish won't fit inside the bag, in which case you can cut off the head. The presentation may not be as impressive but the flavour is just as spectacular.

## But Those TV Commercials Say I Can Use Foil . . .

Recently some high-visibility aluminum foil commercials have touted the technique of filling up a foil package with various tender foods, adding an ice cube, and baking briefly at high heat. You can do this, but as we mentioned above, the packet will not be able to puff up as much due to the stiffness of the foil. The point of the "puffing" is that it creates a miniature convection oven and the hot air swirls efficiently around the food.

Also, water is not a terribly exciting flavouring ingredient—we prefer to add wine, lemon juice, fruit juice, and especially a touch of vinegar. These flavouring ingredients are all

### Toothsome Tips

Serving the whole packet to each diner at the table is quite festive, and inhaling the aroma as you open it can't be beat. It can, however, be a little awkward. If you are faced with a guest whose look seems to say "What on earth am I supposed to do with this package?" there's a solution. Serve the packets in large warmed soup bowls, and show the other diners how to open the packet, inhale the aroma, and slide the contents out into the bowl. Provide a large bowl for the cast-off paper and let the meal commence.

acidic to some degree. Acid in foods (tomatoes are also high in acid) will sometimes react with the metal in the foil, producing an "off" taste.

Therefore, the only results we can really stand behind for this cooking method are those achieved by using parchment paper or oven-roasting bags. The one exception is grilling, when foil-wrapped packets are fine. Parchment would, of course, flare immediately and incinerate the contents.

## Fish in a Packet

Serves 4

*These little packets look like presents on the plate, and your guests will love you for them! Add a few drops of vermouth before sealing, if desired.*

4 16-inch (40-cm) squares of parchment paper

4 paper-thin slices lemon

4 (6-ounce/175 g) fillets of white-fleshed fish, such as sea bass or halibut

4 green onions, white parts only, thinly sliced

1/2 teaspoon (2 mL) dried red pepper flakes

Salt and freshly ground black pepper

4 teaspoons (20 mL) best-quality olive oil

1. Preheat the oven to 450°F (230°C). Fold the paper squares in half and then reopen them to show the centre fold.

2. Place a lemon slice in the centre of one side of each paper and top with a fish fillet. Scatter an even quantity of the green onions over each fillet and sprinkle with the red pepper flakes. Season with salt and pepper to taste, and drizzle the contents of each packet with 1 teaspoon (5 mL) of the olive oil.

3. Fold the opposite, empty side of the paper over the contents and begin crimping and folding at one side of the folded edge. Continue crimping all the way along to the other side of the folded edge, then fold the last corner underneath for added security. Repeat for the other three packets.

4. Place the packets on a large baking sheet and bake for 12 minutes; then serve the packets, still sealed, letting each diner undo the individual packet at the table.

**Nutrition:**

Calories: 343

Protein: 41.9 g

Carbohydrates: 2.07 g

Fibre: .86 g

Total Fat: 17.4 g
 Sat: 2.59 g
 Mono: 7.76 g
 Poly: 5.08 g

Cholesterol: 131 mg

Vitamin A: 66.5 mg RE

Vitamin B6: .605 mg

Vitamin B12: 1.63 mcg

Vitamin C: 5.74 mg

Calcium: 65.2 mg

Iron: 1.06 mg

Potassium: 727 mg

Sodium: 245 mg

Zinc: 2.22 mg

## Paper-Baked Mushrooms

Serves 4

10 ounces (300 g) large firm button
  mushrooms, wiped clean
4 15-inch (38-cm) squares of parchment
  paper
1 medium shallot, thinly sliced
2 teaspoons (10 mL) Pernod, Ouzo, Ricard,
  or other anise-flavoured liqueur

4 teaspoons (20 mL) vermouth or white
  wine
2 teaspoons (10 mL) yogurt-based butter-
  flavoured spread
1/2 teaspoon (5 mL) salt
1/4 teaspoon (1 mL) ground white pepper

1. Preheat the oven to 450°F (230°C). Trim off and discard the stem ends of the mushrooms, and quarter them.

2. Fold the paper squares in half and then reopen them to show the centre fold. Make a mound of 1/4 of the shallot in the centre of one side of each paper square. Top with a quarter of the mushrooms, then the Pernod, vermouth, yogurt spread, salt, and pepper.

3. Fold the other side of the paper over to cover the mushrooms and begin crimping at one corner. Crimp along all three open sides, folding each crimp over the last to create a secure package. Fold the last corner underneath and place on a baking sheet.

4. Bake for 8 minutes, then serve, allowing each diner to open their packet at the table.

**Nutrition:**

Calories: 53.9
Protein: 1.89 g
Carbohydrates: 6.05 g
Fibre: 1.06 g
Total Fat: 2.23 g
  Sat: 1.24 g
  Mono: .585 g
  Poly: .199 g
Cholesterol: 5.18 mg

Vitamin A: 17.8 mg RE
Vitamin B6: .119 mg
Vitamin B12: .003 mcg
Vitamin C: 3.61 mg
Calcium: 10.4 mg
Iron: 1.1 mg
Potassium: 314 mg
Sodium: 272 mg
Zinc: .579 mg

## The Least You Need to Know

➤ Paper-baking is a quick and efficient method of cooking small, delicate ingredients. The liquids, herbs, and spices added to the packet combine for a flavourful, lowfat, instant "sauce."

➤ Aluminum foil can be used, but if acidic liquids or vegetables (like wine or tomatoes) are to be included, there is a risk of an "off" reaction with the foil. Parchment paper is the best choice, unless you plan to grill the packets.

➤ Serving the packets and letting diners unwrap their own is a festive activity, and the aroma "explosion" that results when the packets are torn open is spectacular!

# Eat It Raw!
# Salads, Vegetables,
# Fruit, and Fish

Mention raw food and most people think of carrot and celery sticks, but there's much more to raw food than crudités. The lowfat cook can turn to serving food raw for several reasons: better flavour, increased fibre and nutrient content, no need for added cooking fat, and, of course, ease of preparation.

Naturally, common sense tells us that many foods cannot or should not be served raw, but among the viable candidates are some delicious choices. Vegetables and fruit in season carry oodles more flavour than their insipid, out-of-season selves, and top-quality raw fish, purchased from a source you trust, is one of the great, refreshing joys of summertime dining.

Salads are the most obvious way to eat vegetables raw, and we have all fallen back on crudités as a party-platter standby. There are some vegetables that you may not have thought of serving raw, however. And altering your serving method a little can elevate them from a salad to a more substantial dish. A favourite example is sliced mushrooms scattered with chives and drizzled with lemon juice. An "arranged" salad becomes a real side dish if the vegetables are neatly sliced and layered on a platter with a light dressing or strewn with some fresh herbs and flowers. Lowfat cooking need not be an exercise in self-deprivation—dress up your food and make it look festive and you too will feel special and satisfied.

### Watch Out!

Mushrooms are one of Brigit's favourite raw foods, and not long after she moved to California she was surrounded by at least 30 beautiful, firm white mushrooms, coming up in her lawn. They were so gorgeous she was tempted to whisk them onto a platter, but first called a local chef friend for advice. "Brigit," she said, "If lawn mushrooms were edible, don't you think there would be an annual Los Angeles Lawn Mushroom festival? Instead, every year or so there's a little story about an entire family that was hospitalized because they ate their lawn mushrooms." So advised, Brigit sadly passed up the harvest. Mushrooms are something we always buy.

# Quality, Quality, Quality

Any raw ingredient must be of the highest possible freshness and quality. If your vegetables are looking a bit tired, it's better to cook them. Fish that is not impeccably, luminously fresh should be cooked, too, as long as it has no strong "fishy" odour, in which case it should be discarded.

Choosing vegetables in season is a great way to ensure they'll be top-notch. Also, many vegetables that would need to be cooked at other times of the year can be eaten raw in their season, like peas, shell beans, and corn. Anyone with a vegetable garden knows the great joy of munching on a handful of fresh baby peas while attending to garden chores. If you can get enough of them to the kitchen, toss them with a little soy sauce, sesame oil, and sliced scallions for before-dinner nibbles.

# Vegetables Revealed

Vegetables are chock full of fibre, vitamins, and minerals. Unfortunately, cooking tends to destroy most of those wonderful attributes to one degree or another. In Chapters 9 and 13 we discussed cooking methods that minimize loss of fibre and nutrients, but to really conserve nutrients, don't cook vegetables at all. Use your judgement and your senses to determine if a vegetable is a candidate for raw presentation. Smaller vegetables are usually sweeter, and all should be firm and crisp, not soggy, and completely unblemished. If not, they're in the pot!

## Table 14.1: Vegetables to Serve Raw

| Vegetable: | Comments |
| --- | --- |
| Bell Peppers | cored, seeded, and excess ribs trimmed away from inside |
| Bok Choy | baby-size, core and separate leaves |
| Broccoli | small florets, peeled stalks |
| Brussels Sprouts | the rare tiny sprouts are superb |
| Cauliflower | small florets |
| Carrots | baby-size (not pre-peeled and shaped) |
| Celery | tender inner stalks with leaves |

| Vegetable: | Comments |
|---|---|
| Corn | in season, best if freshly picked |
| Cucumbers | the seedless European variety has an unwaxed edible skin |
| Fennel Bulb | trim, core, and slice paper-thin |
| Green Beans | baby-size |
| Green Cabbage | thinly slice |
| Herbs | tender leafed herbs like basil, parsley, mint, cilantro, chives, oregano, and dill; woody herbs like rosemary, thyme, and sage are less suitable |
| Kohlrabi | peel off tough outer skin and slice, dice, or grate |
| Lettuces and Greens | endless varieties; all must be well washed and spun dry or dressings will run right off the wet leaves |
| Mushrooms | firm specimens only, wipe with moist paper towel—do *not* wash |
| Napa Cabbage | tops and top half of stalks |
| Radish | mildest in spring |
| Scallions | trimmed, for the brave |
| Spinach | baby leaves only, wash thoroughly and remove any tough stems |
| Summer Squash | small green and yellow zucchini, crookneck, and patty pan, sliced into disks or sticks (discard the inner, woody core from larger squash and use only the outer $1/2$-inch/1 cm) |
| Tomatoes | save ripe tomatoes to eat raw; use less than perfect ones for cooking |
| Zucchini | avoid larger ones that will be woody, or treat as for summer squash, above; disks or sticks |

### Watch Out!

With the mania for baby vegetables, many markets have started stocking finger-sized carrots in a bag. There's nothing wrong with baby vegetables, as long as they're in season and don't cost a king's ransom, but these carrots are not really babies. They are full-sized carrots that have been sculpted by a machine into unnatural shapes, and they're just as tough and woody as a full-sized carrot. Cook them if you must, but don't serve them raw.

## Pantry Asian Vinaigrette

*If you have a lime lurking in the bottom of the fridge, whip up this vinaigrette from your well-stocked pantry shelves and use it over a salad, or as a quick sauce for grilled fish, poultry, or pork.*

1 teaspoon (5 mL) rice vinegar

1 tablespoon (15 mL) low-sodium soy sauce

1 tablespoon (15 mL) lowfat vegetable or
chicken broth

1 tablespoon (15 mL) fresh lime juice

$^1/_2$ teaspoon (2 mL) chile paste

$^1/_2$ teaspoon (2 mL) minced pickled ginger

$^1/_2$ small clove garlic, finely chopped

1 tablespoon (15 mL) finely chopped fresh
coriander or mint

In a blender, purée all ingredients until smooth. Place in an airtight jar and keep, refrigerated, for up to 1 week.

**Nutrition** (per tablespoon/15 mL):

Calories: 6.58

Protein: .459 g

Carbohydrates: 1.15 g

Fibre: .060 g

Total Fat: .078 g
  Sat: .018 g
  Mono: .025 g
  Poly: .019 g

Cholesterol: .078 mg

Vitamin A: .732 mg RE

Vitamin B6: .007 mg

Vitamin B12: 0 mcg

Vitamin C: 1.86 mg

Calcium: 2.18 mg

Iron: .035 mg

Potassium: 12 mg

Sodium: 143 mg

Zinc: .010 mg

# Onions: A Matter of Opinion

There are many people on the earth who eat raw onions and love them, and many who can't imagine anything worse. (Those who don't love them unfortunately can often smell those who *do* a mile away.) Onions can vary in strength according to season and variety, being mildest in the spring when they have a higher water content. Of the larger onions, white are the strongest, yellow come next on the taste-o-meter, and red onions are the mildest.

Yellow onions have the best keeping power of all, so are available year-round, but don't confuse them with sweet onions. Vidalia and Bermuda onions are completely different animals, with a sweet, mild flavour and crunchy texture that is out of this world when eaten raw or barely cooked. These sweeties are highly perishable, only available in season (normally winter and spring), and can be very expensive. The Vidalia onion producers reserve much of their harvest for individual buyers months ahead of time, but you'll often see them in better markets during the season. Beware of large-scale buying, though, because even refrigerated they don't last more than a few days.

Other members of the onion family, like leeks, shallots, pearl onions, and garlic are considered too strong to eat raw, but raw scallions have long been a common item on a crudité platter. The bunching onions that are starting to show up in farmers markets around the country (widely used in Japanese cooking) are more fiery than scallions. They have swollen bulbs, white or tinged with red, and long scallion-like greens.

# Fruit—Not Just for Dessert

Many wonderful fruits can be eaten raw, and they make a superb addition to salads, or a garnish for high-protein dishes like chicken, turkey, and pork. Tomatoes are officially a fruit, but we have included them above with the vegetables since most people think of tomatoes as a savoury food.

## Citrus

Citrus fruits are one of the best fruits to serve raw, particularly grapefruit, which has a tart and refreshing, acidic bite. Citrus fruit is one of the best choices for breakfast because of its Vitamin C, but it is also wonderful in salads and vegetable dishes. Lemon juice is one of the most basic cooking ingredients—it's used by virtually every culture in the world. In Mexico, cooks pair lemon juice with chiles, and in the Mediterranean it's often joined with olive oil.

Lemon is the ideal flavour to cut the oiliness of fish, poultry, and meat. One of the most successful and persistent flavour pairings of all time is lemon and chicken. Throw in a little black pepper and you could be standing on a Greek island; some soy sauce and you've jumped to Japan; chopped oregano—you're in Italy; chile powder and it's a quick trip to Mexico; add garlic and you've landed in France.

## To Every Thing There Is a Season

Using food in season is always the best choice. But with fruit the rule is, if possible, even more important. Have you ever eaten a strawberry that, with eyes closed, you might have believed was cardboard? No discernible strawberry taste whatever? Farmers have access to wonderful technology these days, and they can pick fruit when it's under-ripe and ship it in that nice, safe (read *tough*) condition. No unattractive bruising to alienate the potential buyer, true, but fruit ripened in a box or on a shelf has little flavour.

Educate yourself on the local seasons for your favourite fruits and make an effort to buy them only in their true season—you'll find that suddenly everything tastes as it should (and as a bonus, the price will be substantially lower). Yes, it's true that food out of season where you live may be *in* season in Florida or Chile, but when you see it on the shelves, remember that it has travelled. Trucks and planes bring it to us, and in this way we may be better off than our grandparents, but to survive the journey most of this fruit is picked when it is far from ripe. If your great-grandmother tasted a blueberry from

South America in November, she might wonder not only where it came from, but also how it lost its flavour during the trip.

# Soft Fruit

A ripe, juicy apricot needs no preparation. It should be eaten quickly and with great pleasure. For a more formal presentation, halve and stone it, and place it in a bowl. Soft fruits are succulent and packed with flavour at the right time of year, but at the wrong time of year they cost a fortune and taste like wallpaper paste.

Fruit salad is deservedly popular, and can be made from virtually any combination. But don't restrict soft fruits only to *fruit* salads, use them in green salads, with vegetables, and on grilled fish and poultry. One great use for raw, soft fruits is salsa (the word simply means "sauce" so it doesn't have to be tomatoes and chiles). Salsa is one of the all-time best nonfat garnishes, and it's just as good over steamed vegetables as it is on steamed or grilled fish, poultry, and meat. Salsa is not only healthy, it's also beautifully colourful—an easy way to liven up the look and taste of a lowfat dinner.

# Fruit Salsa Master Recipe

Salsa is a personal thing, and once you get into the swing of it you'll be inventing salsas out of all kinds of ingredients. You'll learn to vary the spiciness and the onion-garlic content to suit your taste and that of your family, and you'll invent special-occasion salsas, naming them for yourself, a newly discovered fruit, or a memorable occasion (Sam's Birthday Salsa; My Sweet Sixteen Salsa, etc.).

Below is a guide to get you going. When inventing a salsa, keep in mind flavours that complement each other as well as colours and textures. Try plum and grapefruit with pear vinegar and mint, or kumquat and nectarine with lime juice and cilantro. The possibilities are limitless . . .

## Fruit Salsa

Makes about 2 cups (500 mL)

1$^1$/2 cups (375 mL) diced soft, ripe, raw fruit (use 1, 2, or even 3 kinds of fruit, approximately $^1$/2-inch/1-cm dice)

$^1$/4 to $^1$/2 cup (50 to 125 mL) finely diced onion

1 tablespoon (15 mL) fruit juice (either the same as the main fruit, or another juice)

1 tablespoon acid (15 mL) (lemon or lime juice, or fruit vinegar)

2 teaspoons (10 mL) minced fresh chile (optional)

2 teaspoons (10 mL) minced fresh herbs

$^1$/2 to 1 (2 to 5 mL) teaspoon minced garlic (optional)

$^1$/4 teaspoon (1 mL) salt

Fruit options: banana, kiwi, pineapple, mango, papaya, plum, apple, pear, pomegranate seeds, green tomato, grapefruit, orange, peach, nectarine, kumquat, fig, strawberries, blueberries, grapes, melon, watermelon

Herb options (fresh herbs only!): mint, chives, cilantro, basil, oregano, dill, arugula

Combine all ingredients in a small bowl and stir.

**Note:** Cutting exact dice is not imperative, so if you're in a rush you can coarsely chop the main ingredients. That being said, somehow a uniform, small dice makes the salsa really look special (small berries are left whole, grapes are halved lengthwise).

If you plan to use the salsa immediately, use the milder red onion; if you want to store it (up to 6 hours maximum, refrigerated), use white onion, since it stays crisp longer. For white onion, use a little less, as it is much stronger.

**Nutrition** (approximate):

Calories: 49.3

Protein: .608 g

Carbohydrates: 12.4 g

Fibre: 1.9 g

Total Fat: .3 g
  Sat: .022 g
  Mono: .058 g
  Poly: .082 g

Cholesterol: 0 mg

Vitamin A: 33.3 mg RE

Vitamin B6: .055 mg

Vitamin B12: 0 mcg

Vitamin C: 12.7 mg

Calcium: 14 mg

Iron: .275 mg

Potassium: 133 mg

Sodium: 134 mg

Zinc: .136 mg

# Please, Can I Still Eat Avocados?

Most dieters assume that avocados will be only a fond memory. Yes, avocados do pack a lot of fat, but in our new non-dieting regime, everything (virtually) is OK in moderation. Learning to count fat grams and calories is the first step. Once you have mastered that, it's time to make some sacrifices in order to enjoy some treats. The thing to remember about avocados is that they are not only high in fat, they are also high in calories. That means that if you are not very hungry you can lunch on half an avocado drizzled with salt, cayenne pepper, and lemon juice, and eat a lowfat dinner without sending your daily fat consumption off the scale. The avocado will provide you with enough calories to keep your body going through the afternoon. Another benefit: most of the fat in avocados is the "good" monounsaturated fat.

Here are the figures:

1 whole medium Hass avocado (small, rough skinned) contains: 30 grams fat (19.4 are monounsaturated); 306 calories; 4.5 grams protein, and 12 grams carbohydrates.

1 whole medium Fuerte avocado (larger, smooth-skinned variety) contains: 27 grams fat (14.8 are monounsaturated); 304 calories; 4.8 grams protein, and 27.1 grams of carbohydrates.

Because the smooth skinned Fuerte avocados are larger and yet contain *less* fat and *more* energy-giving carbohydrates, they are obviously the better choice for your avocado splurge.

## Avocado and Grapefruit Salad

Serves 1

*This is a visually stunning preparation that can be doubled and shared with a very good friend.*

$^1/_2$ large ripe smooth-skinned avocado
$^1/_2$ pink grapefruit, separated into sections without the membrane
1 teaspoon (5 mL) blanched, slivered almonds

Peel and slice the avocado.

Alternate slices of avocado and grapefruit sections in a circle on a plate and scatter the almonds over the top.

**Nutrition:**

| | |
|---|---|
| Calories: 240 | Vitamin A: 124 mg RE |
| Protein: 4.23 g | Vitamin B6: .484 mg |
| Carbohydrates: 24.2 g | Vitamin B12: 0 mcg |
| Fibre: 6.05 g | Vitamin C: 58.9 mg |
| Total Fat: 16.6 g | Calcium: 45.2 mg |
|   Sat: 2.97 g | Iron: 1.16 mg |
|   Mono: 9.32 g | Potassium: 942 mg |
|   Poly: 2.9 g | Sodium: 8.22 mg |
| Cholesterol: 0 mg | Zinc: .891 mg |

# Raw Fish: The Natural Choice

Raw fish is the ultimate minimalist diet food. Normally, hardly any preparation is necessary and the only fat present is the fish's own natural fat—which happens to be Omega-3 fatty acid, shown to lower the risk of heart disease. All vitamins are intact, and raw fish also just happens to be elegant and very beautiful.

Of course, there is a problem: don't even dream of serving fish raw unless it is absolutely, impeccably fresh. You also want to be certain that it has come from unpolluted waters and is free of toxins. Supermarket fish is not acceptable for serving raw—you must search out a reputable fishmonger who sells fish that is labelled "sushi-grade." If not, ask the fishmonger for fish suitable for making sushi.

Sushi has become ridiculously popular in the last few decades, and for lowfat dining out you can't make a better choice than a sushi bar or restaurant.

But sushi isn't the only way to serve fish raw. In some cultures, raw fish is "cooked" by exposure to certain liquids—usually either lime juice or strong alcoholic spirits. In the Scandinavian specialty gravlax, it's vodka that "cooks" the salmon; in Mexico's ceviche (page 254), it's lime juice that does the "cooking." Remember the liquid changes the texture and colour of the fish but doesn't really cook it so the fish must be extremely fresh and come from unpolluted waters.

> ### What's the Skinny?
>
> Flowers make a beautiful garnish for salads and vegetables. They can be gathered from your garden, that of a kind neighbour, or purchased from a good supermarket. Never use flowers from a flower shop for eating since you never know what they may have been sprayed with. Edible flowers include borage, calendula, chrysanthemums, daisies, dandelions, day lilies, scented geraniums, hollyhocks, honeysuckle, lavender, any herb flowers, marigolds, nasturtiums, pansies, rose petals, squash blossoms, violas, and chamomile.

## Sushi or Sashimi?

The term sushi refers specifically to a finger-shaped piece of raw fish that is placed atop a finger-shaped clump of rice. Making rice of the correct consistency for sushi is a fine craft among the Japanese—it is meant to cling together gently, not clump, and it must be fluffy, not sticky. Unless you plan to turn this into a major hobby, making sushi rice at home is probably not practicable. If you do plan to become adept at sushi-making (not a bad hobby for the lowfat cook), get a book that deals in-depth with the intricacies of sushi rice and sushi-making.

## Watch Out!

At first glance, you might assume that soy sauce labelled "light" in an Asian market means lower in sodium. Sorry, but light soy sauce in Asia refers to soy sauce that is lighter in colour than normal, but it's also *saltier*. Find a soy sauce that's labelled "low-sodium" to be sure—Kikkoman is an excellent choice.

For the home cook, sashimi is a more viable option. Sashimi refers to perfect slices of raw fish, without the rice. The fish is dipped into a sauce with chopsticks and eaten alone, or accompanied by pickled pink ginger (available in Asian markets). Depending on your taste, a small amount of wasabi, the pungent Japanese mustard, can be stirred into the dipping sauce with a chopstick. A tall mound of shredded white radish is traditionally placed on the plate or platter. Sashimi makes a great, guilt-free appetizer, though it's often too expensive to serve as a main course. Allow $1^1/2$ ounces (45 g) of fish per person for a first course; $3^1/2$ ounces (105 g) as a main course.

## Sushi-Dipping Sauce

Makes about $1/4$ cup (1 mL)

2 tablespoons (25 mL) low-sodium soy sauce

2 teaspoons (10 mL) sesame oil

2 teaspoons (10 mL) rice vinegar

$1/4$ teaspoon (1 mL) sugar

2 teaspoons (10 mL) chopped scallions (green parts only)

$1/4$ teaspoon (1 mL) wasabi paste (green Japanese mustard condiment, optional)

Whisk together the soy sauce, sesame oil, vinegar, and sugar.

Pour into small saucers and float the scallions on the top. Provide the wasabi on the side, if using, and stir in to the sauce to taste.

### Nutrition:

Calories: 30.6

Protein: .869 g

Carbohydrates: 1.7 g

Fibre: .026 g

Total Fat: 2.3 g
 Sat: .324 g
 Mono: .902 g
 Poly: .949 g

Cholesterol: 0 mg

Vitamin A: .417 mg RE

Vitamin B6: 0 mg

Vitamin B12: 0 mcg

Vitamin C: .531 mg

Calcium: 2.23 mg

Iron: .049 mg

Potassium: 2.71 mg

Sodium: 253 mg

Zinc: .002 mg

## Gravlax

Serves 8

*An economical alternative to smoked salmon, gravlax is normally served on thin slices of pumpernickel bread, but Brigit likes to sliver it and mound it onto 1-inch (2.5-cm) thick slices of cucumber. This is superb party fare, with all the work (though there isn't much) done in advance. Crush the allspice berries with a heavy glass or the side of a sturdy chef's knife.*

1 pound (500 g) salmon fillet in 1 piece, bones removed but skin left on

2 teaspoons (10 mL) allspice berries, crushed

2 teaspoons (10 mL) kosher salt

1 tablespoon (15 mL) coarsely ground black pepper

2 tablespoons (25 mL) vodka or aquavit

2 tablespoons (25 mL) coarsely chopped scallions (white part only)

2 tablespoons (25 mL) coarsely chopped cilantro

1. Place the salmon skin side down in a shallow glass dish. In a bowl, combine the allspice, salt, and pepper. Rub this mixture evenly over the flesh side of the salmon and sprinkle with half the vodka.

2. Scatter the scallions and cilantro over the fish and sprinkle on the rest of the vodka. Cover the dish securely with two layers of plastic wrap, leaving enough slack in the centre so the wrap will touch the entire area of the fish.

3. Place a small cutting board or tray on top of the fish and weight it with several full cans. Refrigerate for 2 days.

4. Unwrap the fish just before serving time and if desired scrape off most of the curing mixture. Thinly slice on the diagonal with a long, sharp knife.

**Nutrition:**

Calories: 92.7

Protein: 11.4 g

Carbohydrates: 1.03 g

Fibre: .366 g

Total Fat: 3.68 g
 Sat: .577 g
 Mono: 1.2 g
 Poly: 1.46 g

Cholesterol: 31.2 mg

Vitamin A: 7.93 mg RE

Vitamin B6: .466 mg

Vitamin B12: 1.8 mcg

Vitamin C: .639 mg

Calcium: 14.8 mg

Iron: .74 mg

Potassium: 298 mg

Sodium: 559 mg

Zinc: .387 mg

**Variation:** To double this recipe, get 2 identical pieces of salmon, 1 pound (500 g) each. Sandwich them together with the marinade in the centre and the skin sides outward. Turn over every 12 hours.

**The Least You Need to Know**

➤ Raw food is not only healthy, it's also beautiful, colourful, and easy to prepare. But be sure to choose top-quality ingredients, preferably in season.

➤ Festive and colourful, fruit salsa can be made from almost any fruit, varying the heat and bite to your personal taste. Fruit salsa is one of the best choices for lowfat garnishing, and is especially good on grilled foods.

➤ Raw fish doesn't just mean sushi, though sushi and sashimi are great choices for the lowfat lifestyle. Some raw fish is "cooked" with lime juice or spirits, making it perfectly safe and extra flavourful. Always take care to buy impeccably fresh fish from unpolluted waters. A fishmonger you trust is essential to preparing raw fish.

# Chapter 15

# Equipment You Should Have, and Why

## In This Chapter

➤ Yes, you'll need some new stuff—*if* you're motivated

➤ The necessaries: Nonstick and *its* entourage

➤ Cheers for cast iron

➤ Weighing for accuracy

Hobbies have always been extremely popular. Depending on who you are, where you live, and how much money you have, you might practice woodworking, skydiving, stamp collecting, or any of a hundred other hobbies. If you are a woodworker, you probably wouldn't dream of starting a complicated new project without the appropriate tools. You might borrow them or buy them; you want them because you know the project won't turn out anywhere near as well with inadequate equipment. Skydivers—unless suicidal—obviously ensure the high quality of their equipment. Stamp collectors risk damaging valuable specimens without sturdy notebooks and acid-free paper.

A lowfat cook requires good equipment, too. If you are serious about your commitment to maintaining a healthy lifestyle, this step shouldn't frighten you. After all, the plan is for you to be a lowfat cook for the rest of your life. Now, now, don't get scared. If you've been reading along with us you know that becoming a lowfat cook does not preclude the occasional steak, hollandaise sauce, or carton of Häagen-Dazs. It just means that on a daily basis you'll be cutting down your fat intake. To do that while still keeping your food esthetically pleasing and tasty, you'll need some new gear.

# What About the Stuff I Already Have?

You may be an accomplished cook with a well-equipped kitchen who has decided it's time to adopt a lowfat lifestyle. Or perhaps you're a non-cook who has realized that eating out is expanding your waistline and thinning your wallet, and your kitchen has only a corkscrew and a coffee machine. There are many cookbooks on the market that will help beginners set up their first kitchen, or help middle-level cooks step things up a notch. This is not one of those books. Here, we will address only those items that will make lowfat cooking possible, easier, or more efficient. (Oh, and make sure you have some good knives.)

In Part 3, we explored all the different cooking methods that are lowfat-friendly, and in each chapter we addressed the special equipment, if any, needed in order to steam, grill, braise, etc. The following list is a more general approach toward setting up The Lowfat Kitchen.

# First and Most Important: Nonstick Cookware

In 1938, a new synthetic coating material was developed called Teflon, and it was used to coat the inside of cookware to provide a revolutionary "nonstick" surface. But it wasn't until the 1960s that such cookware was widely available to the public. Since its introduction, Teflon has improved dramatically in its manufacture and in the quality of the products available. Good cooks turned their noses up at the first, flimsy Teflon frying pans and swore they would never be caught dead owning one. It's time to change that tune.

Teflon 2, Silverstone, and the other improved coatings with brand names like T-Fal and Armourcoat are carbon-fluorine polymers (we know, who cares?) that are virtually inert, so they won't react with the acids in food, and nothing will stick to them. For the lowfat cook, this means that a sautéing operation that, in a normal skillet, would require 1 tablespoon (15 mL) of oil to prevent burning, can take place in a nonstick pan with only 1 teaspoon (5 mL) or less of oil. Professional chefs, once as snobby on the subject as anyone, have finally fallen in love with nonstick cook- and bakeware in recent years and often use no oil at all when sautéing.

Most of the recipes in this book that involve sautéing in oil will be possible only with nonstick cookware. This is far and away the easiest way to reduce the fat in a common western-style diet.

**Tidbits!**

Because of the inert, nonstick surface provided by Teflon and Silverstone, they are both commonly used in bearings and other moving-machine parts that benefit from an almost complete lack of friction. There is no such thing as a completely friction-free surface, at least, that is, outside the realm of science fiction.

## What Quality Level Should I Buy? And How Many Pieces Do I Need?

When buying cookware, it's usually the rule to get the heaviest pans you can afford. A good set of cookware should last at least a generation, sometimes two. Cast-iron pans have been known to span even more. The heavier the pan, the better it conducts and retains heat, and heavy pans don't create hot spots that can incinerate one mushroom while the one next to it is gently cooking away. A definite drawback and seemingly insurmountable problem with nonstick pans is that no matter how much you spend, how heavy the pan, and how well you look after it, the pan will probably not last more than 10 years. That may seem like a long time, but if you've seen the high-end prices you'll probably wish they'd last longer. The better quality nonstick cookware will last the longest, but even the pans with triple-coating can never last as long as cast iron or hard-anodized aluminum cookware. For this reason, you might prefer to purchase the middle price range in nonstick cookware. It's fairly heavy and you won't feel so bad when you have to replace it.

### Watch Out!

Anytime you leave an empty pan over high heat, the results can be disastrous. Almost everyone does it once and the memory lasts forever, effectively preventing the mistake from happening again. But with nonstick cookware, the results could be downright deadly. The nonstick coating is inert, meaning that if you accidentally ate some of it, it would not hurt you, but if heated to 500°F (260°C) the coating will begin to deteriorate, and at 650°F (345°C) it gives off toxic fumes. This is unlikely to happen on a home stove, but if it should, be sure to open the windows first before you turn off the heat and cool the pan before discarding it.

You'll still be able to boil water for pasta, blanch and steam vegetables, and make soups in your regular saucepans, so there is no need to replace every pan in the kitchen. If you are single, start with a small skillet; for a larger family you might decide on 1 medium and 1 large skillet. Then, you'll need a large saucepan for starting off stews and vegetable braises. A small saucepan for sautéing garlic and onions is an extra convenience, but you can put off buying that.

Do get at least one nonstick baking sheet and, if possible, a roasting pan. Make sure one of your pans, whether regular or nonstick, has a steamer insert. If you do a lot of roasting and oven-braising, you'll want a covered casserole. Oh, and all your pans should have well-designed, tight-fitting lids. One of the greatest inventions ever is the nonstick roasting rack—a definite must if you plan on roasting poultry without its skin.

**Tidbits!**

Stir-frying has long been touted as a health-conscious cooking method. Unfortunately, at the high heat needed to stir-fry, most foods would scorch in a metal wok without a liberal dousing of cooking oil, which drives the fat content sky high. A nonstick wok requires much less oil, but be certain it doesn't get too hot before the food is added or it could deteriorate the nonstick coating and even give off acrid and toxic fumes. And don't forget to use a nonmetal tool to scoop and fry the ingredients.

# OK, I've Got the Pans— Now What?

Nonstick surfaces can scratch very easily if metal utensils come into contact with them. Not only will food begin to stick to the scratches, but the scratches will also build up an unhealthy amount of bacteria because they cannot be easily cleaned. To avoid scratching the surface, you must never use a scouring pad or abrasive detergent on nonstick cookware—it is designed so that a brief rinse in hot soapy water will remove all trace of food and oil. If the surface has been scratched by using a metal utensil, hot soapy water will not remove the food from inside the scratch, and using a scrubber pad will only make the situation worse. Once a nonstick pan has been scratched it will go downhill fast, and will be unhealthy to cook on as well. It's time for the pan to go. Unfortunately, no cookware manufacturers we know of have started offering a resurfacing service, as do manufacturers of tin-lined copper pans. I'm sure you've often seen nonstick skillets at garage sales and used equipment stores. Don't buy a used one, or you'll be exposing yourself to everything the previous owner had for dinner during the past few years.

## Nonstick Utensils

In the past, utensils designed for use with Teflon pans were flimsy, unattractive, and inefficient. About the only utensil easily found was a nonstick spatula. This was fine if all you needed your nonstick pan for was a fried egg, but we are now talking about converting almost all your cooking processes to nonstick cookware, and a spatula just isn't enough. When you look at the amount of nonstick products currently on the market, it might seem as if the nonstick surface has revolutionized cooking. In a way, it has.

Now, the same companies who have made a huge commitment to manufacturing nonstick cookware have also brought out lines of sturdy, well-designed, and useful implements.

Stovetop Utensils: slotted and solid spoons, ladles, various sizes and shapes of spatulas, skimmers, balloon and flat whisks, potato mashers, stir-fry scoops, tongs, pasta forks, griddles

Grilling Utensils: nonstick baskets for shrimp, herbs, and vegetables; grilling racks

Oven and Baking Utensils: roasting racks, pizza pans and baking sheets; muffin tins, loaf pans, cake, and pies pans, springform pans, Bundt pans, dough scrapers, cooling rack

Specialized Equipment: tortilla press, wafer cookie maker, indoor grills, waffle maker, electric wok

# Cast-Iron Griddle Pan: New But Never Outdated

Cast iron has been around for about as long as we've been cooking food in a vessel. It is reassuringly heavy, sturdy to the point of being indestructible, and inexpensive. Many cast-iron pans are handed down through the generations and their natural nonstick surface is nurtured, developed, and coddled for decades. You may be lucky enough to have such a pan in the family, or you may find a rusty one lurking in your grandmother's garage. It can be rejuvenated! Just scrub the dickens out of it, removing any loose material, and dry it in a low oven. Then brush all surfaces generously with a flavourless vegetable oil like canola. Place the pan in a 350°F (180°C) oven for 2 hours. Again wipe the pan with vegetable oil and return it to the oven, this time reducing the temperature to 200°F (93°C). After 2 more hours, wipe the pan again and return it to the oven. Repeat this a third time, for a total of 6 hours at 200°F (93°C). Your pan is now seasoned, but will always require special care. After cooking in your griddle pan, you will need to rinse it immediately in very hot water, using a scrub brush but, in general, no soap. Rub the cooking surface with a tiny bit of oil on a corner of paper towel. Dry the pan for at least 30 minutes in a turned-off gas oven (if you have a pilot light), or in an electric oven set on the lowest temperature. The pan will not be harmed if it is left in the warm oven for a longer time.

New in the cast iron line-up is the ridged cast-iron griddle pan. This is a pan designed to sit over either one or two burners on the stove top, with a fat-channel running around the outside of the raised griddle area; some have a stay-cool folding handle. You can get it very, very hot, and once the surface is seasoned correctly, you can grill virtually fat-free. The raised ridges serve two purposes: first, they keep the grilling food out of the fat

### What's the Skinny?

If you've browsed through the Grilling chapter, it may appear that we are so enamoured of cast-iron cookware that our kitchens must be equipped with nothing else! As with every kind of cookware, however, there is a drawback. Cast iron can react badly with acid, and does not cook liquids well—the pans can retain the flavours of foods that have been cooked in them before, and pass the flavour on. For this reason, it's best to stock up on well-seasoned cast-iron skillets and take a pass on the saucepans and casseroles.

### Watch Out!

Grilling at high heat has a side effect: smoke. Outside, this is usually no problem, unless you are the beauty that the smoke always follows. But in your kitchen, you will have to get rid of the smoke before the fire department arrives. Opening windows and turning on fans is the only answer. If there is no fan or window nearby, I would think twice about using a cast-iron griddle pan, especially if your kitchen is open-plan. You don't want the sofa to smell like grilled salmon for a month, no matter how good it tasted at the time.

that escapes during cooking, and second, they create attractive parallel grill marks on the food. In the winter, for apartment dwellers, or when you're too tired to fire up the backyard grill, these pans are a godsend (do open all the windows, though).

Some of our most famous chefs have begun to listen to their customers and pay attention to lowfat cooking methods. One of the most common pieces of advice to come from chefs is "Grill Everything!" With a ridged griddle pan, you can grill meat, poultry, fish, and vegetables, all in the cozy comfort of your own kitchen.

# Other Important Gadgets and Gear

## Oil Sprayer

Vegetable-oil spray is OK if you must, but it tends to have propellants and alcohol added. You can't use a normal spray bottle to spray nice, pure oil—the nozzle would clog hopelessly within moments. But finally someone has solved the problem of clogged nozzles. There is a relatively new product available that is made of either stainless steel (preferable) or aluminum. It holds about $1/3$ cup (75 mL) of your favourite oil (hopefully, olive) and must be pumped up every 2 or 3 sprays. It is an easy way to film a pan or grill rack, or to film the food about to be cooked. A 1-second spray contains $1/4$ teaspoon (1 mL) of olive oil, if you're counting.

## Scale

Portion control is one of the most important rules in lowfat cooking. The recommended portion size for red meat is $3^1/2$ ounces (105 g) (after cooking, thank goodness). When dealing with high-calorie, high-carbohydrate foods like potatoes, pasta, and grains, weighing is the only way to ensure you're consuming the correct amount for your daily plan. If you are using a fat-and-calorie-counting guide, the information will be based on weight. Guessing may throw you off to the point where your records become meaningless. Invest in a scale.

Balance and digital scales are excellent, if a little expensive. The spring-loaded models tend to be inaccurate, particularly if anything is left on the scale for longer than a minute or so. Don't be tempted to fill the scale basket with lemons or any other decorative kitchen items—your scale will be thrown off in record time. Many scales have a zeroing feature that allows you to place an empty bowl on the scale, set the counter to zero, and then weigh the food in the bowl. This is really convenient, since you can do it again and again, i.e., zero the scale after adding the zucchini, then zero it again to weigh the cheese. No mess!

## Little Things

A pepper mill is essential for the lowfat kitchen—preground pepper resembles sawdust and, without fat, the flavour of salt and pepper become all-important. Also, how do you know how long that preground pepper has been on the shelf? Cast iron should be handed down over generations, black pepper should not.

An electric coffee grinder that is reserved only for grinding spices is a great tool for those who want to explore spice rubs and grind their own curry powder and other spice mixes (see Chapter 6). These are not expensive, and can be cleaned between spice grindings by running half a piece of fresh white bread through the blades.

Parmesan is full of flavour but low in fat, and it is often used to jazz up lowfat pastas, grains, and even vegetables. Pregrated Parmesan has very little flavour compared to freshly grated, so be sure you have a sturdy, easy-to-use cheese grater.

Have a zester on hand for removing citrus zest, one of the lowfat cook's best garnishing choices, and a basic flavour ingredient in many dishes.

A garlic press is good for making salad dressings, but for sautés it's best to mince the garlic with your *sharp* knife.

If you don't have an oil sprayer, you'll need a pastry brush for lightly coating pans with oil.

Meat thermometers make roasting poultry a breeze, and can be used with beef as well, when appropriate. Overcooking lean protein foods is one of the most common mistakes made in a lowfat kitchen. Since there is little if any fat to keep food moist, the food will begin to dry out at the very moment it's done. If you can figure out the moment *just before* it's done, you can prevent foods from drying out.

Timers go hand in hand with meat thermometers. So does a little notebook. Keep track of your efforts, then next time increase or decrease the time to achieve absolutely perfect results. Sound too obsessive? Watch your family's faces when you serve them a juicy roast turkey breast (as opposed to the look when it's dry and stringy).

A small, manual citrus juicer, with a reamer set above a small dish, should always be on hand for injecting the flavour of the Mediterranean (lemons) into your healthy cooking, without the seeds.

A set of scissors reserved for the kitchen is useful for snipping chives and other fresh herbs directly into a dish without dirtying the cutting board.

Measuring cups and spoons are essential for controlling oil content, and of course for accurately following recipes. You'll need a glass cup to measure the volume of wet

**159**

ingredients (a 1-cup/250-mL or 2-cup/500-mL size works well), and a set of metal cups, which measure dry goods. And at least two sets of heavy measuring spoons. As soon as you get them home, detach them permanently from their connecting ring. What were the manufacturers thinking?

Blenders and food processors can make a thin sauce behave like a thick, luxurious one by puréeing cooked vegetables. They can also emulsify a dressing that doesn't contain much oil, creating the illusion and sensation of a rich, creamy dressing (which will separate quickly, so serve it fast!).

Hand blenders can do many of the tasks of a full-sized blender, are less expensive, and can be immersed right in the pot so there's no extra cleanup. Just make sure the food to be puréed is nice and soft. They are a great tool for puréeing a simple vegetable and broth soup into something creamy and comforting.

A fat separator separates out the fat in sauces, soups, or stock so that it can be easily poured off. This is essential any time you braise food and want to remove every last shred of fat from the liquid or gravy, not just at Thanksgiving. It's excellent for cleansing the sauce for lamb shanks and other fatty meats that are still delicious with all their fat skimmed away.

A "heat-cheater" disk for very low-heat stove-top cooking is invaluable for low-heat, lowfat sweating of vegetables, and stovetop braising. It is placed between the pan and burner and should be made of some solid material—the perforated ones do not work well.

# Things It Might Be Nice to Have Someday

For entertaining, there is nothing more festive than poaching an entire fish. If this sounds like something you would do frequently, invest in a fish poacher, equipped with a handy lift-out rack so the fish always emerges in one piece. A fish poacher will produce a gorgeous, fully intact salmon or other large fish. It is designed to straddle two burners and has handles on either end of the tray insert, making removing the delicate fish a breeze. You can also use it for cooking a large number of fish fillets or boneless chicken breasts, which would get too crowded in the normal steamer basket. You can also use it for cooking asparagus.

A convection oven cooks hotter and faster than a conventional oven because a fan circulates the hot air evenly around the food. It also keeps the temperature constant throughout the oven and stops the transfer of flavours, so you can bake a tray of cookies on the top shelf and some chicken on the bottom (if you can find a large enough oven).

If you want to steam more than one kind of food at a time and already own a wok, invest in a (very inexpensive) multilevel Chinese bamboo steamer. It is attractive enough to bring to the table and will keep the food inside warm for up to $1/2$ hour.

If you are a cake lover and will now be switching to angel-food cake as part of your move to lowfat cooking, some day you will want a copper mixing bowl. Egg whites loft to unheard-of peaks because of some obscure but not dangerous reaction, which also makes the whites more stable than those whipped in a steel or glass bowl.

Canada has been seduced by the bread machine. Even people who can't make a pie crust or whipped cream from scratch are rushing to buy them. If you think it will last at least a year before travelling to the garage, invest.

---

### The Least You Need to Know

➤ This new way of cooking will definitely require some new equipment in the kitchen. It doesn't have to be much, but a few nonstick pans are a necessity.

➤ Materials that are used to make cookware all have some drawbacks; there is no perfect material, even for the lowfat cook. So the well-equipped kitchen will have a *few* of *several* different types of pan—not a full set—to take advantage of the best material for each specific cooking method.

➤ Weighing food is one of the best ways for the lowfat cook to keep control of portion size, an essential when lowering fat and calorie intake.

➤ There are plenty of tools and gadgets to make lowfat cooking easier, more efficient, or just more fun. Choosing the ones that suit you best and planning for future purchases are part of the fun of equipping the new, lowfat kitchen.

---

# Part 4

# Recipes to Live With (and Live On, and On, and . . .)

# Chapter 16

# Slim Soups

SLURP!

---

## In This Chapter

➤ Hot and cold tomato soups

➤ Leftover bread transformed

➤ Lentil soup for the soul

---

A soup can be a meal, and a meal can be a soup. Simple, but true. Fortifying and warming on winter evenings or cool and elegant on a summer afternoon, soups are too often generalized as "boring." One of the highlights of Pamela's day when working as a chef is making the daily soup. Soup has always been one of her favourite foods and it's a wonderful opportunity to have some creative fun mixing flavours and highlighting fresh produce.

Soup can be pure and simple, and this is never more true than in lowfat cooking. Water or light vegetable stock can be the base, bread can be a nondairy, nonfat thickener, and the range of vegetables to choose from is mind-boggling. Veggies that somehow got lost in your vegetable drawer and are a bit past their prime tend to end up in the soup pot and while this makes sense from an economic viewpoint, it doesn't make the best soup. Fresh ingredients will give your soup the best flavour. A box of nonfat garlic croutons in your cupboard is waiting for just this occasion.

## Garbanzo Bean (Chickpea) and Spinach Soup

Serves 4

*If you thaw the spinach several hours in advance, this chunky soup can be ready in only 15 minutes.*

$1/2$ tablespoon (7 mL) canola oil

1 small yellow onion, chopped

2 large garlic cloves, pressed

1 tablespoon (15 mL) mild chile powder, or to taste

1 teaspoon (5 mL) dried thyme, crumbled

$1/2$ teaspoon (2 mL) salt

$1/4$ teaspoon (1 mL) freshly ground black pepper, or to taste

1 14-ounce (398-mL) can chickpeas, rinsed and drained

1 10-ounce (300-g) package frozen spinach, thoroughly thawed and coarsely chopped

4 cups (1 L) light vegetable stock or lowfat chicken broth

Garnish: 4 teaspoons (20 mL) grated Parmesan

In a large heavy saucepan, heat the oil over medium low heat and add the onion. Cook for 4 to 5 minutes, until softened, then add the garlic, chile, and thyme and cook for 1 minute more. Add all the remaining ingredients and bring to a boil.

Reduce the heat slightly and simmer for about 5 minutes, stirring. Serve the soup in warmed bowls and scatter 1 teaspoon (5 mL) of Parmesan over each.

### Nutrition:

| | |
|---|---|
| Calories: 181 | Vitamin A: 621 mg RE |
| Protein: 10.7 g | Vitamin B6: .17 mg |
| Carbohydrates: 27.5 g | Vitamin B12: .029 mcg |
| Fibre: 7.59 g | Vitamin C: 13 mg |
| Total Fat: 5.14 g | Calcium: 193 mg |
|   Sat: .733 g | Iron: 2.92 mg |
|   Mono: 1.27 g | Potassium: 320 mg |
|   Poly: .758 g | Sodium: 1694 mg |
| Cholesterol: 1.64 mg | Zinc: .709 mg |

## Toothsome Tips

Throughout this book we encourage you to garnish, garnish, garnish. Choosing nonfat or lowfat garnishes livens up almost every lowfat dish and gives it a festive feel, too. Herbs are the perfect choice for soups, though you can also choose from nonfat croutons, diced tomatoes, or red peppers, lowfat yogurt, and really good olive oil. See the list of herbs on page 55, and remember that soft-leafed herbs make the best last-minute garnishes. Fresh basil, parsley, chives, mint, dill, and sometimes sage (for a strongly flavoured soup) can be slivered and sprinkled on the top of any soup, with results that far outstrip the effort and expense.

## Chinese Egg Drop Soup

Serves 4

*It seems every culture has a version of this incredibly easy soup—in Italy it is straciatella (the very first dish Brigit ever cooked, aged 8).*

$3^1/2$ cups (875 mL) lowfat, low-sodium chicken broth

$1/4$-inch (5-mm) slice of fresh ginger, peeled

1 teaspoon (5 mL) light soy sauce

1 to 2 drops Tabasco, or to taste

1 large egg, beaten

Garnish: $1^1/2$ tablespoons (20 mL) chopped chives or scallion greens

In a saucepan, combine the broth, ginger, soy sauce, and Tabasco. Bring to a simmer, then drizzle in the beaten egg (it will cook as soon as it hits the hot broth, making adorable little stringy forms).

Ladle the soup into hot bowls and sprinkle the chives over the top. Retrieve and discard the ginger.

### Nutrition:

Calories: 36.3

Protein: 5.36 g

Carbohydrates: 1.9 g

Fibre: .091 g

Total Fat: .794 g
 Sat: .244 g
 Mono: .296 g
 Poly: .111 g

Cholesterol: 32.3 mg

Vitamin A: 19.1 mg RE

Vitamin B6: .018 mg

Vitamin B12: .397 mcg

Vitamin C: .614 mg

Calcium: 5.41 mg

Iron: .53 mg

Potassium: 153 mg

Sodium: 359 mg

Zinc: .101 mg

## Hot Summer Tomato Soup

Serves 4

*Always keep several cans of good-quality canned plum tomatoes in the cupboard for impromptu pasta dishes and soups. It's wise to try them, because quality and flavour can vary between brands. Those from Italy tend to have more flavour and are surprisingly inexpensive at your local Italian grocery. Don't sliver the basil until the last minute, or else it will turn brown.*

1 28-ounce (796-mL) can plum tomatoes, drained
1 small yellow onion, chopped
4 large cloves garlic, sliced
1 sprig fresh rosemary, or a pinch dried, crumbled
1 bay leaf

$1/2$ teaspoon (2 mL) salt
$1/4$ teaspoon (1 mL) freshly ground black pepper
$1^1/2$ cups (375 mL) water
$1/4$ cup (50 mL) tomato paste
6 to 8 leaves fresh basil, slivered

1. In a large saucepan, combine the tomatoes, onion, garlic, rosemary, and bay leaf. Over medium-low heat, cook for about 6 minutes, stirring occasionally until the tomatoes have begun to break down.

2. Add the salt, pepper, water, and tomato paste and stir together. Bring to a simmer and cook for 10 minutes, partially covered. Remove from the heat and allow to cool, uncovered, for 5 minutes.

3. Remove the rosemary sprig and the bay leaf and transfer to a blender or food processor. Purée, in batches if necessary, then return to the saucepan, add the basil, and heat through. Serve in warm bowls.

### Nutrition:

Calories: 75.9
Protein: 3.20 g
Carbohydrates: 16.6 g
Fibre: 3.37 g
Total Fat: .806 g
 Sat: .110 g
 Mono: .109 g
 Poly: .296 g
Cholesterol: 0 mg

Vitamin A: 166 mcg
Vitamin B6: .326 mg
Vitamin B12: 0 mcg
Vitamin C: 40.9 mg
Calcium: 80.9 mg
Iron: 2.12 mg
Potassium: 677 mg
Sodium: 721 mg
Zinc: .591 mg

**Variation:** For *Cold Summer Tomato Soup*, transfer from the blender to a plastic container, cool to room temperature, and then chill for at least 4 but not more than 12 hours. Ladle into chilled bowls, dolloping 2 teaspoons (10 mL) of lowfat yogurt into the centre of each. Sprinkle each one with 1 teaspoon (5 mL) chopped fresh dill and serve.

## Stale Bread and Garlic Soup

Serves 4

*This soup appears throughout the bread-eating world—in Spain as sopa de ajo, in Portugal as açorda, and in France as panade, to name a few. Peasants were not fond of wasting food in the Mediterranean countries, and stale bread usually wound up in a soup of some kind, often with other leftovers. Use a crusty French or Italian bread for this soup—soft white loaves don't work. Note: If your daily fat count is low, this soup really benefits from a last-minute garnish of a teaspoon (5 mL) of extra virgin olive oil.*

5 large cloves garlic, finely chopped

$^1/_3$ cup (75 mL) lowfat, low-sodium chicken broth

2 slices stale country-style bread, broken into rough chunks (see Note)

3 cups (750 mL) water

$^3/_4$ teaspoon (4 mL) salt

1 14-ounce (398-mL) can chopped tomatoes, drained

Garnish: $^1/_2$ teaspoon (2 mL) mild chile powder, or to taste

Freshly ground black pepper to taste

4 teaspoons (20 mL) grated Parmesan

1. In a large saucepan, combine the garlic and the broth. Cover the pan and place over medium-low heat. Let the garlic stew for about 5 minutes, until softened.

2. Gradually add the bread, stirring it into the liquid. Add the water, salt, and tomatoes. Cover the pan and bring to a simmer.

3. Cook, stirring occasionally, for about 10 minutes or until the bread has softened thoroughly but not completely disintegrated. Add a little more water if the soup is excessively thick.

4. Ladle into warmed bowls and sprinkle each with a pinch of mild chile powder, black pepper to taste, and the Parmesan.

Note: If your bread is not stale, dry out 1-inch (2.5-cm) slices in a 350°F (180°C) oven for about 15 minutes.

### Nutrition:

Calories: 80.8

Protein: 3.51 g

Carbohydrates: 13.5 g

Fibre: 1.51 g

Total Fat: 1.79 g
 Sat: .652 g
 Mono: .496 g
 Poly: .421 g

Cholesterol: 2.05 mg

Vitamin A: 66 mg RE

Vitamin B6: .148 mg

Vitamin B12: .029 mcg

Vitamin C: 16.7 mg

Calcium: 75.9 mg

Iron: 1.27 mg

Potassium: 269 mg

Sodium: 777 mg

Zinc: .416 mg

## Tidbits!

In the dark ages, calling for bread in a recipe meant you would most likely reach for the Wonder bread or some similar white, presliced, mushy sandwich loaf. These days, along with our love affair with the heart-healthy Mediterranean diet, we have taken to heart the rustic, earthy breads of France and Italy. Good, coarse-textured loaves are available in most stores now (sliced or unsliced). Combine this increased availability with the great popularity of bread machines, and it means more and more people have good-quality bread on hand.

## French Canadian Soupe au Chou

Serves 4

*The traditional version of this French Canadian classic calls for simmering a beef shank with onion and bay leaves for hours and then making the soup of its stock. If making a beef stock, let it sit in the refrigerator over night and then scrape off the hard, white fat layer before using in the soup. It's still a hearty soup with plenty of flavour when made with chicken stock and it won't eat up precious daily calories.*

1 cup (250 mL) leeks, white only, chopped
1 tbsp (15 mL) olive oil
1 cup (250 mL) celery, diced
2 cups (500 mL) shredded cabbage
$1/2$ cup (125 mL) red wine
4 cups (1 L) lowfat, low-sodium beef or
  chicken stock

1 bay leaf
Salt and fresh pepper
Garnish: $3/4$ cup (175 mL) carrots, grated

1. In a large, heavy nonstick saucepan combine the leeks and olive oil. Place over very low heat and cook gently for 5 minutes, then add the celery and cabbage. Cook for 5 to 10 minutes more, stirring frequently, until the onions and cabbage are completely softened.

2. Stir in the wine, the beef or chicken stock, and bay leaf, increase the heat to high. Stir until the mixture comes to the boil, then reduce the heat again and simmer for 30 minutes. Discard the bay leaf.

3. Pour into four warmed soup bowls and garnish with the grated carrot. Grind black pepper over each bowl and serve.

**Nutrition:**

Calories: 105.8

Protein: 12.3 g

Carbohydrates: 11.0 g

Fibre: 2.1 g

Total Fat: 3.6 g
  Sat: 0.5 g
  Mono: 2.5 g
  Poly: 0.4 g

Cholesterol: 0 mg

Vitamin A:11215 RE

Vitamin B6: 0.20 mg

Vitamin B12:1 mg

Vitamin C:21 mg

Calcium: 64 mg

Iron: 2.1 mg

Potassium: 482 mg

Sodium: 399.5 mg

Zinc: 0.7 mg

## What's the Skinny?

In several of these soup recipes, we have given you the option of using vegetable broth or water. All the nutritional analyses in our recipes are based on the first choice given, usually vegetable broth. How does this choice affect the fat content of the finished soup? Well, canned vegetable broth contains 1 gram of fat per cup (250 mL)—not bad for the added flavour it provides. For a recipe serving four that contains $2^1/_2$ cups (625 mL) of vegetable broth—that's .625 grams of fat. Nothing to get excited about, in other words. Lowfat chicken broth contains 0.5 grams per cup (250 mL), so make your own decision based on your daily allowances.

## Roasted Acorn Squash and Garlic Soup

Serves 4

*This soup is winter-time favourite in Pamela's house. This is the time of year when nothing really grows in Canada so we look to our cold storage for ingredients like squash to cook with. Acorn squash is the small, dark green, and orange squash that is shaped much like an acorn. Roasting the squash before puréeing it in this soup intensifies the flavours and brings out the natural sugar in the vegetable.*

2 small acorn squash

2 bulbs garlic

Pinch sugar

$1/4$ teaspoon (1 mL) olive oil

$3^{1}/2$ cups (875 mL) lowfat, low-sodium chicken stock or replace some of the stock with infused milk (see recipe on page 197)

Garnish: 4 teaspoons (20 mL) lowfat yogurt

1. Preheat oven to 400°F (200°C). Cut squash in half and remove seeds. Chop tops off the garlic bulbs, revealing the tops of the cloves and creating a flat surface to season. Sprinkle with a pinch of sugar and drizzle olive oil on surface of garlic. Place squash and garlic on a tray in the oven for 45 minutes or until the squash is fork tender, the juices are seeping through, and the garlic is browned and bursting from its jacket.

2. In a medium saucepan, heat the stock and add infused milk, if using. Bring to the boiling point, then remove from heat.

3. When the squash is cooked, scrape the meat from the shell and place in a food processor. Carefully remove four cloves of garlic and reserve for garnish. Squeeze the remaining garlic into the food processor. Add half the stock and purée until smooth. Stir the puréed liquid into the remaining stock and warm through. Serve the soup in heated bowls.

Garnish: 1 teaspoon (5 mL) of yogurt with a roasted garlic clove on top.

**Nutrition:**

Calories: 110.3

Protein: 12.3 g

Carbohydrates: 24.5 g

Fibre: 0.3 g

Total Fat: 0.5 g
  Sat: 0.1 g
  Mono: 0.2 g
  Poly: 0.2 g

Cholesterol: 0 mg

Vitamin A: 560 RE

Vitamin B6: 0.47 mg

Vitamin B12: 0 mg

Vitamin C: 23 mg

Calcium: 104 mg

Iron: 2.3 mg

Potassium: 772 mg

Sodium: 232 mg

Zinc: 0.9 mg

## Broccoli-Cheddar Soup

Serves 4

*Cooked potatoes are an easy, nonfat way to thicken vegetable soups. This soup is bright green and full of fibre—the cheese makes a little splash of orange in the intense sea of green. To serve it cold, chill the soup and garnish it instead with 1 teaspoon (5 mL) of lowfat yogurt per serving.*

1 large bunch broccoli
2$^1$/$_2$ cups (625 mL) lowfat vegetable broth
1 large waxy-type potato, peeled and cut
 into 1-inch (2.5-cm) chunks
$^1$/$_2$ small yellow onion, thinly sliced
$^1$/$_2$ teaspoon (2 mL) salt

$^1$/$_4$ teaspoon (1 mL) freshly ground black
 pepper
Garnish: 2 tablespoons (25 mL) grated
 cheddar cheese

1. Separate the florets from the stems of the broccoli and set aside. Halve the stems lengthwise, remove the tough outer skin with a vegetable peeler, and cut stems into 1-inch (2.5-cm) pieces.

2. In a large saucepan, combine the vegetable broth, potato, and onion. Add the salt and pepper and bring to a simmer. Cook gently, partially covered, for 10 minutes, then add the broccoli stems and cook for 5 minutes more.

3. Add the broccoli florets and simmer for about 2 minutes, until all the vegetables are tender. Remove the pan from the heat and let stand, uncovered, for 5 minutes.

4. Purée the soup thoroughly, in batches if necessary, in a blender or food processor. Serve in warmed bowls and sprinkle each with $^1$/$_2$ tablespoon (7 mL) of the cheese.

**Nutrition:**

Calories: 96.2
Protein: 5.8 g
Carbohydrates: 16.9 g
Fibre: 3.78 g
Total Fat: 2.19 g
 Sat: .810 g
 Mono: .359 g
 Poly: .213 g
Cholesterol: 3.72 mg

Vitamin A: 147 mg RE
Vitamin B6: .293 mg
Vitamin B12: .029 mcg
Vitamin C: 88.8 mg
Calcium: 74.5 mg
Iron: 1.01 mg
Potassium: 484 mg
Sodium: 940 mg
Zinc: .630 mg

## Toothsome Tips

Broccoli is such a wonderful vegetable—full of Vitamin C, bright green and incredibly tasty, it's available almost year-round in most parts of the country. Why, then, do many people throw away almost half the head of broccoli? Broccoli stems (once the tough outer skin is removed) should be used along with the florets whenever and however you use broccoli. They do, however, take a little longer to cook, so steam peeled stems for about 5 minutes, then add the florets and steam 2 minutes more. Cut into matchsticks, broccoli stems look fabulous as part of a crudité platter.

## Lentil Soup for the Soul

Serves 8

*There is a fair amount of chopping required for this dish, but take it from us, you'll reap the rewards with the great flavour. Lentil soup can easily make a main course, if backed up by some crusty bread and a green salad. Since this is a great dish for a crowd, we've given quantities for 8 people, but it will freeze well if there are only 2 or 3 of you.*

$2^1/_2$ quarts (2.5 L) light vegetable broth or
  lowfat chicken broth

1 ham hock

2 cups (500 mL) brown lentils, rinsed

1 small yellow onion, finely chopped

1 large carrot, finely chopped

1 rib celery, finely chopped

2 cloves garlic, pressed

$^1/_2$ teaspoon (2 mL) salt

$^1/_4$ teaspoon (1 mL) freshly ground black
  pepper

Garnish: 2 tablespoons (25 mL) finely
  chopped parsley tossed together with
  1 tablespoon (15 mL) finely chopped
  lemon zest

1. In a large saucepan, combine the broth, ham hock, and lentils. Partially cover and bring to a boil, then reduce the heat and simmer, skimming off the foam occasionally, for 1 hour.

2. Remove the ham hock and discard (or discard the fat and skin, dice the meat, and use as garnish for the finished soup).

3. Purée about half of the soup in a blender, then return it to the pan and add the onion, half the carrot, and the celery and garlic. Bring to a simmer and cook for 20 minutes, then taste for seasoning and add salt, if necessary (if the ham hock was salty you may not need to), and pepper.

4. Add the remaining chopped carrot and cook for 10 minutes more. Serve in warm bowls, scattering each serving with some of the parsley-lemon zest mixture.

Note: Adding the diced ham meat to the soup will increase the protein and fat content slightly.

**Nutrition:**

Calories: 236

Protein: 19.4 g

Carbohydrates: 34.5 g

Fibre: 7.10 g

Total Fat: 4.25 g
 Sat: .974
 Mono: 1.18 g
 Poly: .482 g

Cholesterol: 11.5 mg

Vitamin A: 261 mg RE

Vitamin B6: .347 mg

Vitamin B12: .069 mcg

Vitamin C: 7.92 mg

Calcium: 38.9 mg

Iron: 4.7 mg

Potassium: 558 mg

Sodium: 1431 mg

Zinc: 2.26 mg

## Emerald-Green Chilled Pea Soup

Serves 4

*Serve this before a summer dinner for friends—it makes a smashing visual statement (and who's to know it took only 15 minutes to make?). For a truly smooth, sensuous soup, you can strain it before adding the yogurt, but it's not really necessary. Don't use a food processor to purée this soup unless you do plan to strain it—a food processor does a much less efficient job of puréeing than a blender and will leave large pieces of pea skin in your beautiful soup.*

2$^1$/2 cups (625 mL) lowfat chicken broth

$^1$/2 small yellow onion, finely chopped

1 clove garlic, pressed

$^1$/2 teaspoon (2 mL) dried tarragon

4 cups (1 L) frozen baby peas

$^1$/2 teaspoon (2 mL) salt

$^1$/2 teaspoon (1 mL) ground white pepper

$^1$/2 cup plus 2 tablespoons (150 mL) lowfat yogurt

Garnish: 1 tablespoon (15 mL) fresh mint, slivered

1. In a large, heavy saucepan combine the broth, onion, garlic, tarragon, and peas. Bring to a simmer and cook until the peas are tender (this may take up to 15 minutes if the peas were still frozen—test occasionally and be careful not to overcook). Remove the pan from the heat and let stand, uncovered, for 5 minutes. Stir in salt and pepper.

2. Purée the soup, in batches if necessary, in a blender. Transfer the soup to a large bowl or other container which can be refrigerated, and whisk in $^1/_2$ cup (125 mL) of the yogurt.

3. Cool to room temperature, then cover and chill for at least 4 but not more than 8 hours. Ladle into chilled bowls, dollop $^1/_2$ tablespoon (2 mL) of the remaining yogurt in the centre of each and scatter some of the mint on top.

**Nutrition:**

Calories: 169

Protein: 10.4 g

Carbohydrates: 24.5 g

Fibre: 7.3 g

Total Fat: 3.65 g
  Sat: 1.08 g
  Mono: 1.14 g
  Poly: .904 g

Cholesterol: 5.28 mg

Vitamin A: 109 mg RE

Vitamin B6: .223 mg

Vitamin B12: .2 mcg

Vitamin C: 27.5 mg

Calcium: 111 mg

Iron: 2.39 mg

Potassium: 348 mg

Sodium: 1075 mg

Zinc: 1.51 mg

---

## The Least You Need to Know

➤ Making use of creative garnishes can elevate a humdrum soup to the next level of sophistication—or even higher.

➤ All vegetable soups are made in virtually the same manner; only the ingredients change.

➤ Today's prepared lowfat broths mean good news for making lowfat soups that don't skimp on flavour.

➤ Puréeing half the solid ingredients in a soup adds body to the liquid, yet still leaves the star of the soup identifiable.

# Chapter 17

# Shapely Salads

---

**In This Chapter**

➤ Adding body to dressings without oil

➤ Understanding vinegar

---

If you're using this book, our guess is that by now you've progressed past the point where you ordered a salad to be health-conscious and then loaded it up with high-fat dressing. It has always broken Pamela's heart to watch restaurant diners order nothing but a Caesar salad, thinking they were eating light (and feeling deprived) when in reality they were consuming 8 grams of fat for every tablespoon (15 mL) of Caesar dressing. And that's not to mention the Parmesan and the fried croutons! In fact, the McGill University study of Canadian eating habits found that one of the major sources of fat in today's diet is salad dressing.

Salads are healthy choices, but the dressing makes or breaks them. Markets carry plenty of bottled lowfat and nonfat dressings, and you're welcome to use your favourite. But be aware that, in order to make up for the absence of oil most of those dressings contain preservatives, stabilizers, and massive amounts of sugar. Making a dressing with only vinegar wouldn't taste very good—you'd be puckering up as if you'd just bitten into a lemon! There are options, but most mean a little work. Try balancing the tartness of vinegar with reduced fruit juices, roasted vegetables, and small quantities of strongly flavoured ingredients like goat cheese and miso instead of oil.

## Tidbits!

If you have set a target of cutting your intake of calories from fat down to 30 percent of your total (say 60 grams of fat for a 2,000 calories per day regime or 75 fat grams for 2,500 calories a day), counting fat grams is probably the easiest way to monitor your progress. When it comes to salads, don't deprive yourself by searching out oil-free dressings (most are crammed with sugar anyway), but *average* your daily fat intake so that a tablespoon (15 mL) of olive oil in a salad dressing (14 grams of fat) won't send you over the edge. Balance the fat by increasing servings of greens, grains, and proteins up to the total of your target calorie level. Balance is the key—not deprivation.

## Baby Greens with Raspberry Vinaigrette

Serves 4

*It is becoming increasingly easy to find prewashed salads in supermarkets, and the mixed baby greens are a favourite. This salad is so elegant, you'll want to serve it to guests as well as yourself and your family. Of course, this dressing will work well with any salad greens.*

Raspberry Vinaigrette:
2 tablespoons (25 mL) cold water
$1/2$ teaspoon (2 mL) powdered gelatin
$1/4$ cup (50 mL) lowfat chicken or vegetable broth
$1/4$ cup (50 mL) raspberry vinegar
1 medium clove garlic, pressed

$1/2$ teaspoon (2 mL) sugar
$1/2$ teaspoon (2 mL) salt
$1/4$ teaspoon (1 mL) Dijon mustard
Pinch freshly ground black pepper
2 teaspoons (10 mL) extra virgin olive oil
4 cups (1 L) mixed baby greens (frisée, lamb's lettuce, red leaf, mizuma, etc.)

1. Place the cold water in a medium bowl and sprinkle the gelatin over the top. Allow to soften for 5 minutes.

2. While the gelatin is softening, heat the broth to just below the boiling point (on the stove or in a microwave). Whisk the broth into the gelatin and keep whisking until the gelatin is dissolved.

3. Add the vinegar, garlic, sugar, salt, mustard, and pepper and whisk thoroughly. Whisk in the olive oil. You can let the dressing stand for up to 2 hours at room temperature, but whisk it again just before serving to recombine (do not refrigerate this dressing, or it will solidify).

4. Place the baby greens in a large serving bowl, toss with the dressing, and serve on chilled plates.

**Nutrition:**

Calories: 32.3

Protein: 0.71 g

Carbohydrates: 2.03 g

Fibre: .397 g

Total Fat: 2.63 g
 Sat: .38 g
 Mono: 1.76 g
 Poly: .307 g

Cholesterol: .312 mg

Vitamin A: 53.9 mg RE

Vitamin B6: .027 mg

Vitamin B12: 0 mcg

Vitamin C: 6.05 mg

Calcium: 28 mg

Iron: .591 mg

Potassium: 81.2 mg

Sodium: 340 mg

Zinc: .099 mg

## Toothsome Tips

You can rework your favourite salad dressings or adapt dressings from non-lowfat books and magazines: to lower the fat in a salad dressing without losing out on flavour, substitute well-flavoured chicken stock or fruit juice for half the oil. Or purée some leftover vegetables as for baby food and use a tablespoon (15 mL) in place of the same amount of oil. You can even use bottled fruit baby foods. Contrast the flavour and colour of the fruit juice or veggie purée with the salad ingredients. For instance, with chicken salad use some puréed carrots in place of half or most of the oil; for a green salad, use V-8 in place of some of the oil.

## Green Bean and Mushroom Salad with Gruyère

Serves 4

*Mushrooms should never be washed—they are so porous that they absorb lots of water and get mushy. Instead, use a soft brush to remove any dirt that seems to be lurking around the top or under the gills. Many mushrooms are grown in a soil-free environment and are remarkably clean.*

3/4 pound (375 g) tender green beans
Mustard Dressing:
2 teaspoons (10 mL) white wine vinegar
2 teaspoons (10 mL) Dijon mustard
1/4 teaspoon (1 mL) salt
Pinch freshly ground black pepper

1 teaspoon (5 mL) lowfat, low-sodium
 chicken broth
1 tablespoon (15 mL) extra virgin olive oil
1 ounce (30 g) Gruyère or other Swiss
 cheese, coarsely grated
4 medium-sized, firm white mushrooms,
 brushed clean and sliced

1. Bring a large saucepan of lightly salted water to a fast boil. Add the beans and cook for 4 minutes for fine French beans, 6 minutes for string beans. Immediately drain in a colander and run cold water over them to stop the cooking. Shake dry and drain on a towel.

2. Make the dressing by whisking together the vinegar, mustard, salt, pepper, and chicken broth. Whisk in the oil.

3. In a bowl, toss the beans with the dressing until well coated. Add the cheese and the mushrooms and toss gently. Serve immediately.

**Nutrition:**

Calories: 71.0

Protein: 2.63 g

Carbohydrates: 7.43 g

Fibre: 3.17 g

Total Fat: 4.33 g
 Sat: .819 g
 Mono: 2.74 g
 Poly: .456

Cholesterol: 1.86 mg

Vitamin A: 61.9 mg RE

Vitamin B6: .083 mg

Vitamin B12: .028 mcg

Vitamin C: 14.7 mg

Calcium: 53.3 mg

Iron: 1.21 mg

Potassium: 255 mg

Sodium: 210 mg

Zinc: .443 mg

## Beet and Apple Cole Slaw

Serves 4 to 6

*The brilliant colour of beets gives this salad a fantastic look. Serve it as a garnish with sandwiches or chicken, or as a brilliant side dish. Buy beets fresh with the leaves attached and use the leaves for a garnish.*

1 teaspoon (5 mL) black peppercorns

2 teaspoons (10 mL) fennel seeds

1/2 teaspoon (2 mL) coriander seeds

1 clove garlic, finely minced

1 teaspoon (5 mL) grated lemon zest

1 teaspoon (5 mL) dried thyme

1. In a medium bowl combine the beet, red onion, and apple. Toss to mix evenly.

2. In a serving bowl, whisk together the yogurt, mustard, vinegar and salt.

3. Add the vegetables and toss together. Serve at once on washed beet greens, if you have them, or refrigerate for up to 48 hours. If the dressing separates, stir it together again.

**Nutrition:**

Calories: 53.0

Protein: 1.4 g

Carbohydrates: 13.1 g

Fibre: 2.3 g

Total Fat: 0.4 g
 Sat: 0.1 g
 Mono: 0.1 g
 Poly: 0.1 g

Cholesterol: 0 mg

Vitamin A: 755 RE

Vitamin B6: 0.08 mg

Vitamin B12: 0 mg

Vitamin C: 8 mg

Calcium: 47 mg

Iron: 0.9 mg

Potassium: 249 mg

Sodium: 134 mg

Zinc: 0.3 mg

## Tabbouleh Salad

Serves 4

*This is a classic Middle Eastern side dish that just happens to be terrifically good for you, refreshing, and easy to make. If the quantity of parsley seems alarming, don't worry—it's the main flavour component of the dish. It will keep, covered, in the refrigerator for a day or two.*

$1/3$ cup (75 mL) medium bulgur

2 fresh or canned plum tomatoes, chopped

3 scallions, white and green parts only,
 finely chopped

1 bunch parsley, washed, well dried, and
 finely chopped

2 tablespoons (25 mL) fresh lemon juice

$1/2$ teaspoon (2 mL) salt

$1/4$ teaspoon (1 mL) freshly ground black
 pepper

$1/4$ teaspoon (1 mL) ground allspice

2 tablespoons (25 mL) extra virgin olive oil

2 tablespoons (25 mL) finely chopped fresh
 mint

1. In a bowl, cover the bulgur with cold water and let stand for 30 minutes. Drain in a fine sieve and then press the excess water out of the bulgur with the palms of your hands. Get it as dry as possible. Spread on a paper towel and let dry for 10 minutes.

2. In a bowl, combine the bulgur with all the remaining ingredients except the mint. Toss together well, then cover and chill for at least 2 hours.

3. Add the mint, toss again, and taste for seasoning. Add more lemon juice, salt, or pepper if necessary.

**Nutrition:**

Calories: 148

Protein: 3.7 g

Carbohydrates: 18.9 g

Fibre: 3.57 g

Total Fat: 7.4 g
 Sat: 1.02 g
 Mono: 5.08 g
 Poly: .806 g

Cholesterol: 0 mg

Vitamin A: 101 mg RE

Vitamin B6: 117 mg

Vitamin B12: 0 mcg

Vitamin C: 30 mg

Calcium: 34.8 mg

Iron: 2.03 mg

Potassium: 258 mg

Sodium: 279 mg

Zinc: .843 mg

## Watch Out!

Many earnest dieters order salad in a restaurant and think they're shaving calories—then load on the creamy dressing, croutons, bacon, and cheese. A recent study concluded that salad dressing is one of the major sources of fat in the Canadian diet. You might as well eat a stick of butter! Salad is only a lowfat dish if you keep the dressing light and garnish with sprouts, herbs, or some shaved carrots.

## Toothsome Tips

The ratio of vinegar to oil in most salad dressings is 1:3. Cutting too much of the oil would make the dressing very tart and acidic, but using a low-acid vinegar like balsamic or rice vinegar means you can make a dressing of 1 part vinegar to 1 or $1\frac{1}{2}$ parts oil without the mouth-puckering result. Check the acidity of vinegars before you buy: many wine vinegars can be as much as 8 percent, while balsamic vinegar is only 6 percent. The higher the acidity, the more it'll make your mouth pucker (and the more oil you'll have to add to make a palatable dressing).

## Sliced Summer Tomatoes with Balsamic Vinegar

Serves 4

*Growing up in Essex County, Ontario, Pamela enjoyed some of the best summer field tomatoes in the world. The natural sweetness of ripe tomatoes marries perfectly with the slightly sweet balsamic vinegar—leaving no need for any oil at all on this super-simple salad. Don't bother making this salad unless you can lay your hands on good, ripe, juicy summer tomatoes and never, never put these gifts from nature in a refrigerator—it destroys both their taste and their texture.*

1 pound (500 g) large, ripe beefsteak tomatoes
$1/2$ teaspoon (2 mL) salt
$1/4$ teaspoon (1 mL) freshly ground black pepper
1 tablespoon (15 mL) balsamic vinegar
4 leaves fresh basil, slivered

With a sharp knife, slice the tomatoes about $1/4$ to $1/3$ inch (5 to 7 mm) thick. Place, overlapping slightly, on side plates and season with the salt and pepper.

Drizzle the vinegar evenly over the tomatoes and scatter the basil on the top. Serve immediately.

### Nutrition:

Calories: 27.5

Protein: 1 g

Carbohydrates: 6.16 g

Fibre: 1.21 g

Total Fat: .385 g
 Sat: .053 g
 Mono: .060 g
 Poly: .157 g

Cholesterol: 0 mg

Vitamin A: 72.5 mg RE

Vitamin B6: .091 mg

Vitamin B12: 0 mcg

Vitamin C: 21.8 mg

Calcium: 7.76 mg

Iron: .620 mg

Potassium: 256 mg

Sodium: 278 mg

Zinc: 0.108 mg

## White Bean and Watercress Salad

Serves 4

*This salad is an adaptation of a recipe from the Ontario White Bean Producers Web site. Their rendition weighed in at a whopping 13 grams of fat per serving. This is a perfect example of how a few easy tricks can help you adapt many recipes you find into lowfat versions. We have increased the ratio of greens to beans and substituted a dressing more suitable to our healthful tastes.*

Dressing:

$1/2$ teaspoon (2 mL) salt

1 tablespoon (15 mL) balsamic vinegar

1 clove garlic, minced

2 tablespoon (25 mL) extra virgin olive oil

2 tablespoon (25 mL) chicken or vegetable stock

1 teaspoon (5 mL) Dijon mustard

Small pinch white pepper

1 cup (250 mL) white pea beans, precooked or canned, drained

2 cups (500 mL) watercress, large stems removed

1 stalk celery, sliced

$1/2$ small red onion, thinly sliced

$1/2$ red pepper, sliced

1 tablespoon (15 mL) fresh chives, chopped

1. In a medium serving bowl, dissolve the salt in the balsamic vinegar. Whisk together the remaining dressing ingredients set aside.

2. To prepare the salad, if cooking the beans, soak overnight in 4 cups (1 L) of water and then bring the same water to boil. Add beans and reduce to simmer and let simmer until soft, about 1 hour. Never salt beans until after they are cooked or they will stay hard. Rinse the watercress well and spin or pat dry. Place the beans, watercress, celery, onion, and red pepper into the serving bowl and toss well to mix. Sprinkle the chopped chives over the top and serve.

### Nutrition:

Calories: 244.3

Protein: 12.8 g

Carbohydrates: 33.7 g

Fibre: 8.8 g

Total Fat: 7.4 g
  Sat: 1.0 g
  Mono: 5.1 g
  Poly: 0.8 g

Cholesterol: 0 mg

Vitamin A: 1307 RE

Vitamin B6: 0.24 mg

Vitamin B12: 0 mg

Vitamin C: 27 mg

Calcium: 152 mg

Iron: 5.6 mg

Potassium: 1045 mg

Sodium: 254 mg

Zinc: 2.0 mg

## Mediterranean Chicken Salad

Serves 4

*Usually when you buy "bulb" fennel in the market, it still has some of its feathery green tops attached—don't throw them away! Chopped, they make a terrific garnish. If you can't find fennel, feel free to substitute celery, in which case you could use chopped dill for the garnish.*

Mediterranean Dressing:

$1/4$ cup (50 mL) canned chick peas, drained

$2^1/2$ tablespoons (35 mL) lemon juice

1 medium clove garlic, pressed

1 teaspoon (5 mL) honey

$1/2$ teaspoon (2 mL) salt

$1/4$ teaspoon (1 mL) ground cumin

Pinch freshly ground black pepper

1 tablespoon (15 mL) olive oil

$1^1/2$ tablespoon (20 mL) lowfat chicken broth

2 cooked boneless, skinless chicken breasts, cut into $3/4$-inch (2-cm) dice (about 2 cups/500 mL) diced)

1 cup (250 mL) seedless green grapes, halved

1 cup (250 mL) seedless red grapes, halved

1 fennel bulb, trimmed, cored, and coarsely chopped

Garnish: 1 tablespoon (25 mL) chopped fennel greens (see above)

In a blender, combine all the ingredients for the dressing and purée, scraping down the sides of the jar once or twice, until completely smooth. Transfer to a jar and refrigerate, if desired, for up to 2 days.

In a large serving bowl, combine the chicken, grapes, and fennel and add just enough dressing to coat all the ingredients. Toss together gently and serve immediately, garnished with the fennel greens.

### Nutrition:

Calories: 194

Protein: 15.8 g

Carbohydrates: 23.4 g

Fibre: 3.58 g

Total Fat: 5.02 g
  Sat: .848 g
  Mono: 2.72 g
  Poly: .617 g

Cholesterol: 34.3 mg

Vitamin A: 17.6 mg RE

Vitamin B6: .455 mg

Vitamin B12: .224 mcg

Vitamin C: 21 mg

Calcium: 53.1 mg

Iron: 1.33 mg

Potassium: 560 mg

Sodium: 406 mg

Zinc: .655 mg

## Table 17.1: Fat Content of Cheese

News Flash! Not All Cheeses are Created Equal! Many people love to liven up their salads with a little grated cheese, and it's always a feature of salad bars. What's the fat count of some favourites? (Remember, most of the fat in cheese is saturated fat, the worst kind if you're watching your cholesterol.) Parmesan comes out the clear winner, which is handy since it also packs the biggest flavour punch!

**1 Tablespoon (15 mL) each of the following, grated or crumbled = grams of fat**

Blue cheese = 4 g

Cheddar = 4.7 g

Feta = 3 g

Hard goat cheese = 5 g

Soft goat cheese = 3 g

Gruyère = 4.6 g

Monterey Jack cheese = 4.5 g

Mozzarella (whole milk) = 7.5 g

Mozzarella (low moisture) = 3.5 g

Mozzarella (part skim) = 2.25 g

Parmesan = 1.5 g

## Asparagus and Tofu with Sesame Dressing

Serves 4

*Although it might sound intensely boring, peeling the bottom 2 inches (5 cm) of a stalk of asparagus makes a lot of sense. If you don't, the tender tips will be mushy by the time the ends of the stalks have cooked through enough to be edible. Sure, you can cut or snap them off, but then you're wasting about 1/3 of your asparagus—and it's not cheap. We just bite the bullet, as it were, and do it (use a nice, sharp, vegetable peeler).*

Sesame Dressing:

1$^1$/$_2$ tablespoons (20 mL) low-sodium soy sauce

2 tablespoons (25 mL) mirin (sweet Japanese wine) or dry sherry

$^1$/$_2$ teaspoon (2 mL) sesame oil

1 teaspoon (5 mL) minced fresh ginger

Small pinch cayenne pepper

2 small shallots, finely chopped

12 medium asparagus

4 ounces (120 g) firm tofu

5 pale inner leaves of romaine lettuce, cut into $^1$/$_4$-inch (5-mm) strips

1 teaspoon (5 mL) sesame seeds

1. In a steamer basket set over lightly salted boiling water, steam the asparagus, covered, for 4 to 5 minutes, until tender. Place on a plate and set aside.

2. In a small bowl, whisk together all the ingredients for the dressing and pour it over the asparagus. Cover the plate with plastic and refrigerate for at least 1 hour.

3. Just before you are ready to serve, cut the tofu into long sticks, like carrot sticks. On each of four chilled plates arrange four asparagus and a few tofu sticks, crisscrossing them if desired.

4. Pour the remaining dressing from the plate over the salads and top with some of the shredded lettuce. Scatter some sesame seeds over the top, and serve immediately.

### Nutrition:

Calories: 82.9

Protein: 6.62 g

Carbohydrates: 6.16 g

Fibre: 1.27 g

Total Fat: 3.56 g
  Sat: .521 g
  Mono: .922 g
  Poly: 1.86 g

Cholesterol: 0 mg

Vitamin A: 69 mg RE

Vitamin B6: .121 mg

Vitamin B12: 0 mcg

Vitamin C: 9.79 mg

Calcium: 83.9 mg

Iron: 3.73 mg

Potassium: 258 mg

Sodium: 196 mg

Zinc: .772 mg

## Mediterranean Orange Salad

Serves 4

*Easy, bright, refreshing, vitamin-rich, and multi-seasonal, this salad is a sure winner. If sweet onions are in season, try substituting them for the red onion, and double the quantity since they are so mild.*

4 oranges, peel and pith removed

2 tablespoons (25 mL) finely chopped red onion

12 black brine-cured olives, pitted and halved

$1/2$ teaspoon (2 mL) salt

2 teaspoons (10 mL) olive oil

Thinly slice the oranges crosswise and arrange on a large platter in concentric circles.

Scatter the chopped onion and the olives evenly over the oranges. Season with salt and drizzle with olive oil.

### Nutrition:

Calories: 126

Protein: 1.75 g

Carbohydrates: 18 g

Fibre: 2.48 g

Total Fat: 6.11 g
  Sat: .768 g
  Mono: 4.54 g
  Poly: .642 g

Cholesterol: 0 mg

Vitamin A: 25.2 mg RE

Vitamin B6: .103 mg

Vitamin B12: 0 mcg

Vitamin C: 80.5 mg

Calcium: 62.2 mg

Iron: .278 mg

Potassium: 257 mg

Sodium: 499 mg

Zinc: .095 mg

---

### The Least You Need to Know

➤ For lowfat dressings without the pucker factor, use broth, fruit juice, vegetable juice, or puréed vegetables to replace half the oil.

➤ With its low acidity and natural sweetness, balsamic vinegar can be a lowfat cook's best ally for salad-making.

➤ A little Parmesan is OK, but lay off high-fat cheeses in salads—you'll shoot the fat grams right off the scale.

➤ Olive oil is good for you (monounsaturated fat has been shown to increase levels of "good" HDL cholesterol).

➤ Remember it is the average of calories that are derived from fat *per day* or even per week that you should pay attention to—*not* the percentage of calories from fat in one individual dish (especially a salad).

# Chapter 18

# Appetizers Above Suspicion

---

### In This Chapter

➤ Dips, toppings, and a wrap

➤ Shrimp in a martini glass

➤ Stuffed veggies with an attitude

➤ Homemade mini-pizzas

---

Appetizers should fulfill the promise of their name—they should be appetizing. A perfect appetizer is something small that sets the mood for the meal to follow. It is counterpoint, not competition. For instance, if the main course is going to be Smoked Turkey Chili you probably would not want to serve smoked salmon as an appetizer—a better choice might be Crab Quesadillas or Frozen Shrimp Cocktail.

So, appetizers should look attractive, smell good, and follow the theme of the entire menu. Naturally, you will not always want to serve an appetizer—lunch for you and the kids does not require one, for example. But when you are entertaining, an appetizer will keep guests out of your hair until dinner is ready and take a little edge off their appetite. If cocktails are served, and if you tend to take an inordinate amount of time getting the main course onto the table, an appetizer can also stop your guests from becoming too tipsy before dinner to appreciate all your hard work.

Be careful of the traditional appetizers like cheeses, dips, quiches, and pâtés—they are all fat-heavy. Before we became more fat conscious, cooks would wow their guests with a fatty, festive starter. But a starter needn't be fatty to be festive—take oysters for instance. Crudités are a healthy, colourful, and inexpensive option—use one of the dips below and don't get stuck with the old standby vegetables—add radishes, asparagus, jicama—anything with colour and crunch.

## Sun-Dried Tomato Tapenade

Yield: 1$^1$/$_2$ cups (375 mL)

Serves 8 (3 crackers each)

*This is a deep, dark, flavourful concoction that belies its own simplicity. To lighten the flavour and make it go farther, stir in 1 cup (250 mL) of lowfat yogurt.*

$^2$/$_3$ cup (150 mL) boiling water

10 sun-dried tomatoes (dry, not oil-packed)

$^1$/$_4$ cup (50 mL) rice vinegar

1 tablespoon (15 mL) olive oil

2 teaspoons (10 mL) molasses

2 teaspoons (10 mL) low-sodium soy sauce

1 clove garlic, pressed

$^1$/$_4$ teaspoon (1 mL) freshly ground black pepper

24 lowfat rusk, or other yeast crackers

Pour the boiling water over the sun-dried tomatoes, cover and let stand for 10 minutes. Scrape the tomatoes and water into the jar of a blender and add all the remaining ingredients. Blend thoroughly, scraping down the blender bowl once or twice. The purée should be quite smooth.

Transfer to a small bowl or ramekin and refrigerate, if desired, or use immediately. The tapenade will keep for up to 3 days, covered and refrigerated. Spread thinly on rusks to serve.

### Nutrition:

Calories: 161

Protein: 5.2 g

Carbohydrates: 27 g

Fibre: 1.50 g

Total Fat: 4.06 g
 Sat: .721 g
 Mono: 2.38 g
 Poly: .54 g

Cholesterol: 9.30 mg

Vitamin A: 10.3 mg RE

Vitamin B6: .052 mg

Vitamin B12: .021 mcg

Vitamin C: 2.90 mg

Calcium: 31.8 mg

Iron: 1.80 mg

Potassium: 361 mg

Sodium: 268 mg

Zinc: .498 mg

## Hot and Smoky Hummus Wrap

Serves 4

*Chickpeas sometimes seem to be evidence for the lowfat cook that there is still a God. Incredibly tasty, full of fibre and vitamins, and with a terrific texture that enhances all sorts of soups and dressings—this is a bean whose time has come. You can cook your own, of course, but the canned ones are just fine. If you are affected by the gas-producing compounds in beans, drain them well before using and add water to adjust the thickness of the spread. Otherwise, use some of the liquid from the can. (Note: the more you eat beans and legumes, the less you will suffer from their, um, gaseous effects.) The hummus here works well as a dip for crudités.*

1 14-ounce (398-mL) can chickpeas

1 chipotle or to taste

1 tablespoon (15 mL) white sesame seeds

3 tablespoons (50 mL) lemon juice

3 cloves garlic, pressed

3 scallions, white and light green parts only, finely chopped

$1/2$ teaspoon (2 mL) salt

$1/4$ teaspoon (1 mL) ground white pepper

$1/4$ teaspoon (1 mL) ground cumin

2 teaspoons (10 mL) chopped fresh mint or cilantro

4 regular flour tortillas

$1/4$ cup (125 mL) alfalfa sprouts, plus extra for garnish

Drain the beans, reserving their liquid. In a blender, combine the beans, chipotle, sesame seeds, lemon juice, garlic, scallions, salt, pepper, and cumin. Blend into a purée, scraping down the sides of the jar as necessary. It should be very smooth. Adjust the consistency to a stiff but not dry paste, using just a little of either the reserved bean liquid or water (see note above). Scrape into a bowl and stir in the mint. Refrigerate for up to 24 hours, if desired.

To serve, spread evenly on a tortilla, leaving a $1/2$-inch (1-cm) border. Scatter with $1/4$ of the sprouts and roll up firmly. Place the wraps seam side down on a plate and chill for at least one hour, then cut into 2-inch (5-cm) lengths on the diagonal. Place on a platter and garnish with a pinch of alfalfa sprouts.

### Nutrition:

Calories: 231

Protein: 8.76 g

Carbohydrates: 38.4

Fibre: 5.5 g

Total Fat: 4.97 g

  Sat: .66 g

  Mono: 1.45 g

  Poly: 1.52 g

Cholesterol: 0 mg

Vitamin A: 219 mg RE

Vitamin B6: .099 mg

Vitamin B12: 0 mcg

Vitamin C: 18.7 mg

Calcium: 112 mg

Iron: 2.72 mg

Potassium: 123 mg

Sodium: 958 mg

Zinc: .536 mg

## Tzatziki (Greek Cucumber Dip)

Yield: 1 cup (250 mL)

*This Greek classic is wonderful with a platter of raw vegetables. For the adventurous, cut off the top quarter of a red cabbage and scoop out a bowl-shaped area using a grapefruit knife and a sturdy spoon. Place the dip inside and surround with carrot, zucchini, celery, pepper sticks, and mushroom slices. Draining the yogurt makes it thicker, but don't use yogurt prethickened with added gelatin, which will not work well. Check the ingredient list on the container.*

1 cup (250 mL) plain lowfat yogurt (without gelatin)

2 teaspoons (10 mL) olive oil

1 teaspoon (5 mL) white wine or cider vinegar

$1/2$ teaspoon (2 mL) salt

1 large clove garlic, pressed

2 teaspoons (10 mL) chopped fresh mint or dill

1 cucumber, peeled, halved, seeded, and chopped

Garnish: 1 teaspoon (5 mL) chopped fresh parsley

1. Drain the yogurt in a fine sieve set over a bowl, in the refrigerator, for 8 hours.

2. In a serving bowl, combine the yogurt, olive oil, vinegar, salt, garlic, and mint. Whisk together with a fork, then add the cucumber and combine thoroughly. Cover and chill for at least 1 and up to 4 hours.

3. When ready to serve, wipe the sides of the bowl with a paper towel and sprinkle the parsley over the top.

### Nutrition:

Calories: 69.9

Protein: 3.81 g

Carbohydrates: 6.77 g

Fibre: .546 g

Total Fat: 3.31 g
  Sat: .95 g
  Mono: 1.92 g
  Poly: .264 g

Cholesterol: 3.72 mg

Vitamin A: 29 mg RE

Vitamin B6: .072 mg

Vitamin B12: .345 mcg

Vitamin C: 5.2 mg

Calcium: 125 mg

Iron: .305 mg

Potassium: 259 mg

Sodium: 311 mg

Zinc: .712 mg

## Frozen Shrimp Cocktail

Serves 4

*This is an elegant but slightly silly presentation that's lots of fun. Shrimp cocktail (secretly still the favourite of many) is updated for the new millennium in a martini glass, topped with a festive stick of celery. If freezing the cocktail sauce is too much for you, just serve it well chilled—it's still streets ahead of store-bought—and you can adjust the flavours to suit your personal taste.*

$1^{1}/_{2}$ cups (375 mL) low-sodium tomato juice

Pinch celery salt

2 drops Tabasco, or to taste

$1^{1}/_{2}$ tablespoons (20 mL) prepared horseradish

$^{1}/_{4}$ teaspoon (1 mL) salt

$^{1}/_{4}$ teaspoon (1 mL) freshly ground black pepper

12 large cooked shrimp, peeled and deveined, tails left on

4 celery sticks, with some of the greens still attached

1. In a metal roasting pan, whisk together the tomato juice, celery salt, Tabasco, horseradish, salt, and pepper. Spread evenly in the pan and freeze for about $2^{1}/_{2}$ hours, until quite firm.

2. Remove from the freezer and scrape the surface with a fork to create a "granita" of icy cocktail sauce (let rest for 5 minutes if it's too firm to start scraping). Mound a generous scoop into each of four martini or other stem glasses.

3. Place three shrimp in each glass, hooking the tails over the edges. Place a celery stick in the tomato ice and serve within about 10 minutes or the ice will get too slushy.

### Nutrition:

Calories: 40.9

Protein: 4.44 g

Carbohydrates: 5.12 g

Fibre: .855 g

Total Fat: .227 g
 Sat: .061 g
 Mono: .042 g
 Poly: .095 g

Cholesterol: 32.1 mg

Vitamin A: 16.3 mg RE

Vitamin B6: .044 mg

Vitamin B12: .636 mcg

Vitamin C: 24.3 mg

Calcium: 33.7 mg

Iron: .837 mg

Potassium: 106 mg

Sodium: 249 mg

Zinc: .354 mg

## Bruschetta with Tomato–Basil "Salsa"

Serves 4

*Bruschetta is simply Italian-style toast. You can use store-bought salsa as a topping, or substitute canned white beans for the tomatoes here to create a bean salsa. The important thing is the bread. Please don't think of using a regular sandwich loaf. A French baguette, rustic Italian bread, or sourdough sandwich loaf, or a country-style unsliced loaf—only these kinds of breads will make this dish a low-effort, lowfat winner. Make this salsa just before serving so the fresh basil doesn't turn brown.*

1 14-ounce (398 mL) can chopped plum tomatoes, drained

2 cloves garlic, pressed

2 scallions, white parts only, finely chopped

6 large leaves fresh basil, slivered

$1/2$ teaspoon (2 mL) salt

$1/4$ teaspoon (1 mL) freshly ground black pepper

2 teaspoons (10 mL) extra virgin olive oil

2 teaspoons (10 mL) balsamic vinegar

4 ($3/4$ inch/2 cm thick) slices French or Italian bread

1 large clove garlic, halved crosswise

Toss together the tomatoes, garlic, scallions, basil, salt, pepper, olive oil, and vinegar.

Preheat a broiler (or outdoor grill, if using for other cooking later). Toast the bread slices until golden on both sides, then place on a large serving platter and rub firmly with the cut sides of the halved garlic clove. Spoon some of the salsa on each slice of bread and serve at once.

**Nutrition:**

Calories: 135

Protein: 3.83 g

Carbohydrates: 22.3 g

Fibre: 2.04 g

Total Fat: 3.58 g
 Sat: .602 g
 Mono: 1.94 g
 Poly: .720 g

Cholesterol: 0 mg

Vitamin A: 65 mg RE

Vitamin B6: .133 mg

Vitamin B12: 0 mcg

Vitamin C: 18 mg

Calcium: 58.7 mg

Iron: 1.78 mg

Potassium: 287 mg

Sodium: 611 mg

Zinc: .467 mg

## Smoked Mackerel with Spicy Garlic Foam

Serves 4

*Smoked mackerel is another example of "good" fat. It is full of Omega-3 fatty acids which current research suggests are beneficial in reducing the risk of breast cancer and may help to combat heart disease. The salad greens are served without dressing because the fish is flavourful enough as a topping on its own.*

$1^1/_4$ cup(300 mL) skimmed milk
1 clove garlic, sliced
$^1/_4$ teaspoon (1 ml) dried mustard
$^1/_4$ teaspoon (1 ml) dried chili pepper flakes

1 large handful mesclun (about 1 oz/30 g)
4 oz (120 g) smoked, peppered mackerel
Salt

1. In a small pot, scald the milk with the garlic, mustard and chili flakes. Use a spoon to strain out the garlic as you pour the hot milk into a stainless steel foamer. Pump until thick and voluminous, then set aside to firm up. Only the foam will be needed and the excess infused milk can be saved to make soup (see page 172). If you have a steam foamer, you will only need to use $^1/_2$ cup (125 mL) of milk.

2. Divide the mesclun among four small plates and lightly salt. Cut the mackerel into strips and arrange on top of the greens.

3. Using a tablespoon, mound a dollop of foam over the mackerel and serve at once.

### Nutrition:

Calories: 59.3

Protein: 8.5 g

Carbohydrates: 4.3 g

Fibre: 0.0 g

Total Fat: 0.8 g
 Sat: 0.2 g
 Mono: 0.3 g
 Poly: 0.1 g

Cholesterol: 16 mg

Vitamin A: 365 RE

Vitamin B6: 0.17 mg

Vitamin C: 2 mg

Calcium: 106 mg

Iron: 0.6 mg

Potassium: 273 mg

Sodium: 321 mg

Zinc: 0.5 mg

## Crab Quesadillas

Serves 4

*This is one time when it's OK to use surimi (the imitation crabmeat made from cod or pollack fish). We usually don't recommend this product because it looks fake, but hidden inside a quesadilla only you and your grocer will know for sure (and real lump crabmeat has become shockingly expensive!). You do need a nonstick skillet for this dish; otherwise you will need to add 1 teaspoon (5 mL) of canola oil for each quesadilla.*

4 regular-sized flour tortillas

4 ounces (120 g) lump crabmeat or surimi, flaked with a fork

1 canned jalapeño, drained, seeded, and finely chopped

1 medium, ripe tomato, cored, seeds squeezed out, and diced

3 ounces (75 g) grated part-skim mozzarella cheese

$1/4$ cup (50 mL) bottled salsa

1. Preheat the oven to low. Place one of the tortillas in a large, nonstick skillet and place the skillet over medium-low heat. Scatter half of the crab or surimi, jalapeño, tomato, and cheese evenly over the tortilla, leaving a $1/2$-inch (1-cm) border, and immediately place another tortilla directly on top. Press down gently.

2. Cook for about 2 minutes, pressing down again occasionally with a flat spatula. When the cheese begins to melt and the underside is speckled golden, flip the quesadilla over and cook for 1 to 2 minutes on the other side, until evenly golden and the cheese is just beginning to ooze out from the edges.

3. Place on a plate or cookie sheet and keep warm in the oven while you repeat the same process with the remaining two tortillas and the rest of the ingredients. Transfer both the quesadillas to a cutting board and cut into four triangles with a large knife or a pizza wheel. Serve at once, giving each guest two triangles and dolloping on a tablespoon (15 mL) of salsa per triangle.

**Nutrition:**

Calories: 215

Protein: 15 g

Carbohydrate: 23 g

Fibre: 1.76 g

Total Fat: 6.62 g
 Sat: 2.79 g
 Mono: 2.13 g
 Poly: 1.28 g

Cholesterol: 36.7 mg

Vitamin A: 67.5 mg RE

Vitamin B6: .11 mg

Vitamin B12: .328 mcg

Vitamin C: 17.7 mg

Calcium: 231 mg

Iron: 1.90 mg

Potassium: 292 mg

Sodium: 601 mg

Zinc: 2.10 mg

## Stuffed Mushrooms

Serves 2

*Stuffed mushrooms are one of those retro foods that go so well with two martinis and a little Sinatra. (Or a little martini and two Sinatras.)*

4 large, firm button mushrooms (about 2 ounces/50 g each)

3 ounces (75 g) small white mushrooms

1 tablespoon (15 mL) fresh lemon juice

$2/3$ cup (150 mL) coarse, dry bread crumbs

$1/2$ oil-packed anchovy fillet, rinsed well, patted dry, and minced

1 clove garlic, pressed

2 small scallions, white parts only, finely chopped

2 tablespoons (25 mL) finely chopped fresh parsley

Pinch salt

Pinch freshly ground black pepper

$1/2$ tablespoon (2 mL) extra virgin olive oil

2 teaspoons (10 mL) lowfat chicken broth

1 tablespoon (15 mL) grated Parmesan

1. Preheat the oven to 450°F (230°C). Remove the stems from the large mushrooms, keeping them intact, and coarsely chop the stems along with the small mushrooms. Sprinkle the large mushroom caps and the chopped mushrooms with lemon juice.

2. In a bowl, toss the chopped mushrooms together with the bread crumbs, minced anchovy, garlic, scallions, parsley, salt, pepper, and olive oil until well mixed. Mound $1/4$ of the mixture into the hollow of each mushroom cap, compressing the mixture slightly.

3. Place the mushrooms hollow side up in a small roasting pan. Add the chicken broth to the pan and cover tightly with foil. Bake for 8 minutes, then remove the foil and scatter a little Parmesan over the top of each.

4. Return to the oven for about 5 minutes more, until the cheese is golden. Let cool for a moment and then serve immediately.

### Nutrition:

Calories: 227

Protein: 8.34 g

Carbohydrates: 34.7 g

Fibre: 3.25 g

Total Fat: 6.96 g
  Sat: 1.16 g
  Mono: 2.84 g
  Poly: .540 g

Cholesterol: 3.39 mg

Vitamin A: 25.4 mcg

Vitamin B6: .14 mg

Vitamin B12: .053 mcg

Vitamin C: 17 mg

Calcium: 150 mg

Iron: 3.77 mg

Potassium: 444 mg

Sodium: 1384 mg

Zinc: .942 mg

## Homemade Mini-Pizzas

Serves 8

*Pizza has recently been declared to be the perfect health food. When will they make up their minds? But seriously, as long as you choose a veggie pizza with only a subtle hint of meat in the topping, and don't go for double cheese, this dish has everything, and in all the right proportions, too. If you have a food processor, pizza dough is exceedingly easy to make, and it freezes well. Just remember to take it out to thaw several hours before you want to roll it out—this is not a defrosting process that can be hurried in the microwave.*

Pizza Dough:

$^2/_3$ cup (150 mL) warm water (between 105°F
  and 115°F/41°C and 46°C)

$^1/_2$ teaspoon (2 mL) sugar

1 teaspoon (5 mL) active dry yeast

$2^1/_2$ cups (625 mL) all-purpose flour

$^1/_4$ cup (50 mL) cornmeal

2 tablespoons (25 mL) whole wheat flour

1 tablespoon (15 mL) finely chopped fresh
  rosemary or 1 teaspoon (5 mL) dried
  rosemary

2 tablespoons (25 mL) extra virgin olive oil

1 teaspoon (15 mL) coarse sea salt

2 cups (500 mL) good-quality store-bought
  tomato sauce

2 slices peameal bacon, chopped

4 ounces (120 g) lowfat mozzarella cheese,
  cut into small cubes

2 tablespoons (25 mL) grated Parmesan

1. To make the dough: In a glass measuring cup with a lip, combine the water and the sugar and stir to mix. Sprinkle the yeast over the top and allow to stand for 10 minutes until it has a frothy head. If no froth forms, the yeast is bad and you will need to start again with fresh yeast, water, and sugar.

2. In the bowl of a food processor fitted with the metal blade, combine the all-purpose flour with the cornmeal, whole wheat flour, rosemary, olive oil, and salt. Process briefly just to blend. With the motor running, pour the yeast mixture steadily through the feed tube and process until the mixture forms a rough ball on the central stem. If the dough has not formed a ball within 20 seconds, remove the cover and sprinkle a spoonful of water over the dough, then process again. The dough should be processed for a total time of about 45 seconds.

3. Replace the feed tube cover so that no air will get in, and leave the dough in the processor to rise for 1 to $1^1/_2$ hours, or until it has doubled, puffed, and softened.

4. Process the dough in the food processor again for 5 seconds, then turn it out onto a lightly floured board. With the palms of your hands, work the dough together into a smooth mass and form into eight equal-size balls. Place the dough balls on a lightly oiled, large baking sheet, cover with a towel, and allow to rest for 15 minutes. Press each ball out into a 3-inch (8-cm) round.

5. Preheat the oven to 500°F (260°C).

**200**

6. In a saucepan, bring the tomato sauce to a low simmer over medium heat. Cook, stirring frequently, until it has thickened and reduced by almost half. Remove from the heat. Spread about 2 tablespoons (25 mL) of the sauce evenly on each pizza round, leaving a $1/4$-inch (5-mm) border. Distribute the bacon evenly among them, then divide the mozzarella among the pizzettas. Scatter the Parmesan on top.

7. Bake for 10 to 12 minutes, or until the edges are golden and the cheese has melted. Serve immediately.

## Nutrition:

Calories: 251

Protein: 11 g

Carbohydrates: 35.4 g

Fibre: 2.37 g

Total Fat: 7.33 g
 Sat: 2.54 g
 Mono: 3.6 g
 Poly: .615 g

Cholesterol: 12.3 mg

Vitamin A: 91 mg RE

Vitamin B6: .156 mg

Vitamin B12: .200 mcg

Vitamin C: 9.55 mg

Calcium: 146 mg

Iron: 2.57 mg

Potassium: 317 mg

Sodium: 833 mg

Zinc: 1.06 mg

## Tidbits!

You may recently have seen pizza described as "a perfect health food." That came as a shock to many people, but the announcers in this case were sure to specify no meat and little cheese to make it healthy. Once you accept that fact, it's easy to see why pizza is perfect: it combines high-energy bread dough with low-carbohydrate, vitamin-rich tomatoes, with a tiny amount of fat from the cheese. Many nutritionists call that combination perfect, and pizza just happens to fall into exactly this category.

## The Least You Need to Know

➤ Appetizers don't need to be fatty and rich like quiche and pâté, they simply have to "appetize" the diner. Fresh flavours and bright colours do that every bit as well, and even better.

➤ Crudités are a healthy choice and there are several lowfat dips to choose from. If you're feeling adventurous, hollow out a red cabbage (using a stiff spoon and a grapefruit knife) and serve the dip inside.

➤ Once you master the simple art of pizza-making there should always be a lump of dough in the freezer, which can be thawed in a few hours. Use imagination and the contents of your lowfat pantry to create new pizzas in appetizer-size.

# Chapter 19

# Pass the Pasta

---

## In This Chapter

➤ Canned tomatoes rule

➤ Pasta isn't just from Italy

➤ Homemade Ravioli in a flash

---

Pasta has been the mainstay of many of our dinners for longer than most of us care to remember, but take a new look at this incredibly versatile dish. Now that we know we can't load up on complex carbohydrates (starches) and expect to drop pounds, we must start looking at pasta as a feature player, not the star. It couldn't be any simpler: use more sauce or vegetables, and less pasta. Remember that it isn't just fat grams you need to count to maintain your goals, it's calories, too, and complex carbs like pasta are one of the biggest sources of calories, even if they are fat-free.

The key to great pasta is in stocking your pantry—a well-stocked pasta pantry can produce some amazing results without even a trip to the market. Luckily, pasta marries well with lots of ingredients that are actually better in their nonperishable forms, like great canned Italian plum tomatoes, anchovies, canned tuna, dried bread crumbs, frozen peas, garlic, onions, and last but definitely not least, good, fruity olive oil. Olive oil is one of our best sources for those monounsaturated fats that do such a good job of lowering "bad" LDL cholesterol and increasing the "good," artery-scouring HDL cholesterol.

## What's the Skinny?

Almost all Italian and many North American recipes for pasta specify cooking the noodles until they are "al dente." This literally means "to the teeth," but in practical terms it means draining the pasta before it becomes completely mushy. The only way to determine al dente is to test—not by throwing it at the ceiling, but by grabbing a strand a little before the end of the cooking time (specified on the package). There should still be a little resistance left in the noodle. When you have just reached this stage, it's time to drain the pasta immediately.

## Spaghetti with Barely Cooked Tomato Sauce

Serves 4

*Sure, this simple pasta dish is good with fresh tomatoes, if they're in season—but it's every bit as good with canned, chopped plum tomatoes (an item your lowfat pantry should always have in stock). Some people don't even warm the sauce first, just letting the hot pasta gently cook the sauce, but we like to cook it briefly to soften the "bite" of the garlic.*

1 28-ounce (796 mL) can chopped plum tomatoes, drained

2 cloves garlic, finely chopped

1 tablespoon (15 mL) extra virgin olive oil

1 teaspoon (5 mL) balsamic vinegar

2 tablespoons (25 mL) finely chopped parsley

3 to 5 leaves fresh basil, chopped

1/2 teaspoon plus 1 tablespoon (17 mL) salt

1/2 teaspoon (2 mL) freshly ground black pepper

1/2 pound (250 g) dried spaghetti or linguine

1. In a small saucepan, combine the tomatoes, garlic, and olive oil. Over low heat, bring to a simmer and cook for 2 minutes. Remove from the heat and stir in the vinegar, parsley, basil, 1/2 teaspoon (2 mL) salt, and pepper. Let stand while you cook the pasta.

2. Bring a large pot of water to a boil and add the remaining salt and the spaghetti. Cook, stirring occasionally, until al dente or according to the package instructions.

3. Drain the pasta in a colander and return it to the pan. Toss with half the tomato sauce, then serve immediately, topping with the remaining sauce.

**Nutrition:**

Calories: 229

Protein: 7.7 g

Carbohydrates: 41.3 g

Fibre: 3.45 g

Total Fat: 5.1 g
 Sat: .533 g
 Mono: 2.57 g
 Poly: .49 g

Cholesterol: 0 mg

Vitamin A: 132 mg RE

Vitamin B6: .200 mg

Vitamin B12: 0 mcg

Vitamin C: 33 mg

Calcium: 59.2 mg

Iron: 2.92 mg

Potassium: 562 mg

Sodium: 693 mg

Zinc: .365 mg

## What's the Skinny?

Fresh pasta or dried pasta—which is better? Well, they're both good for what they're good for. How's that for an answer? The difference lies in the texture: dried pasta (please search out the really good Italian varieties made with durum wheat flour) is much better for tomato and other vegetable sauces, whereas fresh pasta is ideal for sauces containing butter and cream. You make a decision depending on what you'll be saucing them with. And since you don't cook with butter and cream anymore, you probably won't need to use fresh pasta at all, right?

## Penne with Zucchini and Ricotta

Serves 4

*This is a classic Italian dish that can be thrown together from the contents of the pantry and garden. If you don't have zucchini growing your garden, you'll need to purchase some.*

Salt

2 pounds (1 kg) small young zucchini, untrimmed

$^1/_2$ pound (250 g) dried penne pasta

2 tablespoons (25 mL) olive oil

4 garlic cloves, finely chopped

8 ounces (250 g) part-skim ricotta cheese

Freshly ground black pepper

15 leaves fresh basil, finely sliced

$^1/_3$ cup (75 mL) freshly grated Parmesan

1. Bring a large pot of salted water to a boil (1 tablespoon/15 mL salt per quart/litre of water). Add the whole zucchini, and boil for 2 minutes. Remove with a slotted spoon, cool and slice at an angle into $^1/_2$-inch (1-cm) thick slices.

2. Bring the water back to a boil. Add the penne to the boiling water, and cook according to the package instructions, until al dente. Drain well and return to the pot.

3. In a large heavy saucepan (that will hold all the pasta), heat the olive oil over very low heat. Add the garlic, and cook until softened but not brown, about 2 minutes. Add the zucchini slices and increase the heat to medium low. Cook, tossing gently, 4 to 5 minutes, until zucchini is lightly browned on the edges. Remove from the heat.

4. Add the penne to the zucchini, then stir in the ricotta. Season to taste with salt and pepper, add the basil and Parmesan, and toss to mix. Serve immediately.

### Nutrition:

Calories: 409

Protein: 19.5 g

Carbohydrates: 50.6 g

Fibre: 4.69 g

Total Fat: 15 g
 Sat: 5.48 g
 Mono: 7.14 g
 Poly: 1.3 g

Cholesterol: 24 mg

Vitamin A: 163 mg RE

Vitamin B6: .31 mg

Vitamin B12: .28 mcg

Vitamin C: 21.7 mg

Calcium: 320 mg

Iron: 3.42 mg

Potassium: 707 mg

Sodium: 233 mg

Zinc: 2.28 mg

## Tidbits!

These days, many recipes ask for ripe tomatoes—after all, in lowfat cooking the flavour of your ingredients is more important than ever, because the fat is not there to make up for lackluster tomatoes or bland vegetables. Penne with Zucchini and Ricotta calls for small zucchini because these have the best flavour, and when using tomatoes for pasta or sauce, we almost always call for canned plum tomatoes. Unless you are lucky enough to pick a sun-warmed tomato off your own vine, the flavour of good-quality canned tomatoes is likely to be superior to fresh tomatoes out of season. Added bonus: you don't have to peel them.

## Baked Fideo

Serves 4

*This is a baked noodle dish from Mexico, and it is almost like a toasted rice pilaf, except that it's made with fine, delicate noodles. It makes a great side dish for grilled poultry, and is substantial enough to make a light supper when paired with a green salad.*

$^1/_2$ 28-ounce (796-mL) can plum tomatoes, drained

8 cloves garlic, peeled and halved

1 small onion, coarsely chopped

$^1/_2$ cup (125 mL) water

1 teaspoon (5 mL) salt

2 tablespoons (25 mL) olive oil

$^1/_2$ pound (250 g) fideo, vermicelli, or angel hair pasta, broken into 1-inch (2.5-cm) pieces

1 jalapeño (canned), drained and chopped

$1^1/_2$ cups (375 mL) lowfat, low-sodium chicken broth

1 tablespoon (15 mL) fresh cilantro, finely chopped

1. In a blender jar, combine the tomatoes, garlic, onion, water, and salt. Purée until smooth and set aside.

2. Preheat the oven to 350°F (180°C) and lightly oil an 8-inch x 12-inch (3.5 L) (or approximate) baking dish. In a large heavy saucepan, heat the olive oil over medium-low heat. Add the noodles and sauté, stirring frequently, until golden brown, about 8 minutes. Be careful not to burn them—the idea is to give them a lovely golden colour and toasted flavour.

3. Add the jalapeño and continue stirring over the heat for 2 minutes more. Add the chicken broth and the blended tomato purée to the pan and stir together until the liquid comes to a simmer, then transfer to the baking dish.

4. Cover with aluminum foil and bake for 30 minutes, until all the liquid has been absorbed and the noodles are tender. Serve with a sprinkling of cilantro.

**207**

**Nutrition:**

Calories: 375

Protein: 15.5 g

Carbohydrates: 57.8 g

Fibre: 4.15 g

Total Fat: 10.8 g
 Sat: 2.30 g
 Mono: 5.02 g
 Poly: .716 g

Cholesterol: 7.59 mg

Vitamin A: 99.6 mg RE

Vitamin B6: .218 mg

Vitamin B12: .143 mcg

Vitamin C: 20.2 mg

Calcium: 142 mg

Iron: 3.25 mg

Potassium: 529 mg

Sodium: 1095 mg

Zinc: .32 mg

## Fresh Soba Noodles with Spinach and Miso Broth

Serves 4

*This is a simple dish that takes advantage of the wonderfully versatile Japanese bean paste, miso. It is a soy product, so it's a cancer-fighter and a good source of protein, too. Miso is a bit high in salt, so be careful using it if you must follow a low-sodium diet. It is also a superb source of flavour and protein that is very low in fat.*

5 cups (1.25 kg) loosely packed spinach
 leaves, washed well but not dried (about
 1 bunch)

1 tablespoon (15 mL) canola oil

6 scallions, white and light green parts only,
 thinly sliced

3 cloves garlic, finely chopped

$1/4$ cup (50 mL) miso shiro (white miso)

1 cup (250 mL) hot vegetable stock

2 cups (500 mL) hot water

12 ounces (360 g) fresh soba noodles

$1/2$ teaspoon (2 mL) red pepper flakes

1. Place the damp spinach leaves in a medium saucepan. Cover the pan and place over medium-low heat. Cook for 2 to 3 minutes, remove the lid and turn the mass of spinach over so the other side can cook. Cover again and cook until the spinach is tender, about 2 more minutes. Drain well, pressing out excess water.

2. Wipe out the pan with a paper towel and add the oil. Over medium-low heat, sauté the scallions for 3 minutes to soften, then add the spinach and garlic and cook for 1 minute more. Stir in the miso, vegetable stock, and water, stirring well to break up the miso.

3. Add the noodles and bring the liquid to a simmer. Cook for 3 to 4 minutes, until tender. Use kitchen tongs to place a quarter of the noodles and spinach in each of four warmed, shallow bowls, making a nest by twisting them in a circle. Spoon over the broth and scatter the pepper flakes over the top. Serve immediately. (This is best eaten with chopsticks and a spoon.)

**Nutrition:**

Calories: 247

Protein: 10.6 g

Carbohydrates: 41 g

Fibre: 4.76 g

Total Fat: 6.23 g
  Sat: .447 g
  Mono: 2.25 g
  Poly: 1.73 g

Cholesterol: 0 mg

Vitamin A: 482 mg RE

Vitamin B6: .203 mg

Vitamin B12: 0 mcg

Vitamin C: 26 mg

Calcium: 91.3 mg

Iron: 4.1 mg

Potassium: 557 mg

Sodium: 1037 mg

Zinc: 1 mg

## Linguine with Spicy Bread Crumbs

Serves 4

*This dish is very earthy and flavourful—it makes a fine accompaniment to grilled fish, poultry, or meat. Since it's not shy on flavour, pair it with another dish that's powerful, like Lamb Loin with Shallot Jus (page 289).*

$3/4$ pound (375 g) dried linguine

3 tablespoons (50 mL) extra virgin olive oil

4 cloves garlic, finely chopped

1 cup (250 mL) fresh bread crumbs

4 anchovy fillets, rinsed, patted dry, and chopped

$1/2$ teaspoon (2 mL) freshly ground black pepper

3 tablespoon (50 mL) finely chopped fresh parsley

1. Bring a large saucepan of salted water to the boil (1 tablespoon/15 mL per quart/litre of water) and add the linguine. Cook according to the package directions, until al dente.

2. Meanwhile, in a large nonstick skillet heat the oil over medium heat and add the garlic, bread crumbs, and anchovies. Stir frequently for a few minutes, until the bread crumbs begin to turn golden. Don't allow the garlic to burn. Add the pepper and taste for seasoning. Remove from the heat.

3. When the pasta is done, drain it briefly, leaving a fair amount of water still attached to the noodles, and quickly transfer them to the skillet. Add the parsley and toss for a minute, so that the "sauce" is evenly distributed. Taste for salt—depending on how salty the anchovies are you may not need to add any. Serve immediately on hot plates.

**Nutrition:**

Calories: 477

Protein: 14.2 g

Carbohydrates: 75.8 g

Fibre: 4.07 g

Total Fat: 14.4 g
 Sat: 1.46 g
 Mono: 7.61 g
 Poly: .963 g

Cholesterol: 3.4 mg

Vitamin A: 15.5 mg RE

Vitamin B6: .048 mg

Vitamin B12: .035 mcg

Vitamin C: 4.68 mg

Calcium: 105 mg

Iron: 4.73 mg

Potassium: 203 mg

Sodium: 1301 mg

Zinc: .171 mg

### Toothsome Tips

Anchovies are one of the greatest lowfat flavour boosters available. If you have a fear or even a suspected dislike of anchovies, this is the moment to confront and get over it. Don't think of anchovies as fishy—think of them as a sort of rustic salt-substitute. We have to wonder how Caesar salad became so popular if anchovies are really so widely dreaded. Most people never guess that a dish contains anchovies. An ounce (30 g) of drained anchovy fillets contains 60 calories, just over 2 grams of fat, and plenty of Vitamin A. Use them to your heart's content, but remember to rinse and pat them dry before using to get rid of the oil they are packed in and the excess saltiness.

## Paglia e Fieno
## (Straw and Hay Pasta)

Serves 4

*This is a classic Italian dish that can easily serve as a main course. As a side dish, this quantity serves six. (The nutritional values were computed for four servings.)*

1 teaspoon (5 mL) olive oil

1 small onion, finely chopped

2 cloves garlic, finely chopped

5 ounces (150 g) white mushrooms, thinly sliced

1 cup (250 mL) thawed frozen peas

1/4 pound (125 g) lean cooked ham, slivered

1/2 teaspoon (2 mL) salt

1/4 teaspoon (1 mL) freshly ground black pepper

Pinch nutmeg

4 ounces (120 g) fettucine

4 ounces (120 g) spinach fettucine

1 cup (250 mL) evaporated nonfat milk

1/2 teaspoon (2 mL) lemon juice

2 tablespoons (25 mL) grated Parmesan

1. Bring a large pot of salted water to the boil.

2. Heat the oil in a large nonstick skillet and sauté the onion over medium-low heat for 4 to 5 minutes, until very soft. Add the garlic and cook for 1 minute more. Add the mushrooms and continue cooking until they are tender and have given up their liquid, about 3 minutes. Add the peas and ham and stir just until heated through. Add the salt, pepper, and nutmeg, and reduce the heat to low.

3. Cook the pasta in the salted water according to the package directions, until al dente. Drain well and add to the vegetables. Stir in the milk and lemon juice and toss until all the ingredients are evenly distributed and the noodles have soaked up some of the milk. Stir in the cheese and serve on heated plates.

**Nutrition:**

Calories: 381

Protein: 23.3 g

Carbohydrates: 60.5 g

Fibre: 8.92 g

Total Fat: 5.09 g
  Sat: 1.58 g
  Mono: 2.01 g
  Poly: .823 g

Cholesterol: 19.5 mg

Vitamin A: 132 mg RE

Vitamin B6: .516 mg

Vitamin B12: .443 mcg

Vitamin C: 11.8 mg

Calcium: 284 mg

Iron: 2.8 mg

Potassium: 790 mg

Sodium: 891 mg

Zinc: 3.47 mg

## Spaghetti with Roasted Red Pepper and Truffle Oil

Serves 4

*In Italy, truffles are generously shaved onto pasta and the taste is so good, it's worth the flight. Flying to Italy is just a little less expensive than buying truffles here, but some of the flavour of Umbria can be brought to your pasta with truffle oil. The truffle is preserved in olive oil, which is a good fat, and the amount of flavour it packs is amazing. Yes, it's expensive but a little goes a long way.*

| | |
|---|---|
| 4 large red peppers | 1 tablespoon (15 mL) olive oil |
| 12 ounces (340 g) dried spaghetti | 1 tablespoon (15 mL) truffle oil |
| 2 anchovies, minced | 2 tablespoon (25 mL) parsley, chopped |
| 1 clove garlic, minced | $^1/_4$ teaspoon (1 mL) freshly ground black |
| $^1/_2$ teaspoon (2 mL) salt | pepper |

1. Preheat the oven to 450°F (230°C) and place the red peppers on a baking tray. Let roast for 25 minutes or until the skin is browned and blistering. Remove from the oven and place in a stainless steel bowl. Cover the bowl tightly with plastic wrap and let the peppers cool slightly. Peel the peppers and remove the seeds but retain the juice for the sauce. You may need to strain out some of the seeds.

2. Bring a large saucepan of salted water to the boil. Cook the spaghetti, according to package directions, until al dente.

3. Meanwhile, in a medium-sized bowl, combine the peppers with the pepper juice, the anchovies, the garlic, and salt and stir until the salt has dissolved. Stir in the olive oil and the truffle oil.

3. Drain the pasta well and add it to the bowl, tossing to combine. Check the seasonings, add pepper, and serve in warm bowls, sprinkled with the fresh parsley. Fresh Parmesan can be offered at the table for guests to shave onto the pasta as their daily fat allowance permits.

### Nutrition:

| | |
|---|---|
| Calories: 404.3 | Vitamin A: 1307 RE |
| Protein: 12.4 g | Vitamin B6: 0.30 mg |
| Carbohydrates: 69.6 g | Vitamin B12: 0 mg |
| Fibre: 4.0 g | Vitamin C: 143 mg |
| Total Fat: 8.4 g | Calcium: 54 mg |
| Sat: 1.2 g | Iron: 5.6 mg |
| Mono: 5.2 g | Potassium: 352 mg |
| Poly: 1.2 g | Sodium: 234 mg |
| Cholesterol: 1 mg | Zinc: 1.3 mg |

## Orzo with Spinach and Pine Nuts

Serves 4

*What's orzo? Yes, it belongs in this chapter, because it is a pasta, though it looks like some kind of oversized rice. It's ubiquitous in Greek cooking, and this wonderful Mediterranean pasta dish features the woodsy taste of pine as well as lots of healthy greens. Serve with a tumbler of the pine-scented Retsina for a true cultural experience (Retsina is never served in wine glasses).*

1 tablespoon (15 mL) pine nuts

1 large bunch spinach, leaves only, washed well

$1/2$ teaspoon (2 mL) salt

$1/4$ teaspoon (1 mL) freshly ground black pepper

1 tablespoon (15 mL) olive oil

2 cloves garlic, finely chopped

2 plum tomatoes, cored, seeded, and diced

$1^1/4$ cups (300 mL) dried orzo pasta

1. In a small, dry skillet spread the pine nuts evenly. Over medium heat, toast until only just golden, watching carefully and shaking the pan occasionally to toast all sides evenly (this will only take a minute or two). Set aside.

2. Heat a large nonstick skillet over medium-high heat. When it is hot, add the spinach with the water still clinging to its leaves from washing. Cover and cook for 2 minutes, then remove the lid and turn the spinach over with tongs. Replace the lid and cook for 2 minutes more. Repeat until all the spinach is wilted and tender, and add the salt and pepper.

3. Transfer the spinach to a colander set over a bowl and drain. When cool enough to handle, press down on the spinach to extract as much liquid as possible. Chop the spinach coarsely and reserve the juice.

4. Wipe the skillet dry and add the olive oil. Heat over medium heat and add the pine nuts and the garlic. Cook, stirring, for 1 minute, until the garlic gives off its aroma. Stir in the diced tomatoes and the spinach, cook for 1 minute more, and remove from the heat.

5. In a large saucepan, bring a generous amount of salted water to a boil (1 tablespoon/15 mL salt per quart/litre of water). Cook the orzo, stirring occasionally to stop it from sticking, for about 9 minutes or until tender.

6. Drain thoroughly, shaking the colander to get rid of most of the water, and transfer the orzo to the skillet with the spinach mixture and the reserved spinach juice. Toss to mix the ingredients evenly, taste for seasoning and reheat gently before serving.

**Nutrition:**

Calories: 189

Protein: 6.02 g

Carbohydrates: 28.6 g

Fibre: 2.58 g

Total Fat: 6.3 g
 Sat: .901 g
 Mono: 3.38 g
 Poly: 1.5 g

Cholesterol: 0 mg

Vitamin A: 257 mg RE

Vitamin B6: .15 mg

Vitamin B12: 0 mcg

Vitamin C: 16.3 mg

Calcium: 47.3 mg

Iron: 2.63 mg

Potassium: 352 mg

Sodium: 36 mg

Zinc: .793 mg

### Toothsome Tips

Everybody loves ravioli and making your own is easier than you think. If you use wonton wrappers, it's a snap, and just wait till you see your friends' and family's reaction! Any combination of finely chopped, well-drained ingredients can be stuffed inside ravioli. Just remember that cooking time in the water is brief, so all ingredients should be fully cooked before you assemble the ravioli. A little secret only you will know: inside a ravioli wrapper is the perfect place to put chopped leftovers.

## Roasted Eggplant and
## Goat Cheese Ravioli

Serves 4

*This is an elegant-looking dish with a rustic filling, and if you have help filling the ravioli it's a breeze to make. Kids seem to get a real kick out of making these little packages. Even though we always specify warming bowls or plates for pasta, in this case it's really important, because otherwise the ravioli will be cold by the time you serve it. Since ravioli must be cooked in batches, it's a good idea to keep the first two filled bowls in a low oven while you finish cooking the rest of the ravioli.*

| | |
|---|---|
| 1 medium eggplant, peeled | Pinch cayenne pepper |
| $1/2$ cup (125 mL) fresh goat cheese | 1 package round wonton wrappers |
| 20 leaves fresh basil, slivered | (sometimes called gyoza) |
| $1/2$ teaspoon (2 mL) salt | 1 cup (250 mL) lowfat chicken broth, hot |
| $1/4$ teaspoon (1 mL) freshly ground black | 2 teaspoons (10 mL) extra virgin olive oil |
| pepper | |

1. Preheat the oven to 350°F (180°C). Roast the eggplant on a baking sheet for about 25 minutes, or until quite softened and deflated. Scoop the eggplant flesh into a bowl and mash it into a fairly smooth purée. Stir in the goat cheese, $3/4$ of the basil, salt, and peppers.

2. Making two ravioli at a time, place two wonton wrappers on a dry work surface. Spoon about $1^{1}/2$ teaspoons (7 mL) of filling into a mound in the centre of each wrapper and brush the edges lightly with water. Wet the edges of two more wrappers and place them, one at a time, over the fillings, matching up the edges. Press the mound of filling down gently and then press the edges of the wrappers firmly together, easing out any air that might be inside. Press the tines of a fork all the way around the edges to make a firm seal. Repeat with the remaining wrappers and filling, making a total of 16 ravioli. Wrap the remaining wonton wrappers tightly and freeze for your next ravioli experiment.

3. Bring a large skillet of lightly salted water to a gentle simmer. Cook the ravioli in batches to prevent overcrowding, for 3 to 4 minutes, until they rise to the surface and look slightly translucent.

4. As they are cooked, remove the ravioli with a slotted spoon and rest the spoon on folded paper towels briefly to drain away the excess water. Transfer four of the ravioli to each of the warm bowls, drizzle with $1/4$ cup (50 mL) of the hot chicken broth and $1/2$ teaspoon (2 mL) of the extra virgin olive oil. Scatter the remaining basil on the top and serve immediately.

**Nutrition:**

Calories: 321

Protein: 13.1 g

Carbohydrates: 42.5 g

Fibre: 2.13 g

Total Fat: 10.9 g
 Sat: 5.24 g
 Mono: 3.65 g
 Poly: 1.06 g

Cholesterol: 21.1 mg

Vitamin A: 163 mg RE

Vitamin B6: .165 mg

Vitamin B12: .074 mcg

Vitamin C: 1.94 mg

Calcium: 83 mg

Iron: 3.06 mg

Potassium: 259 mg

Sodium: 998 mg

Zinc: .878 mg

## The Least You Need to Know

➤ Pasta packs a real punch of carbohydrates and calories, so conventional thinking dictates more sauce on less pasta.

➤ If your lowfat pantry is well stocked with Italian and Asian nonperishables and semi-perishables (like garlic, lemons, and Parmesan), many pasta dishes can be created without even a trip to the store.

➤ Making ravioli out of wonton wrappers is easy and relatively quick. Luckily, kids love to help out.

# Chapter 20

# Virginal Vegetables

## In This Chapter

➤ Cut calories by substituting low-carb veggies for high-carb starches

➤ Roasting veggies for deep, rich flavour

➤ Getting your greens

Vegetables are carbohydrates, just like starches such as bread and pasta, but they are much, much lower in calories. It's fairly easy to overdose on starches and consume more calories than you want to. With vegetables, it's hard to have too many. In fact, wherever possible you should try to replace high-carb foods like bread, pasta, rice, and potatoes with low-carb items like vegetables. Counting fat grams is important, yes, but it's also important to count your daily calorie intake and make sure it stays within your target range.

Vegetables carry an extra bonus: they're high in vitamins, minerals, and often fibre—all things that will help you maintain a strong healthy body. Fresh vegetables are, of course, the best choice, but frozen are pretty good, too, especially peas and, in the winter, corn. Occasionally you might want to use a canned vegetable—beans are great and hearts of palm make a good treat—but canned green vegetables have lost so many of their vitamins and minerals that it's a shame to use them if there is any possible way to use fresh.

Try using only vegetables in season—revolutionary, we know, although it's what our forebears did for generations. Bonus: vegetables in season are less expensive and taste better than those purchased out of season. They also have more vitamins because they've ripened naturally.

## Vegetable Gratin

Serves 6

*Use your judgement and select whatever looks nice at the market for this tasty vegetable dish. It can be made ahead of time and reheated, and we like to use it as a main course, accompanied by bread and salad, even when there aren't any vegetarians in the group.*

| | |
|---|---|
| 6 medium zucchini, trimmed | $^1/_3$ cup (75 mL) grated Parmesan |
| 1 tablespoon (15 mL) coarse sea salt | 1 egg, lightly beaten |
| 2 tablespoons (25 mL) olive oil | 2 tablespoons (25 mL) chopped fresh parsley |
| 1 tablespoon (15 mL) lowfat chicken broth | 1 14-ounce (398-mL) can chickpeas |
| 1 medium onion, coarsely chopped | $^3/_4$ teaspoon (3 mL) salt |
| 3 cloves garlic, finely chopped | $^1/_2$ teaspoon (2 mL) freshly ground black |
| 1 10-ounce (300 g) package frozen chopped spinach, thawed and squeezed dry |   pepper |

1. Cut the zucchini into $^1/_2$-inch (1-cm) dice. Place in a colander and sprinkle with the salt. Let drain for 20 minutes.

2. In a large nonstick skillet, heat half the olive oil and the chicken broth and sauté the onion over medium-low heat for about 20 minutes, until it is completely softened and translucent. Pat the zucchini dry with paper towels and add it to the onions. Cook for 10 minutes more, stirring occasionally, and add the garlic and spinach. Cook for 2 minutes, then transfer to a large bowl to cool.

3. Preheat the oven to 375°F (190°C). When the vegetable mixture is cool, stir in all but 2 tablespoons (25 mL) of the Parmesan, the egg, parsley, chickpeas, salt, and pepper and transfer to a lightly oiled 8-inch x 12-inch (3.5 L) baking dish. Smooth the top and sprinkle evenly with the remaining Parmesan and olive oil. Bake for 45 minutes to 1 hour, until a nice brown crust has formed. Serve hot, warm, or at room temperature.

**Nutrition:**

| | |
|---|---|
| Calories: 185 | Vitamin A: 440 mg RE |
| Protein: 9.99 g | Vitamin B6: .247 mg |
| Carbohydrates: 19.7 g | Vitamin B12: .172 mcg |
| Fibre: 5.89 g | Vitamin C: 20.3 mg |
| Total Fat: 8.3 g | Calcium: 202 mg |
|   Sat: 2.09 g | Iron: 2.24 mg |
|   Mono: 4.20 g | Potassium: 507 mg |
|   Poly: .689 g | Sodium: 997 mg |
| Cholesterol: 44.5 mg | Zinc: .938 mg |

## Caramelized Winter Vegetables

Serves 4

*Parsnips are a much-ignored and misunderstood vegetable. Many people seem to feel they're boring and old-fashioned, but obviously these people have never tasted a roasted parsnip. Sweet and nutty, this will be a flavour revelation if it's been some years since you crossed paths with a parsnip.*

3 medium carrots, about $1/2$ pound (250 g), ends trimmed

$1/2$ pound (250 g) small to medium parsnips, ends trimmed

$1/2$ pound (250 g) rutabaga or turnips, ends trimmed

$1^1/2$ tablespoons (20 mL) olive oil

$1/2$ teaspoon (2 mL) freshly ground black pepper

2 tablespoons (25 mL) balsamic vinegar

$3/4$ teaspoon (4 mL) coarse sea salt

1 tablespoon (15 mL) chopped fresh parsley or basil

Preheat the oven to 450°F (230°C) and place the rack at its lowest level. Cut the carrots in half lengthwise and slice crosswise into $1/2$-inch (1-cm) chunks. Cut the parsnips and turnips into similar-sized chunks. In a medium, metal roasting pan, toss the vegetables with the olive oil and pepper.

Roast for 15 minutes, then toss the vegetables around with a metal spatula. Roast for 15 minutes more, then remove from the oven and add the vinegar and salt. Toss again, cool slightly, and sprinkle with parsley before serving.

### Nutrition:

Calories: 132

Protein: 1.88 g

Carbohydrates: 20.5 g

Fibre: 5.28 g

Total Fat: 5.45 g
 Sat: .748 g
 Mono: 3.82 g
 Poly: .540 g

Cholesterol: 0 mg

Vitamin A: 885 mg RE

Vitamin B6: .193 mg

Vitamin B12: 0 mcg

Vitamin C: 25.9 mg

Calcium: 63.4 mg

Iron: 1.22 mg

Potassium: 496 mg

Sodium: 442 mg

Zinc: .654 mg

## What's the Skinny?

Ever wondered what caramel had to do with vegetables? Always thought caramel was something made with lots of sugar? Some vegetables, particularly root vegetables, are quite high in natural sugars. When roasted at high heat, or slowly braised for a long time, the sugars migrate to the surface of vegetables like onion, garlic, parsnips, rutabaga, beets, and carrots. At the surface, they are exposed to the heat and turn golden brown. The naturally sweet flavours of the vegetables are enhanced, hence terms like "caramelized onions," which are often found on pizza.

## Slow-Roasted Tomatoes

Serves 4

*Though they do take a little advance planning, these tomatoes are very versatile: they can be served as a side dish alongside fish or fowl, used as a topping for toasted wedges of country bread or baguette, or dumped atop a pile of freshly cooked pasta. Roasting really brings out the rich flavour of good-quality canned plum tomatoes, but do try to find the Italian ones, if possible.*

1 28-ounce (796-mL) can peeled plum
  tomatoes (preferably Italian), drained
1¹/₂ tablespoons (20 mL) olive oil
1 medium onion, coarsely chopped
2 cloves garlic, thinly sliced

1 sprig fresh rosemary, or ¹/₂ teaspoon
  (2 mL) dried, crumbled
¹/₂ teaspoon (2 mL) coarse sea salt
¹/₄ teaspoon (1 mL) freshly ground black
  pepper

Preheat the oven to 275°F (135°C). Gently squeeze the seeds and some of the liquid out of the tomatoes, but don't squeeze too hard or they'll turn into purée! Into a baking dish, drizzle half the olive oil and evenly scatter half the onions and all the garlic. Scatter in the rosemary, salt, and pepper.

Arrange the tomatoes in the dish and scatter the remaining onion and olive oil over the top. Roast for 3 hours, until shrivelled, juicy, and concentrated.

**Nutrition:**

Calories: 103

Protein: 2.43 g

Carbohydrates: 12.6 g

Fibre: 2.42 g

Total Fat: 5.64 g
Sat: .768 g
Mono: 3.81 g
Poly: .651 g

Cholesterol: 0 mg

Vitamin A: 120 mg RE

Vitamin B6: .244 mg

Vitamin B12: 0 mcg

Vitamin C: 33 mg

Calcium: 64.8 mg

Iron: 1.42 mg

Potassium: 510 mg

Sodium: 591 mg

Zinc: .42 mg

## Grilled Corn on the Cob with Vegetable Medley

Serves 4

*Nothing says "summer" like fresh sweet corn on the cob, grilled simply out of doors. The next time you fire up the barbecue, how about forgetting about the thick slabs of steaks and making a meal out of local vegetables? We've suggested a few, but your best bet is to go to your local farmers market, buy what looks nice and hurry it home for grilling. You're sure to come out with a feast you'll remember.*

| | |
|---|---|
| 4 ears of corn in their husks | 1 fennel bulb, top trimmed flush to the bulb |
| 1 eggplant | 2 red peppers |
| Olive or vegetable oil spray | 4 portobello mushrooms |
| 1 teaspoon (5 mL) salt | 2 zucchini, sliced in rounds |
| 1 teaspoon (5 mL) freshly ground black pepper | 8 artichoke hearts |

1. Soak the ears of corn in their husks, in cold water, for 3 hours. Remove as much of the silk as will easily come away, before grilling. Any left in the husk will come away when you remove the husk. Grill on a hot grill for 2 to 3 minutes per side. The fresher the corn the better, and the less it needs to be grilled.

2. Cut the eggplant into 1-inch (2.5-cm) rounds and sprinkle with salt. Place a weight over the rounds and let drain for 1 hour. Rinse and pat dry, then spray with oil and lightly season. Place on hot grill and cook for 5 to 7 minutes on each side.

3. Remove any bad spots from the fennel bulb, or if the outer layer is badly marked, remove it. Halve the fennel lengthwise, then cut each half into two or three pieces, depending on their size. Trim the core slightly on the diagonal, but do not remove or the wedges will fall apart. Spray with oil, season with salt and pepper and place on the hot grill for 5 to 8 minutes per side.

221

4. Place the red peppers on the grill whole, and turn when each side has turned dark and is blistering. Remove skin and seeds before serving.

5. Remove stems from mushrooms and reserve for stock. Brush clean tops, spray with oil and grill until soft and dark. The time will vary with the size and density of the mushrooms.

6. Lastly, spray zucchini and artichoke hearts with oil and lightly season. Place on hot grill and cook until grill marks are dark brown, 3 to 5 minutes per side.

**Nutrition:**

Calories: 195.4

Protein: 10.9 g

Carbohydrates: 43.2 g

Fibre: 14.9 g

Total Fat: 1.7 g
  Sat: 0.2 g
  Mono: 0.2 g
  Poly: 0.6 g

Cholesterol: 0 mg

Vitamin A: 2893 RE

Vitamin B6: 0.50 mg

Vitamin B12: 0 mg

Vitamin C: 104 mg

Calcium: 121 mg

Iron: 4.0 mg

Potassium: 1461 mg

Sodium: 737 mg

Zinc: 11.7 mg

### Toothsome Tips

Many classic and not-so-classic recipes begin with the words "heat the oil and sauté the onion." On a day when you really want to cut fat (say, because you had a steak the night before), start such a recipe not with oil but with water. You'll need a heavy nonstick pan with a tight-fitting lid; combine the sliced or chopped onions with a tablespoon or two (15 to 30 mL) of lowfat chicken broth or water and cook over low heat, covered all the time, for about 20 minutes. Stir occasionally and check that they aren't scorching. If done carefully, you'll have nice soft onions without any oil and be ready to finish the dish as directed.

## British Columbia–Style
## White Potatoes and Green Beans

Serves 4

*This recipe was adapted from one that appeared on the B.C. Vegetable Marketing Commission's Web site. Their recipe weighed in at 18.6 grams of fat per serving and 316 calories, so we did a little doctoring of the ingredients. We cut the potatoes by half, increased the green beans, and substituted stock for most of the oil. Once again, we see how easy is it to adapt recipes to suit our lowfat lifestyle.*

Dressing:

1 pound (500 g) B.C. or other white potatoes

2 cups (500 mL) fresh green beans

1/2 teaspoon (2 mL) salt

3 tbsp (50 mL) shallot vinegar

2 green onions, sliced

1 clove garlic, minced

1 yellow pepper, sliced

1/4 cup (50 mL) fresh chopped basil

3 tbsp (50 mL) chicken or vegetable stock

2 tbsp (25 mL) extra virgin olive oil

1/2 teaspoon (2 mL) freshly ground pepper

1. In a large pot, cover potatoes with cold, salted water and bring to a boil. Reduce heat slightly and let simmer rapidly until soft, about 20 minutes. Drain, let cool and cut into bite-sized pieces.

2. Clean beans by snipping off the fibrous ends, cut into 2-inch (5-cm) lengths and then plunge them into salted, boiling water until the green colour becomes brilliant, about 3 to 5 minutes. Immediately refresh under cold water and drain. Cut each bean in half and set aside.

3. In a large serving bowl, make the dressing by dissolving the salt in the shallot vinegar. Then whisk in remaining ingredients. Add the vegetables and toss until well mixed and coated with dressing.

Garnish: Black pepper and basil.

**Nutrition:**

Calories: 180.9

Protein: 4.7 g

Carbohydrates: 27.7 g

Fibre: 5.0 g

Total Fat: 7.2 g
 Sat: 1.0 g
 Mono: 5.0 g
 Poly: 0.7 g

Cholesterol: 0 mg

Vitamin A: 759 RE

Vitamin B6: 0.37 mg

Vitamin B12: 0 mg

Vitamin C: 109 mg

Calcium: 87 mg

Iron: 2.7 mg

## Tidbits!

Broccoli is a real powerhouse when it comes to nutrition—it has twice as much Vitamin C as an orange, and almost as much calcium as milk. Broccoli also features lots of Vitamins A and E, and potassium. The fact that it is available virtually all year round makes it a natural choice for a healthy, lowfat diet. If you don't mind peeling the stalks, the whole head can be used. It's a nice addition to a raw vegetable platter, as well as being very tasty when cooked.

## Steamed Broccoli with Gremolata

Serves 4

*Yikes! Don't throw out the broccoli stems. What a waste! With a teensy amount of extra effort (to peel them), you increase the yield of this cancer-fighting vegetable by about 2/3, and actually, many people think the peeled stems taste better than the florets. Gremolata is a classic Italian garnish for veal and other heavy meat dishes, but we think it's even better as a nonfat topping for all steamed vegetables. Try it on asparagus, too.*

1 clove garlic, minced
1$^1$/$_2$ teaspoons (7 mL) minced fresh
  lemon zest

1$^1$/$_2$ teaspoons (7 mL) finely chopped parsley
1 pound (500 g) broccoli

1. Prepare the gremolata: Mix the minced garlic, lemon zest, and parsley together and set aside (there should be approximately the same quantity of each, so adjust for the size of the garlic).

2. Separate the florets and peel the stems of the broccoli. Halve the stems lengthwise and cut into chunks about the same size as the florets. Place the stems into a steamer basket and put the florets on top of them.

3. Steam, covered, for 5 to 7 minutes, until the tip of a sharp knife will easily pierce the stems. The broccoli should still be bright green. Serve immediately, scattering the gremolata over the top.

**Nutrition:**

Calories: 33.3

Protein: 3.46 g

Carbohydrates: 6.35 g

Fibre: 3.52 g

Total Fat: .407 g
 Sat: .063 g
 Mono: .029 g
 Poly: .192 g

Cholesterol: 0 mg

Vitamin A: 177 mg RE

Vitamin B6: .191 mg

Vitamin B12: 0 mcg

Vitamin C: 108 mg

Calcium: 57.5 mg

Iron: 1.05 mg

Potassium: 376 mg

Sodium: 31 mg

Zinc: .469 mg

## Corn and Garlic Confetti

Serves 4

*This dish was inspired by the chef/owner of a great, tiny restaurant in rural southern Spain, where Brigit lived during the late 1980s. Maître d' and chef both, this ex-bullfighter always managed to make her feel pampered in his three-table dining room. He'd bring this dish out as a gift while she was looking at the menu, then rush back into the kitchen to fetch the specials —a rabbit, some quail, or a huge hunk of swordfish.*

2 teaspoon (10 mL) olive oil

4 ears fresh corn, shucked, or 2 cups (500 mL) frozen corn kernels, thawed

2 cloves garlic, finely chopped

$^1/_2$ teaspoon (2 mL) salt

$^1/_4$ teaspoon (1 mL) freshly ground black pepper

2 scallions, green parts only, thinly sliced

2 tablespoons (25 mL) chopped canned pimiento

In a large nonstick skillet, heat the olive oil. Add the corn and sauté over medium-high heat for 2 minutes.

Add the garlic, salt, and pepper, and cook for 1 minute more. Remove from the heat and stir in the scallions and pimiento. Serve at once.

**Nutrition:**

Calories: 91.4

Protein: 2.73 g

Carbohydrates: 15.7 g

Fibre: 2.44 g

Total Fat: 3.21 g
 Sat: .453 g
 Mono: 1.93 g
 Poly: .641 g

Cholesterol: 0 mg

Vitamin A: 41.7 mg RE

Vitamin B6: .076 mg

Vitamin B12: 0 mcg

Vitamin C: 13.3 mg

Calcium: 7.18 mg

Iron: .661 mg

Potassium: 235 mg

Sodium: 280 mg

Zinc: .388 mg

## Spinach with "Rustic Salt"

Serves 4

*Since some people have a silly aversion to anchovies, Brigit usually refers to them by her code name, "rustic salt." That's really all an anchovy is, and it certainly doesn't taste fishy when used in moderation. Try this dish on anchovy-phobic friends (as long as they aren't allergic, of course), and see if they can tell.*

1 tablespoon olive oil

3 cloves garlic, finely chopped

2 canned anchovy fillets, rinsed, patted dry, and minced

2 pounds spinach leaves, well washed, and shaken dry

$1/4$ teaspoon freshly ground black pepper

In a large nonstick skillet, heat the oil over low heat. Cook the garlic and anchovy together, stirring, until the anchovy melts into the oil, about 2 minutes.

Add the spinach and increase the heat to medium. Sauté and toss the spinach just until it wilts. Don't overcook, or the spinach will lose its lovely bright green colour. Add the pepper and serve warm.

### Nutrition:

Calories: 53.3

Protein: 2.77 g

Carbohydrates: 3.32 g

Fibre: 1.99 g

Total Fat: 3.84 g
  Sat: .543 g
  Mono: 2.57 g
  Poly: .445 g

Cholesterol: 1.7 mg

Vitamin A: 476 mg RE

Vitamin B6: .170 mg

Vitamin B12: .018 mcg

Vitamin C: 20.6 mg

Calcium: 79.4 mg

Iron: 2.1 mg

Potassium: 416 mg

Sodium: 130 mg

Zinc: .455 mg

## Sesame-Soy Snow Peas

Serves 4

*Toasting nuts and seeds brings out a wonderful new level of flavour that the untoasted item just can't match. Brigit always used to do it under the broiler, but the number of nuts she burned with that method doesn't bear repeating. Much easier is to use our favourite piece of equipment, the nonstick skillet.*

2 teaspoons (10 mL) sesame seeds

1 pound snow peas (500 g), ends trimmed

3 teaspoons (15 mL) sesame oil

2 teaspoon (10 mL) low-sodium soy sauce

1. Heat a small, dry nonstick pan over medium-low heat. Spread the sesame seeds evenly in the pan and shake now and then to toast the seeds evenly, 2 to 3 minutes, until golden. Watch out, as they can scorch quickly.

2. Bring a large saucepan of lightly salted water to a boil. Boil the snow peas for about 2 minutes, then drain thoroughly (and shock in cold water, if desired—see the next page). Let drain for up to 10 minutes, if desired, before continuing.

3. In a nonstick pan over low heat, toss the snow peas with the sesame oil and the soy sauce. Sprinkle with the toasted sesame seeds, and serve.

**Nutrition:**

Calories: 133

Protein: 6.67 g

Carbohydrates: 17.1 g

Fibre: 5.92 g

Total Fat: 4.6 g
 Sat: .669 g
 Mono: 1.67 g
 Poly: 1.96 g

Cholesterol: 0 mg

Vitamin A: 72.6 mg RE

Vitamin B6: .203 mg

Vitamin B12: 0 mcg

Vitamin C: 45.4 mg

Calcium: 43.6 mg

Iron: 1.89 mg

Potassium: 284 mg

Sodium: 90 mg

Zinc: 1.53 mg

### What's the Skinny?

If you've been around a restaurant kitchen, professional cook, or read any gourmet cookbooks, you may have come across the terms "blanch and shock." Don't be afraid, it's actually just a method of preserving super-bright green colour in vegetables. First you boil the vegetable briefly (blanching) in lots of lightly salted water. Then you plunge the slightly undercooked vegetable into a large bowl of ice water (shocking). The vegetables can then be patted dry and used for salad, eaten cold, or reheated just before serving in a little butter or olive oil—perfect for avoiding those last-minute flurries at a dinner party.

### The Least You Need to Know

➤ Many vegetables are almost "free" foods, since they have so few calories it hardly counts. Load up on green and orange vegetables to your heart's content.

➤ Fresh vegetables are streets ahead of frozen or canned in flavour and vitamin content. Some frozen vegetables like peas and corn are so small that they're frozen in moments, and retain most of their nutrients, so they're handy to keep in the freezer. Lazy people like us often use frozen spinach to avoid washing and stemming large quantities.

➤ Try to serve vegetables in season where possible—they'll taste better, cost less, and provide more vitamins and minerals than their out-of-season cousins.

# Chapter 21

# Bud the Spud

---

**In This Chapter**

➤ New potatoes = Simple goodness

➤ Great gratins

➤ Doing the healthy mash

---

Potatoes have been the staple of many cultures, and they've even had an influence on our country's history. In 1765, the potato became the most popular food in Europe. And it hadn't taken long: in 1553, Ponce de León first wrote of seeing the potato in Chile, an amazing discovery; in 1621, potatoes were planted in Europe for the first time; and by 1765, they were the most popular food on the continent. In less than 150 years, the potato had taken Europe by storm, similar to another New World import, the tomato. The Irish had quickly become so dependent on their potato crop that when there was a potato blight in Ireland in the 1840s, it caused a famine that started many Irish emigrating. Most of them came to North America and helped to create and shape our unique culture.

Potatoes alone are a good source of carbohydrates and energy, but they are relatively high in calories, so it's a good idea to balance potatoes with an equal amount of low-carb foods such as other vegetables (but not corn, peas, or legumes, which are also high in calories).

During the 1980s, there was a misconception that a high-carbohydrate, lowfat diet meant automatic weight loss. Now we know that high carbs, if they are starches, mean high calories. And high calories mean weight gain, whether there is fat present or not. Of course, fat does make a difference, and potatoes have traditionally been paired with high-fat items like butter, milk, cream, and deep-frying oil. The challenge is to find ways to enjoy potatoes and the energy they provide while watching total calorie intake and keeping your vegetable consumption about equal.

## Steamed New Potatoes with Butter and Chives

Serves 4

*What? Butter? Yes, you can use butter occasionally, as long as you use it in moderation and remember to think of it as a seasoning rather than an ingredient. This is one of those cases where the clean and simple flavour of the potatoes really showcases the rich flavour of butter, so a little goes a long way.*

2 teaspoons (10 mL) butter

$3/4$ teaspoon (4 mL) salt

$1/4$ teaspoon (1 mL) ground white pepper

$1^3/4$ pounds (875 g) small red, "new" potatoes

1 tablespoon (15 mL) snipped fresh chives

Place a small heatproof serving dish in an oven set to its lowest heat. Add the butter, salt, and pepper and let it warm while you cook the potatoes so the butter will melt.

Scrub the potatoes under running water and if they are larger than a golf ball, cut them in $1/2$ crosswise. In a steamer basket set over 1 inch (2.5 cm) of simmering water, steam the potatoes for 10 to 12 minutes, or until tender but not falling apart. Transfer the potatoes to the baking dish, add the chives, and toss until evenly coated with the butter and seasonings.

### Nutrition:

Calories: 137

Protein: 2.88 g

Carbohydrates: 27.1 g

Fibre: 2.63 g

Total Fat: 2.34 g
  Sat: 1.3 g
  Mono: .59 g
  Poly: .25 g

Cholesterol: 5.18 mg

Vitamin A: 21.1 RE

Vitamin B6: .375 mg

Vitamin B12: .003 mcg

Vitamin C: 10.6 mg

Calcium: 12 mg

Iron: 2.56 mg

Potassium: 458 mg

Sodium: 935 mg

Zinc: .563 mg

## What's the Skinny?

Baby vegetables are often referred to as "new," but it is only the new potato that most of us are likely to encounter in markets. Most other "new" vegetables are unavailable to anyone without a private vegetable garden, or are ridiculously expensive. The new potato has a unique, nutty flavour and extremely tender skin, and is available in spring and early summer. In England, new potatoes are considered a delicacy on a par with lobster or caviar, with which they are often served.

## Celery Root and Potato Gratin

Serves 6

*Celery root is a little-known vegetable in some parts of the country, but it deserves more attention. When cooked like this with its best friend, the potato, it develops a melting, creamy consistency that's very welcome in a lowfat gratin.*

3 large potatoes (about 1³/₄ pounds/875 g), either Yukon Gold or russet, peeled

1 small celery root (about 1 pound/500 g), peeled

³/₄ teaspoon (4 mL) salt

¹/₂ teaspoon (2 mL) freshly ground black pepper

1 large onion, sliced

¹/₂ teaspoon (2 mL) dried thyme, crumbled

¹/₂ cup (125 mL) lowfat chicken broth

¹/₃ cup (75 mL) white wine or vermouth

1 tablespoon (15 mL) extra virgin olive oil

1. Slice the potatoes and celery root about ¹/₈ inch (3 mm) thick with a sharp knife or in a food processor with the slicing blade.

2. Preheat the oven to 375°F (190°C). In a baking dish, layer the vegetables as follows, seasoning each layer with salt and pepper as you go: ¹/₂ the onion slices sprinkled with ¹/₂ the thyme, ¹/₂ the potato and celery root slices, the remaining onions, and finally the remaining potato and celery root slices (arrange the top slices in an overlapping pattern for a professional look).

3. Drizzle the chicken broth and white wine over the gratin, and then drizzle the olive oil evenly over the top. Scatter on the remaining salt, pepper, and thyme. Cover with aluminum foil and bake for 40 minutes.

4. Remove the foil and press the vegetables down with the back of a spatula so the cooking liquid moistens the top layer. Bake for about 15 minutes more, until tender (test with a sharp knife to be sure the potatoes are done through), and serve.

**Nutrition:**

Calories: 126

Protein: 3.30 g

Carbohydrates: 21 g

Fibre: 6.34 g

Total Fat: 3.03 g
  Sat: .472 g
  Mono: 1.81 g
  Poly: .459 g

Cholesterol: .417 mg

Vitamin A: 0 mg RE

Vitamin B6: .322 mg

Vitamin B12: 0 mcg

Vitamin C: 22.5 mg

Calcium: 78.4 mg

Iron: 2.18 mg

Potassium: 547 mg

Sodium: 796 mg

Zinc: .779 mg

## Mediterranean Potato Gratin

Serves 4

*Some dishes are seasonal, and there's no changing them. Canned plum tomatoes are wonderful, but save this dish for a time when you can locate some really good fresh tomatoes—the canned ones would break down into mush in this gorgeous dish and you would lose the integrity of each vegetable.*

Olive oil spray

1 pound (500 g) boiling potatoes, well washed and thinly sliced

2 red bell peppers, cored, seeded, and cut into $1/2$-inch (1-cm) strips

6 ripe plum tomatoes, cored and sliced $1/4$ inch (5 mm) thick

$1/2$ teaspoon (2 mL) salt

$1/4$ teaspoon (1 mL) freshly ground black pepper

3 cloves garlic, finely chopped

1 tablespoon (15 mL) chopped fresh basil

2 teaspoons (10 mL) dried oregano, crumbled

2 tablespoons (25 mL) olive oil

2 tablespoons (25 mL) lowfat chicken broth

1. Spray a large baking dish lightly with olive oil spray and preheat the oven to 400°F (200°C).

2. Layer the vegetables as follows: a thin layer of potatoes, then peppers, then tomatoes. Season with $1/2$ the salt and pepper, $1/2$ the garlic and herbs. Continue layering until you've used up all the vegetables and seasonings and drizzle the olive oil and chicken broth over the top.

3. Cover with foil and bake for 35 minutes, checking a few times to see if there is still liquid in the dish. Add a spoonful or two of water if it appears dry. Remove the foil and cook for 10 minutes more. Serve hot, warm, or at room temperature.

**Nutrition:**

Calories: 172

Protein: 3.29 g

Carbohydrates: 25 g

Fibre: 4.06 g

Total Fat: 7.6 g
 Sat: 1.06 g
 Mono: 5.08 g
 Poly: .884 g

Cholesterol: .156 mg

Vitamin A: 345 mcg

Vitamin B6: .442 mg

Vitamin B12: 0 mcg

Vitamin C: 119 mg

Calcium: 41.6 mg

Iron: 2.48 mg

Potassium: 569 mg

Sodium: 603 mg

Zinc: .499 mg

## A Mash for All Seasons

Serves 4

*Don't forgo the anchovies, which add a salty, not fishy, flavour. Remember to rinse them well and pat dry to remove excess oil.*

4 medium boiling potatoes, peeled and cut into 2-inch (5-cm) chunks

1/2 cup (125 mL) lowfat chicken broth

2 canned anchovy fillets, well rinsed, patted dry, and finely chopped

2 cloves garlic, minced

1/4 teaspoon (1 mL) salt

1/4 teaspoon (1 mL) freshly ground black pepper

1/3 cup (75 mL) 1% or nonfat milk

2 teaspoons (10 mL) chopped fresh parsley

1. Bring a large saucepan of lightly salted water to a boil and add the potatoes. Simmer for 10 to 12 minutes, until quite tender, then drain in a colander and let stand while you prepare the base.

2. Dry the pan and add the chicken broth, anchovies, and garlic. Over medium-low heat, simmer, stirring, until the anchovies melt into the liquid.

3. Add the potatoes, salt, pepper, and milk and mash with a hand-held blender or potato masher. Keep mashing and stirring until the potatoes are thickened to your liking (add extra chicken stock if desired to reach the right consistency). Serve sprinkled with the parsley.

**Nutrition:**

Calories: 135

Protein: 3.77 g

Carbohydrates: 28.6 g

Fibre: 1.85 g

Total Fat: .891 g
  Sat: .300 g
  Mono: .267 g
  Poly: .207 g

Cholesterol: 2.92 mg

Vitamin A: 15.6 mg RE

Vitamin B6: .395 mg

Vitamin B12: .092 mcg

Vitamin C: 11.5 mg

Calcium: 44.5 mg

Iron: .625 mg

Potassium: 499 mg

Sodium: 440 mg

Zinc: .519 mg

## Oven-Baked Fries

Serves 4

*There are days when nothing but fries will do and when that day comes, this recipe can save you from trashing your commitment to healthy eating. It's still high in carbohydrates and calories, so keep portions modest.*

2 large baking potatoes

1 egg white

2 teaspoon (5 mL) sugar

2 teaspoon (5 mL) chile powder

2 teaspoon (5 mL) paprika

2 teaspoon (5 mL) salt

2 tablespoon (15 mL) flour

1. Preheat the oven to 450°F (230°C). Wash potatoes and cut into strips 1 inch (2.5 cm) in diameter.

2. Mix together dry ingredients and spread on the bottom of a wide, flat baking dish.

3. Beat the egg in a large bowl until it begins to foam, then toss potatoes in egg. Pour potatoes into the baking dish and coat with the dry ingredients. Spread on a nonstick baking tray and bake for 30 to 35 minutes or until potatoes are browned.

**Nutrition:**

Calories: 78.2

Protein: 2.8 g

Carbohydrates: 16.6 g

Fibre: 1.6 g

Total Fat: 0.1 g
  Sat: 0.1 g
  Mono: 0.0 g
  Poly: 0.1 g

Cholesterol: 0 mg

Vitamin A: 1134 RE

Vitamin B6: 0.14 mg

Vitamin B12: 0 mg

Vitamin C: 13 mg

Calcium: 11 mg

Iron: 1.1 mg

Potassium: 373 mg

Sodium: 571 mg

Zinc: 0.3 mg

## Broccoli and Parmesan Stuffed P.E.I. Potatoes

Makes 4

*Bud the Spud hails from the bright red mud of Prince Edward Island. Those wonderful, dirty, table potatoes have been a welcome staple in Canadian kitchens for as long as modern memory. Now, P.E.I. is also producing an equally good Idaho-style baking potato, ideal for this recipe. It is best to buy the potatoes from a bulk display so you can pick through them and choose not only the best, but also the smallest potatoes you can find. This will naturally reduce portion sizes.*

4 small baking potatoes (about 4 ounces/ 120 g each)

1 cup (250 mL) broccoli florets

1/2 cup (125 mL) nonfat yogurt

1 tablespoon (15 mL) horseradish

2 tablespoons (25 mL) Parmesan

1. Preheat the oven to 375°F (190°C). Wash the potatoes and place directly on oven rack. Bake for 40 minutes or until soft to the touch.

2. Ten minutes before the potatoes are ready, steam the broccoli florets until they are brilliant green. If you don't have a steamer, they can be dropped into 4 cups (1 L) of rapidly boiling, salted water and cooked until their colour intensifies. Unfortunately, boiling destroys more vitamins and leaches out flavour.

3. Stir together yogurt and horseradish. When potatoes are finished baking, cut the skin away from one side. Scoop out the flesh and mix it with the Parmesan, then return it to the potato jacket. Arrange the broccoli over the potato with excess broccoli spilling over onto the plate. Serve with horseradish yogurt.

**Nutrition:**

Calories: 129.1

Protein: 6.2 g

Carbohydrates: 2.5 g

Fibre: 3.1 g

Total Fat: 1.1 g
 Sat: 0.6 g
 Mono: 0.2 g
 Poly: 0.1 g

Cholesterol: 2 mg

Vitamin A: 573 RE

Vitamin B6: 0.38 mg

Vitamin B12: 0 mg

Vitamin C: 50 mg

Calcium: 117 mg

Iron: 1.2 mg

Potassium: 796 mg

Sodium: 86 mg

Zinc: 1.0 mg

## A Potato and Mushroom Gift

Serves 2

*We've given this recipe for two servings because the packets are quite large and it's difficult to fit more than two on a baking sheet. The other reason, of course, is that this is definitely romance food. Opening the packets and breathing in the heady aroma of herbs, wine, and mushrooms is quite sensual. Brigit likes to serve this at a beautiful, candlelit table with a poached salmon steak topped with a little tapenade, or just lemon juice and chives. Live a little.*

$1/2$ pound (250 g) small boiling-style potatoes, washed

2 11- x 16-inch (27.5- x 40-cm) sheets parchment paper

4 medium button mushrooms, stems removed, quartered

3 scallions, white and light green parts only, finely chopped

1 sprig fresh, or pinch dried sage, crumbled

1 sprig fresh, or pinch dried thyme, crumbled

$1/2$ teaspoon (2 mL) salt

Pinch freshly ground black pepper

1 teaspoon (5 mL) extra virgin olive oil

1 tablespoon (15 mL) dry white wine or vermouth

1. In a medium saucepan of lightly salted boiling water, cook the potatoes for about 10 minutes, until almost tender. Let cool and set aside for up to 2 hours, if desired, before finishing the recipe.

2. Preheat the oven to 400°F (200°C). Cut the potatoes into quarters and assemble all the remaining ingredients. Fold each piece of parchment in $1/2$ lengthwise. Place $1/2$ of the assembled ingredients on one side of each parchment sheet. Fold the paper over the contents so that the edges meet, and start crimping at one end, folding the crimped edges over each other and continuing around all three open sides until you have a secure packet. Tuck the last corner underneath to seal.

3. Place both the packets on a large baking sheet and bake for 20 minutes. Serve immediately, opening the packets at the table.

**Nutrition:**

Calories: 115

Protein: 2.5 g

Carbohydrates: 20 g

Fibre: 4.26 g

Total Fat: 2.75 g
  Sat: .384 g
  Mono: 1.67 g
  Poly: .342 g

Cholesterol: 0 mg

Vitamin A: .03 mg RE

Vitamin B6: .248 mg

Vitamin B12: 0 mcg

Vitamin C: 8.06 mg

Calcium: 52.7 mg

Iron: 4.3 mg

Potassium: 381 mg

Sodium: 831 mg

Zinc: .544 mg

## Grilled Potatoes

Serves 4

*The next time you have the grill fired up, try these as an accompaniment to green salad and grilled fish. The flavour of the fire combines beautifully with the mild, slightly garlicky potatoes.*

3 large or 4 medium boiling-style potatoes, well scrubbed

2 teaspoons (10 mL) olive oil

1 teaspoon (5 mL) lowfat chicken broth

1 clove garlic, minced

Pinch dried oregano, crumbled

$1/4$ teaspoon (1 mL) salt

Pinch freshly ground black pepper

1. Steam the potatoes over lightly salted boiling water until tender throughout, but not mushy (a sharp knife should penetrate easily). This will take from 15 to 20 minutes.

2. Remove from the steamer and let the potatoes cool. Slice them lengthwise about $3/8$-inch (9-cm) thick. In a small bowl, whisk together the oil, chicken broth, garlic, oregano, salt, and pepper.

3. Brush each side of the sliced potatoes lightly with the oil mixture and grill over medium-hot coals or on a ridged cast-iron griddle pan until nicely charred on both sides and tender in the centre, 7 to 10 minutes. Serve at once.

### Nutrition:

Calories: 142

Protein: 2.74 g

Carbohydrates: 28.2 g

Fibre: 2.81 g

Total Fat: 2.45 g
  Sat: .348 g
  Mono: 1.67 g
  Poly: .256 g

Cholesterol: .026 mg

Vitamin A: .013 mcg

Vitamin B6: .416 mg

Vitamin B12: 0 mcg

Vitamin C: 18 mg

Calcium: 19 mg

Iron: .6 mg

Potassium: 519 mg

Sodium: 144 mg

Zinc: .419 mg

## Toothsome Tips

The reader may have noticed that whenever we call for dried herbs in a recipe, we specify "crumbled." In most cases, fresh herbs are preferable (except oregano, which is actually better in its dried form for most cooking). But dried herbs can be great too, as long as they are less than a year old (if in doubt, dump 'em). Use about $1/3$ of what you would use fresh, since the flavour is so concentrated. And crumble the dried herbs between your fingers before you add them to the dish—this activates the essential, aromatic oils.

## Potato Cakes with Salsa

Serves 4

*These are cute little crunchy cakes that look more difficult to make than they are. If you have a few extra grams of fat for the day, use lowfat sour cream instead of nonfat. We don't find the texture of nonfat dairy products to be very appealing, but sometimes you want a little dairy to round out a dish. Don't attempt this in a regular pan—nonstick is the only option unless you are willing to double or triple the quantity of frying oil.*

$1^1/_2$ pounds (750 g) baking-style potatoes

3 scallions, white and light green parts, finely chopped

2 tablespoons (25 mL) all-purpose flour, sifted

$^1/_2$ teaspoon (2 mL) salt

$^1/_4$ teaspoon (1 mL) freshly ground black pepper

1 egg, lightly beaten

2 teaspoons (10 mL) canola oil, for frying

2 tablespoons (25 mL) spicy, store-bought salsa

2 tablespoons (25 mL) nonfat sour cream or lowfat yogurt

1. Boil the potatoes in lightly salted water for about 20 minutes, until still slightly firm when you cut into the outside. Cool and peel the potatoes, then grate them on the largest hole of a grater or in a food processor.

2. In a large bowl, combine the potatoes, scallions, flour, salt, pepper, and egg. Mix together well and form into little cakes about 4 inches (10 cm) in diameter and $^1/_2$-inch (1-cm) thick.

3. Heat 1 teaspoon (5 mL) of the oil in a large nonstick skillet and fry $^1/_2$ the cakes until golden brown. Turn and crisp the other side, then transfer the first batch to a plate lined with paper towels and keep warm in a low oven while you use the remaining oil to fry the remaining cakes. Serve the potato cakes warm, topping each with a little salsa and sour cream.

### Nutrition:

Calories: 168

Protein: 5.13 g

Carbohydrates: 28.3 g

Fibre: 2.5 g

Total Fat: 4.1 g
 Sat: .703 g
 Mono: 1.89 g
 Poly: 1.04 g

Cholesterol: 60.2 mg

Vitamin A: 49 mcg

Vitamin B6: .35 mg

Vitamin B12: .168 mcg

Vitamin C: 12 mg

Calcium: 27.3 mg

Iron: 2.62 mg

Potassium: 445 mg

Sodium: 762 mg

Zinc: .678 mg

**Tidbits!**

In Italy it's tortino or tegame; in Canada it's called scalloped potatoes; in England it's simply potato gratin, and in France it's the estimable gratin dauphinoise (and opinionated French cooks have been known to come to blows on the issue of whether or not to include cheese). All are dishes in which sliced potatoes are layered in a dish and then baked, with, of course, various and sundry accompaniments. For such an international vegetable, the potato comes up in surprisingly similar preparations. Perhaps it's because the potato was a latecomer to Europe, arriving from South America about midway through the 17th century. What did they do without it?

**Toothsome Tips**

Tapenade is a condiment widely used in the Mediterranean that consists of some or all of the following ingredients (all finely chopped): 1 cup (250 mL) brine-cured black or green olives, pitted, 2 tablespoons (25 mL) anchovies (rinsed and patted dry), 2 tablespoons (25 mL) capers (rinsed), 2 tablespoons (25 mL) fresh parsley, 1 tablespoon (15 mL) garlic, and just enough olive oil to bind all the ingredients into a paste. You can make your own if someone in the household can be convinced to pit the olives, or buy one of the excellent prepared products that are now widely sold in glass jars. Or try Sun-dried Tomato Tapenade on page 192—our olive-free variation. Tapenade makes a piquant garnish for steamed, grilled, and roasted vegetables, and for fish, poultry, and meat. It packs quite a few fat and sodium grams, but it's also very strong and a little goes a long way!

### The Least You Need to Know

➤ Potatoes are a carbohydrate, but they are much, much higher in calories than other carbohydrates like green vegetables. Great for energy, but be sure to count your daily calories and balance them for the day with plenty of low-calorie foods. Weight loss isn't just about counting fat grams—it's counting calories, too.

➤ Potatoes come in lots of varieties, and depending on where you live they may even have different names. We have called for either baking-style (P.E.I.–Idaho type or Russet; larger potatoes with a floury-looking skin), or boiling-style (Yukon Gold or New Potatoes; usually smaller and with a shinier skin than baking-style).

➤ Everyone loves mashed potatoes, but many think they're just no good without the usual milk, cream, and butter. Experiment with chicken broth, nonfat and soy milks, minced anchovies, prepared tapenade, and roasted garlic to liven up and loosen up mashed taters.

WANTED

WILD RICE
Steamed or Alive

# Chapter 22

# Grains Not to Grow With

---

## In This Chapter

➤ A staple from antiquity

➤ Tomatoes plus grains = The perfect combination

➤ Taming wild rice

➤ Grains in the melting pot

---

Grains are a staple food that contains protein, fibre, vitamins, and minerals. Some civilizations have existed almost entirely on grains, with very little, if any, animal protein. Many grains, paired with legumes, are capable of providing a complete protein, which puts the lie to the saying "Man cannot live on bread alone." In fact, man could, and woman too, of course, with some help. Cornmeal, however, cannot provide a complete diet, since it is lacking several essential amino acids.

Nutrition-wise, grains are a starchy, complex carbohydrate so they are relatively high in calories. This means that for weight loss it's important to watch portion size and to balance grains with vegetables and lean sources of animal protein, like chicken and fish. If you are a vegetarian, portion size is not a worry because you will be getting protein and many of your calories from grains and other complex carbs.

Don't fall into the easy rut of blaming starches like pasta, bread, grains, and potatoes for weight gain—if you've been reading diligently up to now, you'll know good nutrition is unfortunately a little more complicated than that. Just be sure to count not only fat grams but also total calories for the day or week and you'll soon learn how often you can include starches in your meal planning.

## Wild Rice with Mushrooms

Serves 4

*It's always good to add vegetables to a starch dish in order to lower the carb count. Here, the mushrooms are softened with a hint of lemon flavour and no fat before being stirred into the nutty, chewy rice. Wild rice is fairly expensive, so save this dish for the holidays, when you'll really need a lowfat, low-carb dish to balance the rest of the menu.*

$1/4$ pound (125 g) button mushrooms, wiped clean and chopped

2-inch (5-cm) piece lemon peel

Pinch freshly ground black pepper

$2^2/3$ cups (650 mL) water

$3/4$ teaspoon (4 mL) salt

1 teaspoon (5 mL) fresh lemon juice

$3/4$ cup (175 mL) wild rice, well rinsed

2 teaspoons (10 mL) extra virgin olive oil

1 tablespoon (15 mL) chopped fresh parsley

1. In a small nonstick skillet, combine the mushrooms, lemon peel, and pepper. Add 2 tablespoons (25 mL) of water, partially cover the pan, and cook over medium-low heat until the mushrooms are softened, about 5 minutes. Set aside.

2. In a medium saucepan, bring the water to a boil and add the salt and lemon juice. Add the rice slowly, stirring, and bring the water back to a boil. Cover the pan and reduce the heat so the water is simmering, and cook for about 40 minutes, until tender (taste to see).

3. Drain in a sieve and return to the pan. Cover and let stand off the heat for 5 minutes, then add the mushrooms and olive oil and toss to mix. Taste for seasoning and warm through before serving, sprinkled with the parsley.

**Nutrition:**

Calories: 122

Protein: 4.37 g

Carbohydrates: 21.5 g

Fibre: 2 g

Total Fat: 2.71 g
  Sat: .369 g
  Mono: 1.7 g
  Poly: .441 g

Cholesterol: 0 mg

Vitamin A: 4.99 mg RE

Vitamin B6: .155 mg

Vitamin B12: 0 mcg

Vitamin C: 4.90 mg

Calcium: 8.4 mg

Iron: 1.15 mg

Potassium: 204 mg

Sodium: 404 mg

Zinc: 1.5 mg

## Tomato Couscous

Serves 4

*Although couscous isn't technically a grain (it's made from semolina wheat flour, and more resembles a pasta), it looks and tastes more like a grain than a pasta, so we've included it here. It's quick and easy to make, and also delicious. Most couscous that's sold commercially in this country is instant, but do make sure you read the package. If it's not instant, you'll be disappointed with a very tough kernel.*

2 teaspoons (10 mL) vegetable oil

¹/₄ small onion, finely chopped

1 clove garlic, finely chopped

1 cup (250 mL) lowfat, low-sodium chicken broth

1 cup (250 mL) low-sodium tomato juice

Scant ¹/₂ teaspoon (2 mL) chile paste

¹/₄ teaspoon (1 mL) salt

Pinch freshly ground black pepper

1 cup (250 mL) medium-grain instant couscous

1 tablespoon (15 mL) chopped fresh parsley

1. In a medium saucepan, heat the vegetable oil over medium-low heat and sauté the onion until translucent, about 4 minutes.

2. Add the garlic and cook for 1 minute more, then add the broth, tomato juice, and chile paste. Increase the heat and bring to a boil. Reduce the heat so the liquid is simmering and cook uncovered for about 10 minutes, until the liquid is reduced by half. Add the salt and pepper.

3. Place the couscous in a metal bowl and pour the liquid over it. Blend well (it should be quite juicy) and cover with a plate. Let sit for 10 to 15 minutes, then fluff with a fork, sprinkle with parsley, and serve immediately.

### Nutrition:

Calories: 175

Protein: 5.28 g

Carbohydrates: 30.6 g

Fibre: 2.22 g

Total Fat: 3.53 g
 Sat: .457 g
 Mono: 1.75 g
 Poly: 1.01 g

Cholesterol: 1.25 mg

Vitamin A: 38.9 mg RE

Vitamin B6: .158 mg

Vitamin B12: 0 mcg

Vitamin C: 14 mg

Calcium: 21.5 mg

Iron: .914 mg

Potassium: 249 mg

Sodium: 614 mg

Zinc: .434 mg

## Bulgur in Savoy Cabbage Leaves

Serves 4

*These rolls are a tasty lowfat take on traditional cabbage rolls. One of Pamela's favourite childhood family feasts was cabbage rolls and perogies from the local Polish delicatessen, served with gobs of fattening sour cream. These rolls offer the same satisfying heartiness. Take the time to make the roasted garlic yogurt and you won't even miss the sour cream.*

4 leaves Savoy cabbage

$^3/_4$ cup (175 mL) bulgur

1 clove garlic, minced

$^1/_4$ teaspoon (1 mL) salt

$^1/_4$ teaspoon (1 mL) fresh ground black pepper

Dash Worcestershire sauce

2 tablespoon (25 mL) chopped chives

1 cup (250 mL) canned plum tomatoes with juice

1 anchovy, rinsed and patted dry

1. Preheat oven to 375°F (190°C). Bring 4 cups (1 L) of salted water to boil and plunge the cabbage leaves into the boiling water. Cook until they are soft and pliable, about 5 minutes, then remove from water and refresh under cold running water. Retain 2$^1/_4$ cups (550 mL) of hot water for the bulgur.

2. Bring the water back to the boil and add the bulgur. Let it sit off the heat, covered tightly, for 25 minutes or until all of the water is absorbed and the kernels are tender. Stir the garlic, salt, pepper, Worcestershire sauce, and chives into the bulgur.

3. Divide the mixture equally into 4 parts and spoon into the centre of the cabbage leaves. Roll the leaves as you would for cabbage rolls and place in a small baking dish. Cover with tomatoes and juice and cut the anchovy into four thin strips. Place one strip over each cabbage roll. Place in the hot oven and bake for 30 minutes.

Garnish: A dollop of roasted garlic yogurt is ideal for these rolls (see page 247).

**Nutrition:**

Calories: 280

Protein: 19.5 g

Carbohydrates: 68.6 g

Fibre: 36.1 g

Total Fat: 3.2 g
  Sat: 0.5 g
  Mono: 0.5 g
  Poly: 1.6 g

Cholesterol: 2 mg

Vitamin A: 6251 RE

Vitamin B6: 1.70 mg

Vitamin B12: 0 mg

Vitamin C: 181 mg

Calcium: 274 mg

Iron: 8.5 mg

Potassium: 2164 mg

Sodium: 1064 mg

Zinc: 5.0 mg

## Tomato-Barley Risotto

Serves 4

*Risotto is a wonderful Italian dish that gets its creaminess from the starch on the outside of the rice kernels. This variation is made with barley and has a wonderful nutty flavour as well as a creamy texture. The Parmesan hits just the right note of flavour in this versatile dish.*

$1/4$ cup (50 mL) chopped yellow onion

$1^3/4$ cups (425 mL) lowfat, low-sodium chicken broth

1 cup (250 mL) pearl barley

2 cloves garlic, minced

2 cups (500 mL) water

1 14-ounce (398-mL) can chopped plum tomatoes, drained

$1/4$ cup (50 mL) tomato paste

$1/4$ teaspoon (1 mL) dried oregano, crumbled

$1/2$ teaspoon (2 mL) salt

$1/4$ teaspoon (1 mL) freshly ground black pepper

3 tablespoons (50 mL) grated Parmesan

4 leaves fresh basil, slivered, or 2 teaspoons (10 mL) chopped fresh parsley

1. In a medium nonstick saucepan, combine the onion with 1 tablespoon (15 mL) of the chicken broth. Cover and sweat over low heat until softened, about 5 minutes.

2. Add the barley and the garlic and stir until the grains are coated with the onion and garlic. Add the water and increase the heat to medium. Cook the barley partially covered, stirring frequently, until most of the water is absorbed, about 10 minutes.

3. Add the remaining chicken broth, tomatoes, tomato paste, oregano, salt, and pepper and reduce the heat a little. Cook uncovered for 10 to 15 minutes, again stirring frequently, until most of the liquid is absorbed.

4. Remove from the heat, taste for seasoning, and stir in the Parmesan and basil. Serve immediately. (The barley should be quite plump and more than doubled in size.)

**Nutrition:**

Calories: 257

Protein: 9.20 g

Carbohydrates: 48.1 g

Fibre: 8.78 g

Total Fat: 4.18 g
 Sat: 1.52 g
 Mono: 1.2 g
 Poly: .923 g

Cholesterol: 5.88 mg

Vitamin A: 114 mg RE

Vitamin B6: .32 mg

Vitamin B12: .066 mcg

Vitamin C: 23.6 mg

Calcium: 122 mg

Iron: 2.57 mg

Potassium: 563 mg

Sodium: 1093 mg

Zinc: 1.56 mg

## Rice Pilaf with a Middle Eastern Attitude

Serves 4

*Rice pilaf was one of the first foods Brigit ever learned to cook at her mother's elbow. She still loves it and serves it with all manner of fish, fowl, and meat, especially when she's too lazy to think of anything else. Of course, you could add some diced leftover chicken to this dish and turn it into a protein-rich main course, as long as you remember to provide some vegetables alongside in the form of leafy greens, green beans, carrots, or peas.*

2 teaspoons (10 mL) olive oil
$3/4$ cup (50 mL) finely chopped onion
$3/4$ cup (175 mL) long-grain white rice
Scant 2 cups (500 mL) lowfat chicken broth
$1/2$ teaspoon (2 mL) salt
$1/4$ teaspoon (1 mL) freshly ground black
  pepper

$1/4$ cup (50 mL) currants
1 tablespoon (15 mL) pine nuts, lightly
  toasted and chopped
2 tablespoons (25 mL) chopped fresh parsley
1 teaspoon (5 mL) minced orange zest
  (without any white pith)

1. Heat 1 teaspoon (5 mL) of the olive oil in a medium nonstick saucepan and sauté the onion over medium-low heat for about 5 minutes, until softened.

2. Add the rice and stir frequently for about 5 minutes more, until slightly golden. Add the broth, salt, pepper, and currants. Increase the heat and bring to a boil, then cover the pan and reduce the heat so the liquid is barely simmering. Cook for about 20 minutes.

3. Remove from the heat and let stand, covered, for 5 minutes, then add the pine nuts and remaining olive oil. Fluff with a fork and serve scattered with plenty of chopped parsley and the orange zest.

### Nutrition:

Calories: 198

Protein: 3.58 g

Carbohydrates: 35.7 g

Fibre: 1.37 g

Total Fat: 4.63 g
Sat: .889 g
Mono: 2.53 g
Poly: .814 g

Cholesterol: 2.5 mg

Vitamin A: 10.6 mg RE

Vitamin B6: .098 mg

Vitamin B12: 0 mcg

Vitamin C: 4.24 mg

Calcium: 23.7 mg

Iron: 2 mg

Potassium: 165 mg

Sodium: 770 mg

Zinc: .493 mg

## Grain Patties with Roasted Garlic Yogurt

Serves 4

*Eggs and cheese! Why not? When cooking lowfat, you will have much more success if you allow yourself to use these kinds of ingredients for binding, richness, and flavour. One egg and 1 tablespoon (15 mL) of Parmesan split among four people will contribute less than 2 grams of fat to your daily intake.*

$^1$/2 cup (75 mL) bulgur

$^1$/2 cup (125 mL) couscous

1/4 cup (50 mL) fresh thyme, stemmed

1 egg

$^1$/2 teaspoon (2 mL) salt

1 teaspoon (5 mL) dry mustard

2 tablespoons (25 mL) flour

1 tablespoon (15 mL) Parmesan

Olive oil spray

Roasted Garlic Yogurt:

$^1$/2 cup (125 mL) lowfat yogurt

2 bulbs garlic, roasted (see page 118)

1. In two separate bowls, steam the grains by combining the bulgur with 1 cup (250 mL) of boiling water, and the couscous with $^1$/2 cup (125 mL) boiling water. Cover the bowls tightly with plastic wrap and let the grains absorb the liquid and become tender, 20 minutes for the bulgur and 5 minutes for the couscous. Fluff the couscous with a fork to separate the grains.

2. Mix the egg with the thyme, salt, and dry mustard and stir into the grains. Dust the mixture with the flour and Parmesan and then stir until all is combined. Refrigerate for 2 hours. Form into 2-ounce (50-g) patties.

3. Heat a nonstick griddle or skillet over medium high heat and spray with olive oil. Brown patties on both sides, about 3 to 5 minutes per side.

4. To make yogurt sauce, roast garlic as directed, then purée with yogurt. Heat mixture in a stainless steel bowl over hot, not boiling water and salt to taste. Serve warm over grain patties.

**Nutrition:**

Calories: 174.2

Protein: 6.6 g

Carbohydrates: 26.3 g

Fibre: 4.4 g

Total Fat: 5.8 g
 Sat: 0.7 g
 Mono: 0.6 g
 Poly: 0.4 g

Cholesterol: 46 mg

Vitamin A: 76 RE

Vitamin B6: 0.14 mg

Vitamin B12: 0 mg

Vitamin C: 0 mg

Calcium: 51 mg

Iron: 1.4 mg

Potassium: 156 mg

Sodium: 256 mg

Zinc: 1.0 mg

## Baked Polenta with Not-Your-Own Tomato Sauce

Serves 4

*Polenta is less threatening than you might think. Many cookbooks say polenta must be stirred constantly, like risotto, but actually if the heat is low enough you can get away with a good thorough stirring once every 1 to 2 minutes. Don't leave the kitchen, however, because if you let it go unstirred for more than 5 minutes you'll come back to an impenetrable paste. We have topped the polenta here with bottled tomato sauce because this dish is a little time-consuming to make, and you don't need to be making a sauce, too. You could also top it with salsa, bottled caponata, roasted peppers and basil, or tapenade.*

2 teaspoons (10 mL) olive oil

$1/2$ cup (125 mL) finely chopped onion

2 cloves garlic, minced

3 cups lowfat, low-sodium chicken broth

1 cup (250 mL) nonfat milk

$1/2$ teaspoon (2 mL) salt

1 cup (250 mL) coarsely ground yellow cornmeal

$1/4$ teaspoon (1 mL) white pepper

3 tablespoons (50 mL) grated Parmesan

Vegetable oil cooking spray

2 cups (500 mL) good-quality lowfat tomato sauce

$1/4$ cup (50 mL) crumbled feta cheese

Garnish: sprigs of fresh parsley

1. In a large heavy saucepan, heat the oil over medium heat. Add the onion and sauté, stirring occasionally, for 5 to 6 minutes or until softened. Add the garlic and cook for 1 minute more.

2. Add the broth, milk, and salt and increase the heat to high. When the liquid is simmering, gradually sprinkle in the cornmeal in a very slow, thin stream, whisking constantly in the same direction until all the grains are incorporated and no lumps remain.

3. Reduce the heat to very, very low. Switch to a wooden spoon and stir every 1 or 2 minutes for 25 to 30 minutes, or until the mixture pulls away from the side of the pan and the grains have softened. Stir in the pepper and Parmesan.

4. Rinse an 8- x 12-inch (3.5 L) pan with cold water and shake dry. Pour the polenta into the pan and, using a rubber spatula that is repeatedly dipped in very hot water, spread the polenta evenly in the pan until it is just under $1/2$ inch (5 cm) thick. Cover with a towel and allow to rest for 1 hour at room temperature or up to 24 hours in the refrigerator.

5. Lightly spray an 8-inch (2-L) square or 8- x 12-inch (3.5 L) rectangular baking dish with vegetable cooking spray and preheat the oven to 350°F (180°C).

6. Cut the polenta into 3-inch (8-cm) squares and place them in the baking dish, overlapping, in two rows. Spoon some of the sauce down either side and in the centre, not covering the polenta completely. Sprinkle the feta sparingly over the exposed polenta, cover with aluminum foil, and bake for 40 to 45 minutes, or until the polenta is slightly golden and the sauce is bubbling. Garnish with the parsley sprigs and serve immediately.

**Nutrition:**

Calories: 288

Protein: 11.1 g

Carbohydrates: 41.8 g

Fibre: 2.63 g

Total Fat: 9.68 g
  Sat: 3.50 g
  Mono: 3.56 g
  Poly: 1.59 g

Cholesterol: 14.9 mg

Vitamin A: 174 mg RE

Vitamin B6: .497 mg

Vitamin B12: .328 mcg

Vitamin C: 18 mg

Calcium: 220 mg

Iron: 2.39 mg

Potassium: 771 mg

Sodium: 1903 mg

Zinc: 1.32 mg

### Toothsome Tips

One of the most versatile flavour boosters in the lowfat kitchen is citrus zest. Keep an orange, lemon, and a lime around and you'll always have a source of flavour on hand. But be careful when removing the zest: the coloured zest itself is where the flavour resides; it's not in the bitter white pith just underneath. A good, sharp vegetable peeler is the ideal tool for removing zest, but check the back of each piece as you remove it. If there is a lot of the white pith still attached, you'll have to take it off. Hold a small, sharp knife nearly parallel to the zest, lying horizontal on the cutting board, and gently saw back and forth as you move the knife away from you along the length of the piece, slicing off the pith but leaving the zest. One teaspoon (5 mL) of zest will liven up a dish that serves four admirably.

## Spicy Lentil Salad

Serves 4

*Lentils are a nutritious powerhouse with calcium, iron, phosphorus, and Vitamins A and B. Sadly, lentils somehow got a bad name and became the butt of health food jokes. Actually, they have a woodsy character that goes really well with spicy or meaty flavours. This dish shines served alongside a grilled, lowfat chicken sausage. If you can't find the tiny, green French lentils, use brown lentils and decrease the cooking time by 5 minutes.*

1 cup (250 mL) French green (Puy) lentils, rinsed and picked over

1 medium carrot, halved lengthwise and thinly sliced

3 teaspoons (15 mL) extra virgin olive oil

3 cloves garlic, cut into slivers

$1/4$ teaspoon (1 mL) ground cumin

$1/4$ teaspoon (1 mL) ground coriander

$1/4$ teaspoon (1 mL) curry powder

Pinch cayenne pepper

$1/2$ teaspoon (2 mL) salt

3 tablespoons (50 mL) white wine vinegar

3 scallions, white and light green parts only, thinly sliced on the diagonal

2 tablespoons (25 mL) chopped fresh parsley

Garnish: lemon wedges

1. Bring a generous amount of lightly salted water to the boil in a large saucepan. Add the lentils, reduce the heat to low, and cover the pan. Simmer the lentils for about 10 minutes, then stir in the carrot and again cover the pan. Cook for about 10 minutes more, until the lentils are tender but not mushy. Take care not to overcook them or they will fall apart.

2. While the lentils are cooking, heat a medium nonstick skillet over medium-low heat. Add 1 teaspoon (5 mL) of the olive oil and the garlic and cook gently for 5 to 6 minutes, or until softened and just slightly golden. Do not allow to brown. Remove from the heat combine the garlic in a large mixing bowl with the cumin, coriander, curry, cayenne, and salt. Stir in the vinegar.

3. When the lentils are cooked, drain them in a colander, and immediately transfer to the bowl. Toss together until the lentils are evenly coated with the garlic mixture, then drizzle the remaining 2 teaspoons (10 mL) olive oil over the top and toss again just to mix.

4. Cool to room temperature and stir in the scallions and parsley. Serve immediately, garnished with lemon wedges, or refrigerate for 1 or 2 hours to allow the flavours to combine.

**Nutrition:**

Calories: 211

Protein: 14 g

Carbohydrates: 31.5 g

Fibre: 7.03 g

Total Fat: 3.98 g
 Sat: .538 g
 Mono: 2.6 g
 Poly: .535 g

Cholesterol: .0 mg

Vitamin A: 402 mg RE

Vitamin B6: .314 mg

Vitamin B12: 0 mcg

Vitamin C: 11.5 mg

Calcium: 39.8 mg

Iron: 4.75 mg

Potassium: 536 mg

Sodium: 278 mg

Zinc: 1.85 mg

### Toothsome Tips

Salt and pepper are ubiquitous in the kitchen, yet they are dreadfully misunderstood. Some professional chefs may add too much salt, but they do know how important salt is in bringing out the natural flavours of food. You don't want to overwhelm, true, but undersalted food can taste strangely flat. Always taste for seasoning and correct with a little more salt or pepper just before serving. It can make the difference between a so-so dish and a super dish.

---

## The Least You Need to Know

➤ Grains have a high level of carbohydrates, and thus are high in calories. There are lots of good things about grains, too, so don't leave them out of your diet —just eat them in moderation.

➤ Always make sure to balance high-carb food like grains with low-carb green and orange vegetables to keep calorie intake on target.

➤ Grains are an important source of protein for vegetarians, particularly those who do not eat fish. Adding legumes or some chopped nuts to a grain dish is a great way for vegetarians to increase the protein content.

# Chapter 23

# Fishing
# for
# Compliments

---

## In This Chapter

➤ The raw and the cooked

➤ Top with salsa and ragout to add excitement

➤ Steamin', skewerin', and dippin'

---

Writing fish recipes is such a joy for both of us that we scarcely call it work. Fish is not only a nutritious, naturally lowfat food but also happens to taste marvellous all by itself. Adding flavourings is optional, enjoyable, and easy. Many dietitians and nutritionists recommend three servings of fish per week, and if you follow their advice you'll have little difficulty lowering your fat intake to acceptable levels.

For those concerned about cholesterol, you get a bonus with fish—Omega-3 fatty acids. Certain fish such as salmon may lower the risk of heart attack by 50 to 75 percent if consumed just once a week. Of course, you need to pay attention to how the fish is prepared—deep-fried fish will not do you much good. Grilling, steaming, poaching, and paper-baking are all good options for cooking fish, and most of these methods take just minutes, as long as you have on hand a good, fresh piece of fish and a few crucial pantry items.

Fish is a delicate food and must not be overcooked. Because meat and poultry have much more connective tissues than fish, they are less likely to fall apart in cooking. Fish can also be dry if overcooked, and the lowfat cook will be adding little if any additional fat, so this means timing is all-important for succulent, delicious results. Luckily, the rules for correctly cooking fish couldn't be easier to remember (see page 262).

## Simple Ceviche

Serves 4

*In this classical, refreshing South American dish, the citric acid in the lime juice "cooks" the fish, yielding a piquant and elegant dish for scooping up with tortilla chips.*

12 ounces (340 g) bay scallops, or sea
  scallops cut into quarters
$1/3$ cup (75 mL) fresh lime juice, strained
1 teaspoon (5 mL) minced fresh cilantro
  (coriander)

$3/4$ teaspoon (4 mL) salt
$3/4$ teaspoon (4 mL) ground white pepper
2 drops Tabasco, or to taste
1 small avocado, peeled and diced
4 ounces (120 g) baked tortilla chips

In a glass or ceramic bowl, combine the scallops, lime juice, cilantro, salt, pepper, and Tabasco. Toss gently and cover. Refrigerate for at least 6 hours or overnight, tossing the ingredients occasionally.

When ready to serve, gently stir in the avocado and serve with the tortilla chips for scooping.

### Nutrition:

Calories: 231

Protein: 17.2 g

Carbohydrates: 25.6 g

Fibre: 2.87 g

Total Fat: 7.19 g
 Sat: 1.25 g
 Mono: 3.95 g
 Poly: 1.11 g

Cholesterol: 28.9 mg

Vitamin A: 36.7 mg RE

Vitamin B6: .243 mg

Vitamin B12: 1.69 mcg

Vitamin C: 9.7 mg

Calcium: 71 mg

Iron: 1 mg

Potassium: 466 mg

Sodium: 826 mg

Zinc: .887 mg

## Smelts with Thyme and Pernod

Serves 4

*Some of Pamela's fondest childhood memories are of fishing the smelt run at Point Pelee in southern Ontario. With her grandfather, she would go out into the water late at night and help reel in the big nets. Then came the gruesome job of cleaning hundreds of the tiny fish, but it was all worth it for the fishfry that followed. Of course, the fish were fried in tons of butter, but for this version we are frying them on a nonstick surface with just a spray of oil. Any loss of taste is more than made up for by finishing the fish with a splash of Pernod.*

3 tablespoons (50 mL) flour

2 tablespoons (25 mL) fresh thyme, stemmed

1/4 teaspoon (1 mL) ground sea salt

1 egg white egg white

16 smelt, cleaned, head off

Olive oil spray

3 tablespoons (50 mL) Pernod

2 lemons, cut in wedges

1. In a flat-bottomed, shallow bowl, combine the flour, thyme, salt, and pepper. In a second bowl, whisk the egg white until frothy. Dredge the fillets through the egg white and then lightly coat with the flour mixture.

2. Heat a nonstick skillet or griddle, preferably large enough to fry all the fish, over medium high heat and spray with olive oil. Quickly fry the smelts until browned on both sides, about 3 to 5 minutes. When the smelts are browned on both sides, add the Pernod and cook until absorbed. The Pernod may flame but it will extinguish itself in a second. If you are frying the fish in batches, wipe the griddle or pan clean between batches to remove any bits that may burn. Keep cooked smelts hot in a warm oven. Serve immediately, with wedges of fresh lemon.

### Nutrition:

Calories: 382.7

Protein: 62.1 g

Carbohydrates: 10.6 g

Fibre: 0.0 g

Total Fat: 9.4 g
 Sat: 1.6 g
 Mono: 2.2 g
 Poly: 3.1 g

Cholesterol: 238 mg

Vitamin A: 186 RE

Vitamin B6: 0.58 mg

Vitamin B12: 12 mg

Vitamin C: 42 mg

Calcium: 247 mg

Iron: 3.8 mg

Potassium: 1095 mg

Sodium: 338 mg

Zinc: 5.7 mg

## Salmon and Mandarin Oranges in a Paper Bag

Serves 4

*Paper-bag cookery is covered in depth in Chapter 13, and is one of the prime choices for cooking fish. Here, fresh black bean sauce and shallots are paired together for a piquant surprise. The orange cuts the oiliness of the salmon in a charming fashion. This is an eye-opening dish, suitable for your gourmet friends.*

| | |
|---|---|
| 4 16-inch (40-cm) square pieces parchment paper | 4 teaspoon (20 mL) black bean sauce |
| | 4 shallots, sliced |
| 4 1-inch (2.5-cm) salmon steaks | 4 mandarin oranges, segmented |

1. Preheat the oven to 450°F (230°C). Fold the paper squares in half and then reopen them to show the centre fold.

2. Place one steak in the centre of one side of each square. Rub in black bean sauce and sprinkle shallots over the surface of each steak. Cover with orange segments.

3. Fold the opposite, empty side of the paper over the contents and begin crimping and folding along one open side. Continue crimping all the way along to the other side of the folded edge, then fold the last corner underneath for added security. Repeat for the other three packets.

4. Place the packets on a large baking sheet and bake for 12 minutes, then serve the packets unopened, letting diners undo their own packets at the table.

Garnish: Serve on a bed of mesclun tossed in a shallot vinaigrette.

### Nutrition:

| | |
|---|---|
| Calories: 257.9 | Vitamin A: 3641 RE |
| Protein: 35.3 g | Vitamin B6: 0.47 mg |
| Carbohydrates: 12.6 g | Vitamin B12: 5 mg |
| Fibre: 1.7 g | Vitamin C: 21 mg |
| Total Fat: 6.9 g | Calcium: 43 mg |
| Sat: 1.1 g | Iron: 1.8 mg |
| Mono: 2.0 g | Potassium: 746 mg |
| Poly: 2.6 g | Sodium: 304 mg |
| Cholesterol: 88 mg | Zinc: 1.2 mg |

## Southeast Asian–Style Whitefish Fillets

Serves 4

*Cooking lowfat style is much more fun once you start experimenting with Asian flavours. Pantry items like fish sauce will keep virtually forever and add a completely unexpected level of flavour to fish and pork dishes.*

2 tablespoons (25 mL) low-sodium soy sauce

1 tablespoon (15 mL) brown sugar, firmly packed

1 tablespoon (15 mL) fish sauce

1 clove garlic, finely chopped

4 small or 2 large snapper, flounder, or other whitefish fillets

2 scallions, light and dark green parts only, thinly sliced

1 fresh red chile pepper, cored, seeded, and very thinly sliced

1. In a shallow glass or ceramic baking dish, whisk together the soy sauce, brown sugar, fish sauce, and garlic. Add the fish and brush both sides with half of the marinade. Cover and let stand, refrigerated for 1 hour.

2. Prepare a medium fire or preheat the broiler to medium heat (or place the broiler pan at least 4 inches/10 cm from the heat). Let the fish come to room temperature for 10 minutes, so it will cook evenly.

3. Broil for 10 minutes per inch (2.5 cm) of thickness, until firm, and opaque throughout. Baste occasionally with the remaining marinade. Serve immediately, scattered with the scallions and chiles.

**Nutrition:**

Calories: 156

Protein: 29.9 g

Carbohydrates: 2.97 g

Fibre: .263 g

Total Fat: 1.93 g
 Sat: .407 g
 Mono: .358 g
 Poly: .66 g

Cholesterol: 52.6 mg

Vitamin A: 160 mg RE

Vitamin B6: .538 mg

Vitamin B12: 4.05 mcg

Vitamin C: 30 mg

Calcium: 59.7 mg

Iron: .592 mg

Potassium: 631 mg

Sodium: 656 mg

Zinc: .602 mg

## King Crab with Kuta Beach Dippin' Sauce

Serves 2

*Brigit spent some time in Bali in the 1970s, and she and her friends once splurged on a visit to the "best" Chinese restaurant in Kuta Beach—a thatched-roof affair with no walls, candlelight, and lots of mystery (and probably history, too). The steamed crab was delicious, served with the simplest of dipping sauces. If you don't want to fight with a whole crab (there's too much work involved just to extract the smallest tidbits of succulent flesh), use large frozen king crab legs.*

2 frozen king crab legs, about $1/2$ pound (125 g) each

2 tablespoons (25 mL) soy sauce

2 tablespoons (25 mL) rice vinegar

1 teaspoon (5 mL) minced fresh ginger

1 teaspoon (5 mL) minced fresh garlic

1 teaspoon (5 mL) sliced scallion (white part only)

1. Let the crab legs thaw at room temperature for about 30 minutes over a double thickness of paper towels.

2. In a bowl, mix together the soy sauce, vinegar, ginger, and garlic. Pour into two small saucers or ramekins, and float half of the scallions on top of each.

3. Steam the crab legs over lightly salted boiling water, covered, for 5 minutes, and serve with the dipping sauce.

### Nutrition:

Calories: 183

Protein: 24.2 g

Carbohydrates: 3.2 g

Fibre: .118 g

Total Fat: 7.63 g
  Sat: 1.36 g
  Mono: 2.8 g
  Poly: 2.54 g

Cholesterol: 111 mg

Vitamin A: 77.9 mg RE

Vitamin B6: 224 mg

Vitamin B12: 8.13 mcg

Vitamin C: 4.84 mg

Calcium: 125 mg

Iron: 1.14 mg

Potassium: 385 mg

Sodium: 1148 mg

Zinc: 4.73 mg

258

## Tuna Teriyaki

Serves 4

*Most of us have tasted teriyaki sauce, but have you made your own? It couldn't be simpler and the flavour is on another level from the bottled stuff. People will come running when you add the glaze to the pan, because it smells so good! When cooking Asian food, always use vegetable oil rather than olive oil if oil is required in the recipe. Although the health benefits are better with olive oil, its flavour just does not go with Asian ingredients. Usually, the quantity used is so small that it doesn't make much of a difference to your health anyway.*

12 ounces (340 g) tuna steak, in one piece
$1/2$ teaspoon (2 mL) salt
3 tablespoons (50 mL) soy sauce
3 tablespoons (50 mL) mirin (sweet rice wine) or dry vermouth
3 tablespoons (50 mL) sake (dry rice wine)

1 teaspoon (5 mL) sugar
$1/2$ clove garlic, minced
Vegetable oil cooking spray
$1/3$ seedless English cucumber (about 4 inches/10 cm), washed and finely diced

1. Season the steaks generously on both sides with the salt and let rest in the refrigerator for 30 minutes.

2. In a small saucepan, mix together the soy sauce, mirin, sake, sugar, and garlic. Over medium heat, stir just until the sugar has dissolved, and remove from the heat.

3. Spray a nonstick skillet lightly with vegetable spray and heat over medium-high heat until very hot. Sauté the tuna steak in the hot pan for 5 minutes on one side. Turn to the other side and add the teriyaki sauce.

4. Cook, simmering, for 4 minutes more, tilting the pan and spooning the sauce over the steak to glaze it. Spread a little of the chopped cucumber on each of four heated dinner plates. Cut the steak into four equal portions and place one on each plate, over the cucumber. Drizzle the sauce over the steaks and serve.

### Nutrition:

Calories: 142
Protein: 21.1 g
Carbohydrates: 3.52 g
Fibre: .168 g
Total Fat: 4.22 g
 Sat: 1.08 g
 Mono: 1.16 g
 Poly: 1.45 g
Cholesterol: 32.3 mg

Vitamin A: 562 mg RE
Vitamin B6: .405 mg
Vitamin B12: 8.03 mcg
Vitamin C: 1.43 mg
Calcium: 14 mg
Iron: .988 mg
Potassium: 250 mg
Sodium: 679 mg
Zinc: .565 mg

## Skewered Garlic Shrimp

Serves 4

*Shrimp, garlic, parsley, and lemon. What more could you want in life? For a guilt-free, sophisticated Saturday dinner serve these skewers with some steamed white rice and a few sliced ripe tomatoes drizzled with balsamic vinegar.*

32 medium shrimp (about 1 pound/500 g)

8 bamboo skewers

3 tablespoons (50 mL) dry white wine

2 cloves garlic, finely chopped

$^1/_2$ teaspoon (2 mL) dried oregano, crumbled

1 tablespoon (15 mL) olive oil

$^1/_2$ teaspoon (2 mL) salt

$^1/_4$ teaspoon (1 mL) freshly ground black pepper

2 teaspoons (10 mL) chopped fresh parsley

1 lemon, cut into wedges

1. Peel the shrimp, leaving the tails attached, and devein them if the vein is visible. Thread four shrimps onto each skewer, touching each other to keep them moist.

2. In a glass baking dish, combine the wine, garlic, oregano, olive oil, salt, and pepper. Add the shrimp skewers and let marinate, covered, at room temperature for 20 minutes.

3. Preheat the broiler to medium-high heat. Wrap the ends of the skewers with little pieces of foil to stop them from catching fire. Discard the marinade and grill the skewers for about 2 minutes on each side, until pink throughout. Sprinkle with the parsley and serve two skewers per person, accompanied by a wedge of lemon.

### Nutrition:

Calories: 221

Protein: 28.1 g

Carbohydrates: 3.55 g

Fibre: .629 g

Total Fat: 9.25 g
 Sat: 1.59 g
 Mono: 4.37 g
 Poly: 2.30 g

Cholesterol: 208 mg

Vitamin A: 113 mg RE

Vitamin B6: .169 mg

Vitamin B12: 1.5 mcg

Vitamin C: 11.6 mg

Calcium: 86 mg

Iron: 3.59 mg

Potassium: 293 mg

Sodium: 832 mg

Zinc: 1.56 mg

## Steamed Whitefish
## with Salsa Fresca

Serves 4

*Salsa goes with fish like olives go with martinis. It's a combo you can't escape, and why would you want to? Salsa is bright and refreshing and can be adjusted to suit your personal taste. If you simply must, you could use a top-quality, freshly made store-bought salsa.*

Salsa:

2 small ripe tomatoes, cored, seeded and finely diced

2 tablespoons (25 mL) red onion, minced

1 jalapeño, stemmed, seeded, and minced

1$^1$/$_2$ tablespoons (30 mL) finely chopped fresh cilantro

1 tablespoon (15 mL) fresh lime juice

$^1$/$_2$ teaspoon (2 mL) salt

$^1$/$_4$ teaspoon (1 mL) freshly ground black pepper

1 drop Tabasco (optional)

12 ounces (340 g) white fish (bass, flounder, or sole)

Vegetable oil spray

$^1$/$_4$ teaspoon (1 mL) salt

$^1$/$_4$ teaspoon (1 mL) freshly ground black pepper

$^1$/$_4$ teaspoon (1 mL) dried oregano, crumbled

1. Combine all the ingredients for the salsa in a mixing bowl. Stir and toss well. Store in a covered container in the refrigerator for 2 hours maximum before serving.

2. Cut the white fish into four equal portions. Prepare a steamer according to your equipment and place it over 1 inch (2.5 cm) of lightly salted boiling water. Spray the steamer basket or plate with vegetable spray to stop the fish from sticking. Season both sides of the fish with the salt, pepper, and oregano.

3. Steam for 10 minutes per inch (2.5 cm) of the fish's thickness. Serve immediately, topped with a dollop of the salsa.

**Nutrition:**

Calories: 121

Protein: 20.8 g

Carbohydrates: 4.36 g

Fibre: .96 g

Total Fat: 2.07 g
 Sat: .374 g
 Mono: .617 g
 Poly: .610 g

Cholesterol: 51 mg

Vitamin A: 48.6 mg RE

Vitamin B6: .234 mg

Vitamin B12: 1.47 mcg

Vitamin C: 17.4 mg

Calcium: 30.7 mg

Iron: 1.02 mg

Potassium: 492 mg

Sodium: 354 mg

Zinc: .551 mg

## Tidbits!

Cooking fish is not rocket science; it's a simple matter of the ruler. Yes, all you have to do is measure the fish at the thickest point and cook it for 10 minutes per inch (2.5 cm). Amazingly, this works with virtually any cooking method except very slow braising, which is not something you'd want to do to a delicate little fish anyway. Oven-roasting at 450°F (230°C), grilling, poaching, steaming, and paper-baking will all yield the same great results if you follow this simple rule. If a fish fillet is $3/4$ inch (2 cm) thick, you cook it for $7^1/2$ minutes. Do be sure that your heat source is fully up to speed before you begin cooking, though. Oh, and the fish must be at room temperature, not chilled: 10 minutes out of the fridge for thin fillets, up to 30 minutes for whole fish.

## Roasted Snapper with Garlic Ragout

Serves 4

*This garlic ragout is easy to make and very delicious, and it can be used for a myriad of dishes in the lowfat kitchen. You can mash it to a paste and spread it on toasted country bread, spoon it onto a baked potato, add it to a pasta sauce, use it to fill homemade ravioli (see page 215). Think up your own uses! The ragout or the purée can be covered and refrigerated for up to 3 days before using (if you have a helper to peel garlic, you could even double the recipe).*

Garlic Ragout:

2 teaspoons (10 mL) olive oil

40 cloves garlic, peeled (about 3 ounces/ 75 g)

$3/4$ cup (150 mL) lowfat, low-sodium chicken broth

$1/4$ teaspoon (1 mL) salt

Pinch cayenne pepper

1 teaspoon (5 mL) finely chopped parsley

1 $2^1/2$-pound (1.25 kg) or 2 $1^1/4$-pound (725 kg) whole red snappers, gutted, scaled, and gills removed

$1/2$ lemon, thinly sliced

2 bay leaves

2 sprigs parsley

2 teaspoons (10 mL) olive oil

$3/4$ teaspoon (4 mL) salt

$1/2$ teaspoon (2 mL) freshly ground black pepper

1. To make the ragout: In a small nonstick saucepan, heat the oil over medium heat and sauté the garlic for about 2 minutes, tossing frequently, until golden brown. Watch carefully and do not allow the garlic to scorch.

2. Add half the broth and simmer until it has completely evaporated, about 10 minutes. Add the remaining broth and simmer for about 10 minutes more, stirring occasionally, until the garlic is very soft, golden, and glazed with the syrupy, reduced broth. Stir in the salt, pepper, and parsley. Use warm or at room temperature. Store covered in the refrigerator for up to a week.

3. Preheat the oven to 450°F (230°C). Fill the cavity of the snapper(s) with the sliced lemons, bay leaves, and parsley sprigs. Brush each side with olive oil and season generously with the salt and pepper.

4. Place the fish in a nonstick roasting pan or baking sheet and roast for 10 minutes per inch (2.5 cm) at the thickest part of the fish (one fish will take the same amount of time to roast as two). Fillet the fish in the kitchen or at the table, depending on your filleting prowess. Serve on warm plates with a spoonful of the garlic ragout.

**Nutrition:**

Calories: 290

Protein: 42.6 g

Carbohydrates: 8.50 g

Fibre: .838 g

Total Fat: 8.86 g
  Sat: 1.63 g
  Mono: 4.37 g
  Poly: 1.65 g

Cholesterol: 75.8 mg

Vitamin A: 121 mg RE

Vitamin B6: .745 mg

Vitamin B12: 2.04 mcg

Vitamin C: 12.2 mg

Calcium: 67 mg

Iron: 1.55 mg

Potassium: 1001 mg

Sodium: 723 mg

Zinc: 1.19 mg

### Toothsome Tips

The quality of frozen shellfish seems to be getting better and better. In fact, usually we'd rather buy frozen shrimp and king crab legs because they were flash-frozen in incredibly cold freezers within moments of emerging from the sea. Virtually all shrimp are frozen anyway, so why not thaw them yourself instead of letting your market do it? Who knows how long those shrimp in the case have been thawed, anyway? Plus, it's almost impossible to find king fresh crab legs unless you live in Alaska. Make your own cocktail sauce by mixing $1/2$ cup (125 mL) of ketchup with 1 tablespoon (15 mL) bottled horseradish, a little fresh lime juice, and some chopped parsley or cilantro.

## What's the Skinny?

Fish is a nutrient powerhouse compared to grains and other carbohydrates. It does not contain as much iron and vitamins as meat, but it's a lot lower in fat, too. Shellfish, oily fish, and many kinds of whitefish are high in Vitamin E. Fish are also high in an interesting trace mineral called selenium, which is an antioxidant and is thought by many experts to retard tumour development in breast cancer. The highest concentrations of selenium are found in tuna, oysters, mackerel, flounder, clams, and perch, in that order.

## The Least You Need to Know

➤ Many doctors and nutritionists recommend we eat three servings of fish per week, and it's not difficult when you think of the vast range of fish out there to choose from.

➤ Fish is a superb source of lean protein. Following lowfat fish recipes makes it easy to limit fat and calorie intake.

➤ The oilier fish like salmon and tuna contain high levels of the heart-healthy Omega-3 fatty acids. Studies show the risk of heart disease may be cut by 75 percent by eating just one serving of salmon per week.

➤ Shrimp have a high level of cholesterol, so should be limited to once or twice a month if high blood cholesterol is a concern.

# Chapter 24

# Pure Poultry

## In This Chapter

➤ It's all in the skin

➤ Keeping it moist

➤ Duck the duck and goose

Chicken has gotten a bad rep from countless functions and airline meals, where cheap and cheerful so often end up bland and rubbery. Just because chicken is high in protein, low in cost, and low in fat, why should that mean a bad rep? Jealousy?

For the lowfat cook, white meat from chickens and turkeys is both an invaluable ally and a tough challenge. Most of the fat in chicken and turkey (again, white meat only) is in the skin, so it's easy to get rid of it and still have plenty of meat left for eating. Boneless, skinless chicken and turkey breasts are a dependable source of lowfat protein, but badly cooked, they resemble shoe leather. Many lowfat cooks advocate removing the skin before cooking, but in most cases we advise leaving it on till afterward. It's one important step in keeping the white meat of poultry moist. The other is to be very careful not to overcook.

Turkey gets more respect than chicken but many people can't imagine serving it except at Thanksgiving and Christmas. The dark meat of turkey (the legs and thighs) is slightly higher in fat and packs slightly less protein than chicken, and is consequently much easier to keep moist during cooking. Braised turkey legs and thighs are a great joy—you can use individual pieces and cook them slowly and gently so the succulent meat falls from the bones, and any fat that might have come out during cooking can easily skimmed from the top (see "The Beauties of Braising," Chapter 12).

Unfortunately duck and goose are both so completely inundated with fat that they should be avoided, but Cornish game hens make a festive presentation for a party, as long as you remove the skin before serving. If skinless poultry reminds you of pale bodies on the beach in February, scatter chopped fresh herbs overtop to cover their nakedness.

### Toothsome Tips

Japanese cooking offers a wealth of inspiration for the lowfat cook. Japanese cooks hardly ever use oil in cooking and when they do it is usually only to lightly coat food to be grilled, to prevent it from sticking to the pan. Sauces are made with simple, nonfat ingredients and are often quite delicious to the western palate. Supermarkets stock a wide range of Asian foodstuffs these days, so you can probably find most of the ingredients even if you don't have a specialty market in your area. Luckily, almost all the common ingredients are nonperishable, so once you have them your pantry is always ready to go (see "Stocking a Lowfat Pantry," Chapter 7).

### Watch Out!

The most common cause of less-than-perfect chicken dishes is overcooking. This is especially true for the lowfat cook, since we cannot add oil, wrap with bacon, or use any of the other high-fat solutions for keeping chicken from drying out. But perfectly cooked chicken, even breast meat, is not dry. So the solution is to learn how to tell when the meat is almost cooked, and then quickly remove it from the heat. The chicken will continue cooking (for another few moments or several minutes, depending on the size of the piece) after it comes off the heat and should cook to perfection. Use a combination of sight and touch to determine doneness, use a timer, and keep records!

## Chicken Yakitori

Serves 4

*If you are making this recipe using your oven's broiler, cut the chicken into slightly larger strips—since the heat of an oven broiler is lower than an outdoor grill, the chicken could dry out if it's cut in smaller pieces. Be sure not to overcook! If you soak the bamboo skewers in water for an hour before threading on the food, they'll be less likely to burn during cooking.*

$^1/_3$ cup (75 mL) sake

$^1/_2$ cup (125 mL) dark soy sauce

3 tablespoons (50 mL) mirin (sweet Japanese wine) or sherry wine

2 tablespoons (25 mL) sugar

1 pound (500 g) boneless, skinless chicken breasts

16 scallion whites, root ends trimmed and cut about $1^1/_2$ inches (4 cm) long (reserve the rest of the scallions for another use)

16 bamboo skewers

1. In a small saucepan, combine the sake, soy sauce, mirin, and sugar. Stir together and bring to a boil, then remove from the heat (this eliminates the alcohol and dissolves the sugar).

2. Cut the chicken breasts into $^1/_2$- to $1^1/_2$-inch (1- to 4-cm) strips. The scallion bulbs and the chicken strips should be about the same length. Thread a few of the chicken strips, one scallion, and a few more chicken strips onto the top $^1/_3$ of each skewer, making four skewers per person (the bottom $^2/_3$ of the skewers should be bare).

3. Place the skewers in a shallow baking dish and pour the marinade over them. Turn to coat evenly and let marinate at room temperature, covered, for 20 minutes.

4. Prepare a medium-hot fire for grilling or preheat a broiler. Wrap the uncovered ends of the skewers with small pieces of foil to stop them from catching fire. Grill for 2 minutes, then brush generously with the yakitori sauce. Turn, brush again generously, and grill for 2 minutes on the other sides. Transfer to a platter or individual plates and serve immediately.

### Nutrition:

Calories: 284

Protein: 38.7 g

Carbohydrates: 11.8 g

Fibre: .625 g

Total Fat: 4.13 g
  Sat: 1.17 g
  Mono: 1.43 g
  Poly: .9 g

Cholesterol: 96.4 mg

Vitamin A: 6.83 mg RE

Vitamin B6: .763 mg

Vitamin B12: .385 mcg

Vitamin C: 6.68 mg

Calcium: 34.5 mg

Iron: 2.14 mg

Potassium: 417 mg

Sodium: 1705 mg

Zinc: 1.34 mg

## Asian Noodles with Chicken and Scallions

Serves 4

*The range of versatile Asian noodles is fascinating, but soba noodles have been getting the most attention recently because of their high nutritional value and slightly nutty flavour. There are even green tea–flavoured soba noodles. This dish is not a soup, though it is a brothy main course that must be served in a bowl.*

8 ounces (250 g) dried soba noodles (or linguine)

$1^1/_2$ teaspoons (7 mL) sesame oil

$1/_2$ pound (125 g) chicken breast meat

8 scallions, white and light green parts only, cut into $1^1/_2$-inch (4-cm) lengths

2 cups (500 mL) lowfat, low-sodium chicken broth

1 cup (250 mL) water

1 tablespoon (15 mL) Thai or Vietnamese fish sauce

Pinch cayenne pepper

4 white button mushrooms, wiped clean and sliced

1. Bring a large saucepan of lightly salted water to a boil and cook the noodles until tender, according to package instructions. Drain and rinse well with cold water, then toss with the sesame oil until all the strands are coated. Transfer the noodles to four bowls and keep warm in a low oven.

2. Cut the chicken meat into $3/_4$-inch (2-cm) squares and halve the scallion pieces lengthwise. In a small saucepan, combine the broth, water, fish sauce, and cayenne and bring to a simmer. Add the chicken, cover the pan, and simmer for about 5 minutes. Skim off any foam that rises to the surface, and add the scallions and mushrooms. Simmer for 1 minute more.

3. Spoon some of the hot chicken, mushroom, scallion, and broth mixture over the noodles, distributing the ingredients evenly (the hot broth will warm the noodles). Serve at once.

**Nutrition:**

Calories: 201

Protein: 15 g

Carbohydrates: 23.5 g

Fibre: .685 g

Total Fat: 4.58 g
  Sat: .964 g
  Mono: 1.62 g
  Poly: 1.43 g

Cholesterol: 38 mg

Vitamin A: 7.54 mg RE

Vitamin B6: .355 mg

Vitamin B12: .543 mcg

Vitamin C: 4.69 mg

Calcium: 27.2 mg

Iron: 1.33 mg

Potassium: 285 mg

Sodium: 883 mg

Zinc: .815 mg

268

## Chicken Breasts Escabeche

Serves 4

*Escabeche is a vinegary sauce that originated in Latin America. It can be used with fish, poultry, and vegetables. This is an intense sauce that complements the chicken well—a completely different animal from the Italian-style tomato sauces we are all familiar with.*

2 teaspoons (10 mL) olive oil

4 cloves garlic, minced

1 $1/2$ teaspoons (7 mL) ground coriander

2 tablespoons (25 mL) sherry vinegar

1 tablespoon (15 mL) red wine vinegar

2 teaspoons (10 mL) tomato paste

2 cups (500 mL) tomato juice

2 sprigs fresh cilantro

2 sprigs fresh thyme

1 bay leaf

$1/2$ teaspoon (2 mL) salt

$1/4$ teaspoon (1 mL) freshly ground black pepper

2 dashes Tabasco

4 4-ounce (120-g) individual boneless chicken breasts, skin on

1. Heat a large nonstick skillet over medium-low heat and add the olive oil. Sauté the garlic and the coriander together, stirring, for $1^1/2$ minutes. Don't allow the garlic to brown.

2. Add the sherry and red wine vinegars and deglaze the pan by using a wooden spoon to scrape up any bits from the bottom of the pan. Simmer for about 3 minutes to reduce slightly, then stir in the tomato paste and tomato juice. Add the cilantro, thyme, and bay leaf and bring to a boil, then reduce the heat so the sauce barely simmers.

3. Cook, uncovered over very low heat, for about 20 minutes, until thickened. Remove the herbs and bay leaf. Add half of the salt and pepper, and the Tabasco. Keep warm.

4. Season both sides of the chicken breasts with the remaining salt and pepper and place in a steamer basket over lightly salted, simmering water. Cover and steam for 9 minutes, until firm.

5. Transfer to a plate, cover with foil, and let rest for 1 minute. Discard the skin and slice the chicken breasts $1/2$-inch (1-cm) thick on the diagonal. Place the slices on heated dinner plates and spoon a generous amount of sauce over the top.

**Nutrition:**

Calories: 197.1

Protein: 28.0 g

Carbohydrates: 5.5 g

Fibre: 0.9 g

Total Fat: 5.6 g
 Sat: 3.0 g
 Mono: 1.4 g
 Poly: 0.5 g

Cholesterol: 71 mg

Vitamin A: 813 RE

Vitamin B6: 0.66 mg

Vitamin B12: 1 mg

Vitamin C: 10 mg

Calcium: 162 mg

Iron: 1.4 mg

Potassium: 509 mg

Sodium: 593 mg

Zinc: 1.7 mg

## Emmenthal-Stuffed Chicken Breasts Braised in Tomato Sauce

Serves 4

*Most Emmenthal cheeses weigh in at about 7 percent fat content, so although it is still a saturated fat, you can use it in moderation to make special dishes like this one. And it doesn't have the unpleasant texture of reduced-fat cheeses. Most chicken breasts weight at least 5 ounces (140 g), so trim them down to a 3$^1$/2-ounce (105-g) portion and reserve the trim for another meal.*

4 3$^1$/2-ounce (105-g) chicken breasts, boneless, skinless

2 ounces (60 g) Emmenthal cheese, sliced

$^1$/4 teaspoon (1 mL) ground salt

$^1$/4 teaspoon (1 mL) freshly ground black pepper

1 cup (250 mL) tomato sauce

or

$^3$/4 cup (175 mL) canned plum tomatoes in juice

$^1$/4 cup (50 mL) red wine

1 clove garlic

$^1$/4 cup (50 mL) chopped fresh basil

1. Preheat the oven to 375°F (190°C). When trimming the chicken, leave the thickest part of the breast and the tenderloin (the strip attached to the breast) for this dish. Place the chicken on a cutting surface with the side that would have had the skin on it facing down. Remove the tenderloin. Cut a pocket into the thickest part of the breast and place $^1$/2 ounce (15 g) of the cheese inside. Cover the opening up with the tenderloin and place the breast, tenderloin side down, in a baking dish. Season with salt and pepper.

2. Cover the chicken with store-bought or prepared tomato sauce, or combine the plum tomatoes with the red wine, garlic, and basil and pour this mixture over the chicken.

3. Braise, uncovered, for 20 minutes or until there is no pink left in the breast. Serve hot.

**Nutrition:**

Calories: 197.1

Protein: 28.0 g

Carbohydrates: 5.5 g

Fibre: 0.9 g

Total Fat: 0.9 g
  Sat: 5.6 g
  Mono: 1.4 g
  Poly: 0.5 g

Cholesterol: 71 mg

Vitamin A: 813 IU

Vitamin B6: 0.6 mg

Vitamin B12: 1 mg

Vitamin C: 10 mg

Calcium: 162 mg

Iron: 1.4 mg

Potassium: 509 mg

Sodium: 593 mg

Zinc: 1.7 mg

## Chicken Paillard with Salsa Fresca

Serves 4

*This staple of spa cuisine is a great standby for the lowfat cook. The chicken, pounded into thin pieces called "paillards," cooks evenly since you have flattened it to a uniform thickness; thus there are no dry edges. And it cooks in a flash! For toppings, hit the pantry: fresh salsa, pesto, olive paste, or a teaspoon (5 mL) each of minced lemon zest, minced garlic, and parsley (gremolata). Since the topping isn't cooked, it's worth using your best olive oil.*

4 4-ounce (120-g) individual boneless, skinless chicken breasts

1 28-ounce (796-mL) can best-quality chopped tomatoes, well drained

2 tablespoons (25 mL) slivered fresh basil

2 cloves garlic, minced

2 teaspoons (10 mL) extra virgin olive oil

$1/2$ teaspoon (2 mL) salt

$1/4$ teaspoon (1 mL) freshly ground black pepper

Olive oil spray

1. Place a chicken breast between two sheets of waxed paper or plastic wrap. Gently pound from the centre toward the edge, smoothing the paper and aiming for a uniform thickness of about $3/8$ inch (9 mm). Repeat with the remaining breasts.

2. In a bowl, combine the chopped tomatoes, basil, garlic, olive oil, and half of the salt and pepper. Let sit at room temperature for at least 20 minutes.

3. Pat the chicken dry with paper towels and season both sides of each breast with the remaining salt and pepper. Spray briefly with olive oil to lightly film each side. Preheat a ridged cast-iron griddle pan or outdoor grill to high heat.

4. Grill the chicken breasts for $2^1/2$ to 3 minutes on either side (do this in two batches if the griddle pan isn't large enough to hold them all without touching —if they touch, they'll poach instead of grill). Be sure not to overcook—as soon as the chicken feels quite firm, it's done. Transfer to warmed plates and spoon some of the salsa over the top. Pass the remaining salsa.

**Nutrition:**

Calories: 168

Protein: 27.3 g

Carbohydrates: 5.02 g

Fibre: .93 g

Total Fat: 3.93 g
 Sat: .717 g
 Mono: 2.04 g
 Poly: .615 g

Cholesterol: 65.7 mg

Vitamin A: 71.3 mg RE

Vitamin B6: .736 mg

Vitamin B12: .43 mcg

Vitamin C: 17.4 mg

Calcium: 43.6 mg

Iron: 1.54 mg

Potassium: 527 mg

Sodium: 508 mg

Zinc: 1.10 mg

## Chicken Scallops with Dijon Sauce

Serves 4

*This recipe uses flattened chicken breasts prepared exactly as in the previous recipe, only in this case each one is called a scallop instead of a paillard. (It's a French thing.) For this recipe, a pan sauce is prepared instead of serving the chicken with a chunky, salsa-like topping as before. Be sure to have warmed plates waiting for this dish (you always should anyway!).*

4 4-ounce (120-g) individual boneless, skinless chicken breasts
$1/4$ teaspoon (1 mL) salt
Pinch ground white pepper
1 teaspoon (5 mL) butter

$3/4$ cup (175 mL) white wine or vermouth
$1/4$ cup (50 mL) sherry
1 tablespoon (15 mL) Dijon mustard
4 sprigs fresh parsley
Pinch of ground paprika

1. Place a chicken breast between two sheets of waxed paper or plastic wrap. Gently pound from the centre toward the edge, smoothing the paper and aiming for a uniform thickness of about $3/8$ inch (9 mm). Repeat with the remaining breasts. Season both sides with salt and pepper.

2. Heat a nonstick skillet over medium-high heat and add the butter. When it is nice and hot, sauté the chicken breasts for about 3 minutes on one side, then turn over and cook for about 2 minutes more, until just firm (but not tough) and golden brown. Transfer to a plate in a warm oven.

3. Add the wine and sherry to the pan, increase the heat to high and simmer, scraping with a wooden spoon to get all the flavourful bits into the sauce. Simmer for about 3 minutes, stirring, until the wine is reduced to a few spoonfuls. Remove from the heat and stir in the mustard until smooth.

4. Spoon a little of the sauce over each chicken breast, and serve, garnished with the parsley and a very light dusting of paprika.

**Nutrition:**

Calories: 204
Protein: 26.6 g
Carbohydrates: 3.37 g
Fibre: .217 g
Total Fat: 2.77 g
  Sat: .99 g
  Mono: .753 g
  Poly: .448 g
Cholesterol: 68.3 mg

Vitamin A: 19 mg RE
Vitamin B6: .634 mg
Vitamin B12: .433 mcg
Vitamin C: 2.29 mg
Calcium: 24.3 mg
Iron: 1.23 mg
Potassium: 331 mg
Sodium: 311 mg
Zinc: .999 mg

## Grilled Chicken with Yogurt and Cumin

Serves 4

*The yogurt in this marinade acts as a tenderizer on the chicken, which will really benefit from spending the night in the fridge. If not, 2 hours at room temperature will do it. Serve this dish with the Rice Pilaf with a Middle Eastern Attitude on page 246.*

2 teaspoons (10 mL) ground cumin

2 teaspoons (10 mL) ground paprika

1 small yellow onion, coarsely chopped

4 cloves garlic, finely chopped

2 tablespoons (25 mL) fresh lemon juice

1 cup (250 mL) nonfat yogurt

8 4-ounce (120-g) boneless, skinless chicken thighs

$^{1}/_{4}$ teaspoon (1 mL) salt

$^{1}/_{4}$ teaspoon (1 mL) freshly ground black pepper

1 teaspoon (5 mL) finely chopped cilantro or parsley

1 lemon, cut into 4 wedges

1. In a blender or food processor, combine the cumin, paprika, onion, garlic, lemon juice, and yogurt and purée until almost smooth. Rinse the chicken in cold water and pat dry with paper towels. Place in a medium casserole and pour the yogurt mixture over the top, making sure all the chicken pieces are coated evenly. Cover and refrigerate overnight or let stand at room temperature for no more than 2 hours.

2. If refrigerated, bring the chicken back to room temperature. Prepare a fire for medium-high heat grill or preheat a broiler to high heat.

3. Season the thighs with the salt and pepper and grill or broil for 6 minutes on each side, until firm with no trace of pink remaining. Sprinkle with the cilantro and serve immediately with a wedge of lemon.

**Nutrition:**

Calories: 232

Protein: 31.9 g

Carbohydrates: 12.3 g

Fibre: 1.55 g

Total Fat: 6.02 g
 Sat: 1.51 g
 Mono: 1.74 g
 Poly: 1.49 g

Cholesterol: 116 mg

Vitamin A: 100 mg RE

Vitamin B6: .588 mg

Vitamin B12: .859 mcg

Vitamin C: 16 mg

Calcium: 166 mg

Iron: 2.7 mg

Potassium: 625 mg

Sodium: 303 mg

Zinc: 3.46 mg

## Orange Sage Chicken

Serves 4

*This dish was inspired by Brigit's friend Evan Kleiman, who has overseen the Angeli restaurant empire in Los Angeles since 1984. Evan is the maestro of simple, healthy Italian food, and has been a great influence on Brigit's cooking style.*

4 4-ounce (120-g) individual boneless, skinless chicken breasts

$^1/_4$ teaspoon (1 mL) salt

Pinch freshly ground black pepper

Olive oil spray

2 teaspoons (10 mL) finely chopped fresh sage or 1 teaspoon (5 mL) dried sage, crumbled

1 medium shallot, finely chopped

$^1/_2$ cup (125 mL) orange juice

1 orange, skin and white pith trimmed away

1 teaspoon (5 mL) finely chopped parsley

1. Preheat the oven to 375°F (190°C). Pat the chicken dry with paper towels. Season both sides with the salt and pepper.

2. Spray a small baking dish for 1 second with the olive oil spray and scatter half of the sage and half the shallots in the bottom. Place the chicken on top and scatter the remaining sage and shallots over them. Pour the orange juice around the edges, and cover with aluminum foil.

3. Bake for 10 minutes, then turn the breasts over and recover the dish with the foil. Bake for about 12 minutes more, until the meat is firm. Let cool in the pan for 5 minutes.

4. Slice the whole, trimmed orange in half lengthwise and then again into $^1/_4$-inch (5-mm) thick half-moon shapes. Place a few orange slices on each plate. Cut the chicken breasts crosswise into $^1/_2$-inch (1-cm) thick slices and serve over the orange slices, with the pan juices drizzled over the top. Scatter with the parsley and serve.

**Nutrition:**

Calories: 166

Protein: 26.9 g

Carbohydrates: 8.72 g

Fibre: .82 g

Total Fat: 2.18 g
 Sat: .493 g
 Mono: .789 g
 Poly: .402 g

Cholesterol: 65.7 mg

Vitamin A: 24.2 mg RE

Vitamin B6: .673 mg

Vitamin B12: .43 mcg

Vitamin C: 34.8 mg

Calcium: 40.6 mg

Iron: 1.13 mg

Potassium: 439 mg

Sodium: 208 mg

Zinc: .994 mg

## Turkey-Stuffed Vine Leaves with Yogurt

Serves 4

*Vine leaves packed in a jar are available in any good market, particularly if there is a Middle Eastern population nearby. These dolmades (the Greek name) are spectacular for a party, since they can be made ahead of time, and the recipe can easily be doubled. You can substitute $1/2$ cup (125 mL) of leftover cooked rice for the bread if desired.*

| | |
|---|---|
| 16 to 24 vine leaves, packed in brine | 2 egg whites |
| $3/4$ pound (374 g) ground turkey (white meat) | $1/2$ teaspoon (2 mL) salt |
| 1 large yellow onion, finely chopped | $1/4$ teaspoon (1 mL) freshly ground black pepper |
| 3 cloves garlic, finely chopped | Olive oil spray |
| 2 tablespoons (25 mL) chopped fresh chives | 2 tablespoons (25 mL) fresh lemon juice |
| 2 tablespoons (25 mL) chopped fresh parsley | $1/2$ cup (125 mL) lowfat chicken broth |
| 2 slices sourdough bread, crust removed and finely chopped | 3 tablespoons (50 mL) lowfat yogurt |

1. Rinse the vine leaves and leave them to soak in a bowl of cold water for about 10 minutes. In another bowl, combine the turkey, onion, garlic, chives, parsley, bread, egg whites, salt, and pepper and work together well until evenly blended.

2. Drain the vine leaves, pat them dry with a towel, and trim off the tough stems. Place two or three leaves with the veined side up on a work surface, fanned out and overlapping each other by about an inch (2.5 cm), with the stem ends together. Scoop two rounded spoonfuls of the filling into the centre and press down with the cupped palm of your hand to compact the filling into a ball. Fold the ends of the leaves up and over the filling.

3. Place seam side down in a 9- x 12-inch (3.5-L) baking dish and continue making packets until you have used all the filling. The packets should be touching each other snugly. (At this point the dolmades could be covered and refrigerated for up to 1 day.)

4. Preheat the oven to 350°F (180°C) and bring the dolmades to room temperature. Spray the tops for 2 seconds with the olive oil spray and drizzle the lemon juice and broth around the edges. Cover and cook for about 20 minutes, until almost all of the liquid has been absorbed. Serve two packets per person, garnished with a dollop of yogurt.

**Nutrition:**

Calories: 246

Protein: 21.4 g

Carbohydrates: 16.8 g

Fibre: 2.37 g

Total Fat: 10.9 g
 Sat: 3.26 g
 Mono: 4.19 g
 Poly: 3.05 g

Cholesterol: 70.5 mg

Vitamin A: 367 mg RE

Vitamin B6: .199 mg

Vitamin B12: .098 mcg

Vitamin C: 14.4 mg

Calcium: 126 mg

Iron: 3.6 mg

Potassium: 577 mg

Sodium: 680 mg

Zinc: 3.18 mg

## Moroccan-Style Cornish Hens

Serves 4

*Cornish hens are lovely to work with and their presentation is delightful. Here we have stuffed them with dates and apricots for a Moroccan-type treat. Removing the skin after cooking helps to keep these game hens moist.*

2 Cornish hens

4 dried apricots

6 dates

2 tablespoon (30 mL) nonfat yogurt

Pinch dry mustard

1 clove garlic

$1/4$ teaspoon (1 mL) curry powder

$1/4$ teaspoon (1 mL) paprika

1. Preheat the oven to 400°F (200°C). Rinse the hens under cold, running water. Stuff the apricots and dates into the large cavity of the birds.

2. Combine the yogurt and spices and rub into the flesh of the bird. As much as possible, try to rub the seasonings under the skin so it is not all lost when you remove the skin. This is sometimes easier if you run a knife between the skin and the flesh at looser parts like the breast.

3. Roast the hens breast side down (to keep them juicy) on a roasting rack for 15 minutes. Reduce the oven heat to 325°F (165°C), turn the hens breast side up and roast for an additional 30 minutes or until firm with no trace of pink remaining at the thigh joint.

4. Let rest, loosely covered, on a platter for 10 minutes, then remove the skin, cut the hens in half and serve half per person with the fruits as garnish.

**Nutrition:**

Calories: 261.6

Protein: 24.2

Carbohydrates: 15.0 g

Fibre: 0.9 g

Total Fat: 11.6
 Sat: 3.2 g
 Mono: 4.5 g
 Poly: 2.5 g

Cholesterol: 75 mg

Vitamin A: 1129 RE

Vitamin B6: 0.4 mg

Vitamin B12: 0 mg

Vitamin C: 1 mg

Calcium: 67 mg

Iron: 1.8 mg

Potassium: 419 mg

Sodium: 273 mg

Zinc: 1.8 mg

## The Least You Need to Know

➤ Poultry is a good source of lean protein, but only if you take care to remove the skin. Poultry skin contains about 75 percent of the fat—most of it the nasty, saturated kind—in the whole bird.

➤ Boneless, skinless chicken breasts may bore you, and they may be ubiquitous in every lowfat cookbook, but there's a reason. This cut of poultry is quick and easy to cook and takes on flavour very well. Take care not to overcook and make sure you add lots of flavour by marinating, garnishing, or using a sauce.

➤ Turkey is a good source of lean protein, too, but duck and goose have so much fat in the flesh as well as the skin that they should be avoided. That is, except for special occasions. If you do want to cook duck or goose, you'll need to: (1) use only the breasts, (2) remove the skin before cooking, and (3) grill.

# Chapter 25

# Managing Meat

## In This Chapter

➤ Flank steak rules

➤ Pork changes its act

➤ Skimming and trimming make lamb a viable choice

It's hard to believe now, but steak was once thought to be the dieter's best choice. This was back in the 1950s when *Esquire* magazine published trendy diet suggestions like this:

> Breakfast: 1 piece toast (dry); 1 cup coffee (nothing in)
>
> Lunch: 1 martini (dry); 6 oysters (raw);
>
> Dinner: 1 sirloin steak (medium-rare)

We now know that to satisfy our bodies' need for protein, it's probably better to choose fish three times a week and poultry on a few of the other nights. There are some cuts of beef, however, that are very lean without being tough or dry, most notably the flank steak. If you want to keep beef in your diet, then you have two choices: either make it a special-occasion treat and balance the next few days' fat intake to compensate, or (and this is easier) practice stringent portion control. The cooked weight per portion should be 3 to 4 ounces (75 to 120 g), tops. Choose flank or skirt, round, or sirloin (this includes T-bone but not porterhouse, which has a big piece of the filet attached). Do not choose rib-eye, prime rib, or filet mignon, which tend to have a lot of fat running through the meat. Trim most of the exterior fat before cooking and remove the remainder afterward. The next time you walk past the meat counter, keep in mind that a 6-ounce (170-g) piece of prime rib totes about 45 grams of fat.

Pork has been getting (or has been giving itself) lots of press as "the other white meat." In fact, the fat content of pork has dropped drastically over recent decades due to hard work on the part of pork producers. There are plenty of pork cuts that are less fatty than chicken thighs, particularly the loin. Pork is an excellent source of lowfat protein, iron, B vitamins, niacin, and zinc). It is also a good source of selenium, an antioxidant that studies have shown can defend against cancer.

When it comes to lamb, choose cuts that can be braised, most notably the shanks, so that fat can be skimmed off after the slow, gentle cooking. All the natural gelatin and flavour will still be in the remaining juices. Lamb fat is particularly unpalatable, and it is usually trimmed or skimmed from cooked dishes anyway. So you can use lamb recipes from conventional cookbooks as long as they don't call for adding any additional fat to the dish. Remember to skim and trim thoroughly.

## Chile Vinegar–Marinated Skirt Steak with Onion Cilantro Relish

Serves 4

*This dish packs a flavour punch, so cut the marinating time in half if you prefer a milder touch. The relish tastes fine made with a green or red serrano chile, but we prefer it with green for a fresh green-and-white look—a bit of a change from the usual red salsas. It would be nice with any grilled meat or poultry.*

$1/2$ small white onion, peeled and finely chopped

1 serrano chile, stemmed, seeded and minced

2 tablespoons (25 mL) chopped cilantro

$1/2$ teaspoon (2 mL) salt

2 tablespoons (25 mL) fresh lime juice

1 teaspoon (5 mL) olive oil

4 whole dried red chiles, stemmed and seeded

1 teaspoon (5 mL) ground cumin

2 cloves garlic, minced

$1/2$ teaspoon (2 mL) salt

$3/4$ cup (175 mL) red wine vinegar

1 pound (500 g) trimmed skirt steak

1. To make the relish, in a bowl combine the onion, serrano, cilantro, salt, lime juice, and olive oil, and set aside, covered, in the refrigerator for up to 2 hours.

2. To make the marinade, combine the dried red chiles with enough water to cover in a small saucepan and bring to a boil. Remove from the heat and let stand for 20 minutes, to soften. Drain, discarding the water. In a blender, combine the chiles, cumin, garlic, salt, and vinegar. Purée for 1 to 2 minutes, or until thick and smooth.

3. Place the skirt steak in a shallow glass or enamel dish and cover with the marinade. Set aside, covered, at room temperature for 1 hour, or refrigerate for up to 4 hours. If refrigerated, bring back to room temperature before cooking.

4. Prepare a grill for medium-hot cooking or preheat a broiler. Grill or broil the steak for 3 to 4 minutes per side, or until seared on the outside and pink inside. Do not overcook or it will be tough.

5. Let rest on a cutting board, covered with foil, for 5 minutes. To serve, slice steaks against the grain on the diagonal and fan the slices out on each plate. Place a dollop of the relish on the side and serve.

**Nutrition:**

Calories: 310

Protein: 32.7 g

Carbohydrates: 14.4 g

Fibre: 3.8 g

Total Fat: 14 g
 Sat: 5.12 g
 Mono: 5.46 g
 Poly: .580 g

Cholesterol: 76.3 mg

Vitamin A: 124 mg RE

Vitamin B6: .462 mg

Vitamin B12: 3.7 mcg

Vitamin C: 31.6 mg

Calcium: 35.2 mg

Iron: 4.48 mg

Potassium: 649 mg

Sodium: 500 mg

Zinc: 5.6 mg

## Tidbits!

Beef can definitely be a part of a lowfat diet, with certain restrictions. Portion size should be small, ideally about 3 ounces (75 g) or the size of a pack of cards. The real key to keeping beef in your diet lies in choosing the right cuts, like flank steak, skirt steak, or round, rather than the fattier cuts. Of the luxury steaks, sirloin is the lowest in fat, then comes filet, and the worst culprit is the rib steak. Prime rib is a no-no except for superspecial occasions (and you're not allowed to have one of those every week; that would be cheating).

## Mom's Flank Steak from the 1970s

Serves 4

*During high school, Brigit went hiking in the Grand Canyon for 3 weeks and lived mostly on reconstituted Chicken à la King. She wrote her mother several postcards during that time, mostly in praise of her flank steak. On visits from college, she called ahead to request it.*
*Brigit has somehow now transferred this same obsession to her stepdaughter, who requests it every other weekend. Should there be any leftover, it makes a super steak salad.*

$^3/_4$ cup (175 mL) low-sodium soy sauce

2 tablespoons (25 mL) powdered mustard

1 tablespoon (15 mL) Worcestershire sauce

1 teaspoon (5 mL) granulated garlic

$^1/_4$ teaspoon (1 mL) freshly ground black pepper

1 pound (500 g) trimmed flank steak

1. In a shallow baking dish, combine the soy sauce, mustard powder, Worcestershire sauce, garlic, and pepper. With a pastry brush, squish the mustard granules until they break up. Place the flank steak in the marinade and brush the top liberally with the marinade. Cover and refrigerate for at least 4 hours or overnight, turning and brushing the steak with the marinade occasionally.

2. Bring the steak to room temperature, then remove it from the marinade and pat off the excess liquid with paper towels. Transfer the marinade to a small saucepan.

3. Prepare a grill for medium-high heat cooking or preheat a broiler. This also works well on a ridged cast-iron griddle pan. Bring the marinade to a simmer while the grill or broiler heats up, simmer 1 minute, and remove from the heat.

4. Grill the steak for $4^1/_2$ to 5 minutes per side for medium-rare. Let the steak rest on a cutting board, loosely covered with foil, for 5 minutes. Slice across the grain about $^1/_4$-inch (5-mm) thick and serve immediately with a teaspoon or two (5 to 10 mL) of the marinade to moisten.

### Nutrition:

Calories: 312

Protein: 36.1 g

Carbohydrates: 7.89 g

Fibre: .762 g

Total Fat: 14.1 g
  Sat: 4.96 g
  Mono: 4.62 g
  Poly: .455 g

Cholesterol: 76.3 mg

Vitamin A: .493 mg RE

Vitamin B6: .385 mg

Vitamin B12: 3.7 mcg

Vitamin C: .73 mg

Calcium: 38 mg

Iron: 4.02 mg

Potassium: 505 mg

Sodium: 1147 mg

Zinc: 5.46 mg

**Variation:** Add $^1/_2$ cup (125 mL) orange juice and 1 teaspoon (5 mL) minced orange zest to the marinade.

## What's the Skinny?

Why do our recipes often advise you to bring refrigerated meat, poultry, and fish back to room temperature before cooking? For two reasons: one is that all the cooking instructions here, and in any other cookbook for that matter, are based on room-temperature ingredients. Also, food that is too cold on the inside will char and burn on the outside long before the centre is cooked. If you've had trouble cooking meat, fish, or poultry to the correct doneness in a predictable period of time, this may be why. Engrave this knowledge on the front of the fridge and never suffer a hopelessly delayed dinner again.

## Steak Kebabs with Yogurt Sauce

Serves 4

*This dish takes some time, but not much effort, so you just need to plan ahead. Giving lowfat meat dishes extra flavour takes time, but it's worth it. You'll need bamboo skewers for this one—instead of soaking them, just wrap the ends in aluminum foil to stop them from catching fire.*

$^3/_4$ of a large red onion, thinly sliced

5 sprigs fresh parsley, coarsely chopped

$^1/_2$ teaspoon (2 mL) dried thyme, crumbled

$^1/_2$ teaspoon (2 mL) freshly ground black pepper

$^1/_4$ cup (50 mL) fresh lemon juice

$^1/_4$ cup (50 mL) dry red wine

1 pound (500 g) 1-inch (2.5-cm) thick sirloin steak, fat trimmed

Salt

Yogurt Sauce:

$^3/_4$ cup (175 mL) nonfat yogurt

1 tablespoon (15 mL) finely chopped fresh parsley

$1^1/_2$ tablespoons (20 mL) chopped fresh basil or mint

$^1/_4$ of a large red onion, finely chopped

1 teaspoon (5 mL) fresh lemon juice

$^1/_4$ teaspoon (1 mL) salt

$^1/_8$ teaspoon freshly ground black pepper

8 bamboo skewers

12 medium, firm white button mushrooms

Olive or vegetable oil spray

1. In a glass or earthenware baking dish, combine the onion, parsley, thyme, pepper, lemon juice, and wine. Cut the steak into 1-inch (2.5-cm) cubes, cutting away all fat and gristle. Toss the meat with the onions and the marinade, cover and refrigerate for 6 to 8 hours, or overnight, turning over 2 or 3 times to give the meat even flavour.

2. To make the sauce, combine yogurt, parsley, basil, onion, lemon juice, salt, and pepper in a glass bowl and whisk together well. Cover and refrigerate, if desired, for up to 2 hours before serving (this will improve the flavour).

3. Preheat a grill or broiler for high-heat cooking and bring the steak to room temperature. Thread the steak onto four bamboo skewers, pressing the cubes firmly together. Thread three mushrooms onto each of the remaining skewers and spray them lightly with the oil. Wrap the blunt ends of the skewers, where they are not covered by food, with small pieces of aluminum foil.

4. When the grill is hot, grill the meat for 3 minutes on one side, then turn and cook for the same amount of time on the other side, until just firm, or done to your liking. Salt the meat as it comes off the grill. Grill the mushrooms for about 2 minutes on all four sides, then serve two skewers to each person, with the yogurt sauce on the side.

**Nutrition:**

Calories: 301

Protein: 38.8 g

Carbohydrates: 10.6 g

Fibre: 1.65 g

Total Fat: 10 g
 Sat: 3.72 g
 Mono: 4.34 g
 Poly: .532 g

Cholesterol: 102 mg

Vitamin A: 15.2 mg RE

Vitamin B6: .634 mg

Vitamin B12: 3.52 mcg

Vitamin C: 14 mg

Calcium: 124 mg

Iron: 5.16 mg

Potassium: 872 mg

Sodium: 249 mg

Zinc: 8.36 mg

### Toothsome Tips

Pork and grilling go together like football and beer. Grilling or broiling pork is the ideal way to get rid of fat while adding the smoky, earthy flavour of the fire. Fat drips off into the fire instead of staying in the pan and being served up with dinner. Spice rubs (widely sold if you don't want to make your own) are a quick and simple way to flavour pork for grilling (see page 59). If you trim excess fat and choose small cuts that will cook quickly without drying out you'll find that grilling pork yields some really tasty results. The lowfat cook should choose the leaner cuts like loin and tenderloin.

## Wine-Braised Pork Chops

Serves 4

*Bone-in pork chops are quite fatty, so it's best to use little boneless cutlets for this recipe. Adapt any other chop recipe to use cutlets by reducing the cooking time, and be extra careful not to overcook, or they'll be dry. Brigit found this recipe in an old Italian cookbook, and it needed only the slightest alteration to become a favourite recipe in her lowfat repertoire.*

2 cloves garlic, minced

2 teaspoons (10 mL) minced fresh rosemary

$^1/_2$ teaspoon (2 mL) salt

$^1/_4$ teaspoon (1 mL) mild chile powder

1 teaspoon (5 mL) olive oil

4 boneless pork loin cutlets, about $^3/_4$ inch (2 cm) thick, fat trimmed

Olive oil spray

$^1/_2$ cup (125 mL) dry white wine

$^3/_4$ cup (175 mL) lowfat beef broth

1. In a small bowl, combine the garlic, rosemary, salt, chile powder, and olive oil and mix together into a paste. Pat the chops dry with paper towels and spread a little of the paste on both sides of each cutlet, spreading it very thin and pressing down hard.

2. Spray a nonstick skillet lightly with the olive oil spray and heat over medium-high heat. Sauté the chops for about 2 minutes, or until golden, then turn and sauté for 2 minutes more on the other side. Add the wine and simmer until it has mostly evaporated.

3. Add the broth, reduce the heat to low, and continue simmering for about 6 minutes, turning the chops over once, until reduced by about half. Serve at once, with the pan juices spooned over the chops.

**Nutrition:**

Calories: 141

Protein: 16.3 g

Carbohydrates: .731 g

Fibre: .09 g

Total Fat: 5.62 g
 Sat: 1.94 g
 Mono: 2.74 g
 Poly: .444 g

Cholesterol: 43.9 mg

Vitamin A: 4.26 mg RE

Vitamin B6: .232 mg

Vitamin B12: .327 mcg

Vitamin C: .698 mg

Calcium: 19.5 mg

Iron: .791 mg

Potassium: 256 mg

Sodium: 312 mg

Zinc: 1.4 mg

## Pork and Fresh Ginger Sauté

Serves 4

*Here is an example of a lowfat meat dish that's very quick and easy. If you've stocked your pantry with nonperishable goodies from the Asian market, you'll be able to whip up dishes like this in a flash. If you have fresh chives on hand, they make a great garnish for this dish, but it's just as tasty without.*

2-inch (50-cm) piece fresh ginger, peeled

4 pork loin cutlets, about $1/4$ inch (5 mm) thick

$1/4$ teaspoon (1 mL) freshly ground black pepper

Vegetable oil spray

2 tablespoons (25 mL) sake

1 tablespoon (15 mL) mirin (sweet Japanese wine) or sherry

1 tablespoon (15 mL) low-sodium soy sauce

8 large fresh shiitake or field mushrooms, wiped clean and sliced $1/4$ inch (5 mm) thick

1. Grate the ginger on the finest holes of a grater or on a ceramic ginger grater. Transfer the grated ginger to a fine sieve, set over a small bowl, and push down hard with the back of a spoon to extract the juice. You should have about 1 tablespoon (15 mL) of juice.

2. Season both sides of the pork with pepper. Spray a nonstick pan lightly with the oil spray and heat until very hot. Sauté the pork cutlets for 2 minutes on one side. Reduce the heat to low and cook for 2 minutes more, then turn and cook for 2 to 3 minutes more, until only just firm to the touch. Transfer the cutlets to a plate and keep warm, covered.

3. Wipe the fat, if any, from the pan and add the sake, mirin, soy sauce, and ginger juice. Over medium heat, stir for a minute or two to deglaze the pan. Add the mushrooms and stir to coat them with the liquid.

4. Cook for about 1 minute (they will be nicely glazed); then serve the cutlets on warmed plates with a few spoonfuls of mushrooms poured over each. Pour a bit of the juices that accumulated on the plate over each portion.

### Nutrition:

Calories: 244

Protein: 35.7 g

Carbohydrates: 3.36 g

Fibre: .574 g

Total Fat: 7.66 g
  Sat: 2.58 g
  Mono: 3.1 g
  Poly: .787 g

Cholesterol: 107 mg

Vitamin A: 2.29 mg RE

Vitamin B6: .639 mg

Vitamin B12: 1.15 mcg

Vitamin C: 2.57 mg

Calcium: 10 mg

Iron: 2.16 mg

Potassium: 663 mg

Sodium: 202 mg

Zinc: 3.64 mg

## Braised Lamb Shanks with Pearl Onions

Serves 4

*This is a variation of a recipe Brigit wrote for* Food and Wine *some years ago. Searing the shanks in the oven allowed her to cut out the fat that was required for pan-searing. This may seem like an involved recipe, but in order to get the fat out of meat a few extra steps are required. If you want to keep meat in your lowfat diet, you'll have to do just a little more work!*

4 small, meaty lamb shanks, well trimmed
$^1/_2$ teaspoon (2 mL) salt
$^1/_4$ teaspoon (1 mL) freshly ground black pepper
2 cups (500 mL) dry, white wine

20 cloves garlic, unpeeled (2 ounces/50 g)
2 cups (500 mL) lowfat, low-sodium chicken broth
2 sprigs fresh rosemary
$^1/_2$ pound (125 g) pearl onions

1. Preheat the oven to 500°F (260°C). Season the shanks generously with salt and pepper. In a large heavy casserole, sear the shanks in the oven, uncovered, for 30 minutes, turning once. Turn the oven down to 325°F (165°C) and open the door for a moment to let some heat escape.

2. Transfer the shanks to a plate and wipe the hot pan with a paper towel to get rid of the fat. Return the shanks to the pan and add the wine. On top of the stove, bring the wine to a simmer and cook for 5 minutes. Add the garlic, broth, and rosemary and bring back to a simmer.

3. Cover the pan and braise in the oven for $1^1/_2$ hours, turning occasionally. Transfer the meat with a slotted spoon to a plate and cover with foil.

4. Pour the cooking juices into a fat separator or a large glass measuring cup. To skim the fat from the glass measuring cup, use one of the methods below:

   A. Wait 5 minutes for the fat to separate and skim it from the top of the juices using a large, flat spoon. Drag a paper towel quickly across the surface of the liquid to absorb any fat that was left behind.
   or
   B. Make sure the lamb is tightly covered, cover the glass measuring cup, and refrigerate overnight. Lift off the solidified fat from the cooking juices.

5. When ready to serve, bring a small saucepan of water to the boil and blanch the pearl onions for $1^1/_2$ minutes. Drain and, when cool enough to handle, slide off their skins.

6. Return the lamb shanks to the casserole and strain the juices over them, pressing hard on the garlic to squeeze it out of the skins and force it through the sieve (scrape off the bottom of the sieve, where all the yummy purée will have accumulated). Add the onions, cover the pan, and braise for 1 hour more. Serve the shanks with the juices and onions, in warmed bowls.

**Nutrition:**

Calories: 354

Protein: 34.4 g

Carbohydrates: 12 g

Fibre: 1.66 g

Total Fat: 9.86 g
  Sat: 3.25 g
  Mono: 4.09 g
  Poly: 1.08 g

Cholesterol: 101 mg

Vitamin A: .025 mg RE

Vitamin B6: .475 mg

Vitamin B12: 3.08 mcg

Vitamin C: 7.64 mg

Calcium: 72.4 mg

Iron: 3.4 mg

Potassium: 631 mg

Sodium: 981 mg

Zinc: 6.08 mg

### What's the Skinny?

Protein is an essential nutrient for building and maintaining body tissues. Among other things, protein is vital to the functioning of the immune system. It is also rich in iron, and this is why vegetarians can sometimes become anemic if they don't get enough protein and iron in their diets. Protein is harder to find in the nonmeat food groups, so it is important for vegetarians, especially if they don't eat dairy products, to understand where their protein will come from (usually from grains and legumes like beans, dried peas, and lentils). Meat is also an excellent source of iron, zinc, and Vitamin B.

## Lamb Loin with Shallot Jus

Serves 4

*This is a very easy dish that uses the leaner loin cut of the lamb. The jus will be stronger if made with a lamb or beef stock, but chicken stock is often more convenient and works nicely. Pamela is fortunate enough to be able to buy organic lamb from local Ontario Mennonite farmers and the taste is too good to pass up, so she has devised several lower fat recipes like this one.*

4 4-ounce (120-g) pieces of lamb loin, at
   room temperature
Pinch salt
Pinch freshly ground pepper
Olive oil spray

2 tablespoons (25 mL) shallot vinegar
$1/2$ cup (125 mL) lamb, beef, or chicken
   stock
4 branches fresh rosemary

1. Preheat the oven to 400°F (200°C) and place a baking tray inside. Lamb loins tend to come in about 6-ounce (170-g) portions—too much for one, too little for two. Trim the loins to size and freeze the excess to make medallions of lamb at a later date.

2. Heat a nonstick skillet over high heat and spray with olive oil. Season loins with salt and pepper. When pan is very hot, brown loins on both sides, about 1 minute each side. Add vinegar and 2 tablespoons (25 mL) of the stock to the pan and let simmer for 30 seconds. Lift the loins out of the pan, letting all the liquid drain back into the jus and transfer the loins to the hot baking tray in the oven. Add the remaining stock to the jus and let reduce by half, then set aside.

3. Roast the lamb until it reaches desired doneness then remove from the oven—about 5 minutes for rare and 12 minutes for medium rare. Tent with foil and let rest for 5 minutes, then serve with jus drizzled on top.

Garnish: Place one branch of rosemary on each loin.

### Nutrition:

Calories: 74.1

Protein: 4.3 g

Carbohydrates: 0.8 g

Fibre: 0 g

Total Fat: 5.9 g
  Sat: 2.1 g
  Mono: 2.0 g
  Poly: 0.4 g

Cholesterol: 16 mg

Vitamin A: 0 mg

Vitamin B6: 0.03 mg

Vitamin B12: 1 mg

Vitamin C: 0 mg

Calcium: 19 mg

Iron: 12 mg

Potassium: 90 mg

Sodium: 139 mg

Zinc: 0.8 mg

## The Least You Need to Know

➤ Meat can be a part of the lowfat regime if you follow a few simple rules:

1. Choose lean cuts of beef like flank, skirt, or round; the loin or tenderloin of pork; and lamb shanks.

2. Keep an eye on portion size: it should be 3 to 4 ounces (75 to 120 g) cooked weight—about the size of a pack of cards.

3. If there is a sauce or braising liquid, skim the fat scrupulously.

➤ Grilling is a good option for the lean cuts of meat, since there is no need for added cooking oil. Just be sure not to overcook, since lean meat will dry out quickly after it's done.

➤ Make meat an occasional choice—last in line after fish, lean poultry, and vegetarian meals.

# Chapter 26

# Sweets for the Sweet

## In This Chapter

➤ Focus on fruit

➤ Freezing for texture

➤ Correct cobbler

In the lowfat kitchen dessert generally means fruit, but you'd be amazed at the things you can do with a well-stocked pantry and a little time. Of course, if time is a problem, try to locate really ripe fresh fruit and serve it with a knife and fork for an elegant presentation. Or use the Master Fruit Salsa recipe on page 146, leave out the garlic and onion, and use as a topping for lowfat ice creams or sorbets.

There is a lot of controversy about the role of sugar in a lowfat diet. Most lowfat prepared products (such as salad dressing) are full of sugar. Sugar carries a big wallop of calories (774 calories per cup/250 mL) so you will want to limit it purely from a calorie-counting standpoint.

Sugar is also an "empty" carbohydrate and rushes through your system like a late train. It increases insulin, which will cause the body to transform excess calories to fat. You may get a rush of instant energy, but it'll be gone within half an hour and you'll feel like you've lost a pound and found a penny. Avoid sugary concoctions and stick mostly with natural, fruit-sweetened desserts. And remember, a little bit of sugar won't hurt once in a while.

## Pears Poached in White Wine

Serves 4

*Brigit has been making this dessert, with occasional variations, since she was in college. Sometimes she uses red wine, which gives the pears a lovely ruby-red appearance. In nonslimming days Brigit would remove the cores of the poached pears with a melon-baller and stuff the resulting cavity with gorgonzola for a little unexpected bonus.*

4 small, firm pears (Conference or Anjou),
  just beginning to ripen
3 cups (800 mL) vermouth or other slightly
  sweet white wine

2 tablespoons (25 mL) sugar
Zest of a lemon, removed in 1 piece
1 vanilla bean
2 cups (500 mL) water, or as needed

1. Cut a slice from the bottom of each pear so that it will stand upright. Peel the pears from the bottom up with a vegetable peeler, leaving the stems.

2. In a saucepan just large enough to hold all the pears, combine the wine and sugar and stir over low heat until the sugar dissolves. Add the pears, lemon zest, vanilla bean, and enough water to reach the base of the stems. Partially cover and bring to a slow simmer. Cook gently for 20 to 30 minutes, or until the pears are tender but not mushy (test with a sharp knife). The cooking time will depend on the ripeness of the pears. Transfer the pears to a plate.

3. Reduce the wine mixture over high heat until only about $1/3$ cup (75 mL) syrupy liquid remains, about 30 minutes. Discard the lemon peel, and rinse the vanilla bean under cool running water. Dry and save for another use later. (At this point, you could refrigerate the pears and syrup separately for up to 6 hours, bringing them to room temperature before serving. The sauce may be reheated if desired.) Place the pears on small plates and drizzle with the syrup.

### Nutrition:

Calories: 291

Protein: .799 g

Carbohydrates: 36.7 g

Fibre: 4.09 g

Total Fat: .577 g
  Sat: .033 g
  Mono: .118 g
  Poly: .137 g

Cholesterol: 0 mg

Vitamin A: 3.13 mg RE

Vitamin B6: .049 mg

Vitamin B12: 0 mcg

Vitamin C: 14.7 mg

Calcium: 35.4 mg

Iron: .918 mg

Potassium: 245 mg

Sodium: 25.5 mg

Zinc: .239 mg

## Toothsome Tips

Poaching fruit in a light sugar syrup is a great treatment for slightly underripe pears. You can do the same thing with peaches and apricots, too. With peaches, substitute 1 cup (250 mL) of red wine for part of the white wine in the recipe for Pears Poached in White Wine. Before you reduce the syrup, pour off a cup of it and use as the base for a Champagne cocktail. Place 1 tablespoon (15 mL) of the peach-poaching juice in the bottom of a Champagne glass and fill with the sparkling wine of your choice (there's no need to use an expensive Champagne for this; any decent local sparkler will do).

## Pineapple Frozen Yogurt with Banana Rum Salsa

Serves 4

*Use just barely ripe bananas for this salsa; otherwise they'll fall apart into a mush. For the frozen yogurt, your ripest banana is fine. If desired, you could substitute white grape juice for the rum in this exotic salsa, but it won't be nearly as much fun.*

1 ripe banana, peeled and sliced
$1/2$ cup (125 mL) light brown sugar, firmly
  packed
$1^1/2$ teaspoons (7 mL) vanilla extract
$2^1/2$ cups (625 mL) plain lowfat yogurt
$2^1/2$ cups (625 mL) canned crushed
  pineapple in juice

Salsa:
2 ripe bananas, peeled
2 tablespoons (25 mL) brown sugar
2 tablespoons (25 mL) dark rum
$1/4$ teaspoon (1 mL) ground cinnamon

1. In the bowl of a food processor, combine the banana, sugar, vanilla, and yogurt. Drain pineapple and add, then process until smooth and evenly blended. Pour into a metal roasting pan and cover with plastic wrap. Freeze for 4 hours (it should be almost solid).

2. Remove the pan from the freezer and let rest for 5 minutes. Cut off pieces of the frozen block and place in a food processor. Purée again and either serve immediately or return to the freezer for up to 3 days. When you serve, you might have to purée the mixture again for a pleasing texture. Either way, remove the yogurt from the freezer about 15 minutes before serving, to soften. Any liquid that separates from the yogurt should be discarded.

3. To make the salsa, preheat a broiler. Halve the bananas lengthwise and place cut side up on a baking sheet. Sprinkle with the sugar and broil, watching carefully, until golden and bubbling, about 3 minutes. Cool and dice the bananas; then stir them gently together with the rum and cinnamon. Chill for up to 1 hour before using.

4. Scoop frozen yogurt into chilled bowls and top with a spoonful of the salsa.

**Nutrition:**

Calories: 354

Protein: 9.44 g

Carbohydrates: 72.1 g

Fibre: 2.6 g

Total Fat: 2.89 g
  Sat: 1.70 g
  Mono: .697 g
  Poly: .177 g

Cholesterol: 9.31 mg

Vitamin A: 35.7 mg RE

Vitamin B6: .66 mg

Vitamin B12: .863 mcg

Vitamin C: 19.9 mg

Calcium: 323 mg

Iron: 1.22 mg

Potassium: 918 mg

Sodium: 119 mg

Zinc: 1.66 mg

## Cinnamon Applesauce

Serves 4

*Slow, moist cooking brings out the natural sweetness of "eating" apples like Golden and Red Delicious, so very little added sugar is necessary. This tastes like an apple pie without the crust, and also makes a good lowfat topping for pancakes and French toast. Work quickly when preparing the apples, or they will turn brown.*

4 Red or Golden Delicious apples, peeled, cored and coarsely chopped

$1/4$ cup (50 mL) water

$1/4$ teaspoon (1 mL) ground cinnamon

$1/2$ to 1 teaspoon (2 to 5 mL) granulated sugar

In a medium saucepan, combine the apples with the water. Cover and place over medium-low heat. Simmer until the apples are softened, about 8 minutes.

Remove the lid and simmer for 2 to 3 minutes more to evaporate some of the liquid. Stir in the cinnamon. Taste for sweetness and add up to 1 teaspoon (5 mL) sugar, depending on the sweetness of the apples (which will vary with the time of year). Serve warm, or cool to room temperature, refrigerate, and serve chilled.

**Nutrition:**

Calories: 77.4

Protein: .198 g

Carbohydrates: 20 g

Fibre: 2.5 g

Total Fat: .402 g
  Sat: .066 g
  Mono: .018 g
  Poly: .117 g

Cholesterol: 0 mg

Vitamin A: 5.67 mg RE

Vitamin B6: .06 mg

Vitamin B12: 0 mcg

Vitamin C: 5.16 mg

Calcium: 6.87 mg

Iron: .145 mg

Potassium: 146 mg

Sodium: .048 mg

Zinc: .054 mg

## Pink Grapefruit Granita

Serves 4

*Pepper is often added to lowfat fruit desserts to perk up flavour. The pink peppercorns here are a gourmet item that may be difficult to find. Since they are really just a festive garnish and not crucial to the flavour, omit them if you can't find any (add a grind or two of black pepper instead). If the granita freezes so hard it cannot be stirred, let it sit for 10 or 15 minutes. Then transfer it to a food processor and purée to a slush.*

1 large pink grapefruit, washed and dried
1 cup (250 mL) freshly squeezed pink grapefruit juice
1 12-ounce (350-mL) can frozen pink grapefruit juice, almost thawed
$1/2$ teaspoon (2 mL) pink peppercorns, if available

1. Place a metal roasting pan in the freezer to chill. With a citrus zester, remove about half of the grapefruit zest and set aside. Halve the grapefruit and use a sharp knife to remove the skin and all the white pith, taking care not to remove too much of the fruit itself.

2. Coarsely chop the flesh and place, with any escaped juices, into a food processor. Add the fresh juice and fruit juice concentrate and purée until smooth.

3. Scoop into the chilled roasting pan and return to the freezer, leaving a large metal spoon in the pan. Freeze for about 1 hour, until the edges of the juice have begun to crystallize. Use the spoon to stir the crystals into the centre. Refreeze and stir again after 30 minutes.

4. Repeat the process two more times, for a total freezing time of about $2^1/2$ hours. Scoop into glasses and scatter a few pink peppercorns over the top.

**Nutrition:**

| | |
|---|---|
| Calories: 194 | Vitamin A: 19.8 mg RE |
| Protein: 2.7 g | Vitamin B6: .212 mg |
| Carbohydrates: 46.1 g | Vitamin B12: 0 mcg |
| Fibre: 1.6 g | Vitamin C: 172 mg |
| Total Fat: .662 g | Calcium: 43.7 mg |
|   Sat: .08 g | Iron: .811 mg |
|   Mono: .077 g | Potassium: 691 mg |
|   Poly: .14 g | Sodium: 4.69 mg |
| Cholesterol: 0 mg | Zinc: .258 mg |

## Apple Pizza

Serves 4

*Pizza is a good choice for the lowfat cook, so it's worth finding a source for dough or learning to make it at home (it's easy). There are several options: make your own, buy some risen bread dough from a local bakery, or use the frozen pizza dough available in the chilled section of the supermarket. Make this on an occasion when someone else is making the rest of dinner on the grill outside, freeing you and the kitchen for the project.*
*Double the recipe for a party, if desired.*

Vegetable oil spray

12 ounces (340 g) risen pizza dough
(page 199), frozen pizza dough (thawed), or
a roll of canned pizza dough, at room
temperature

2 large Golden Delicious apples, peeled,
cored, and halved

2 tablespoons (25 mL) sugar

$1/4$ teaspoon (1 mL) ground cinnamon

2 tablespoons (25 mL) sugar-free apricot
preserves

$1/2$ tablespoon (7 mL) orange liqueur
(Grand Marnier, Cointreau, or Triple-Sec)

1. Preheat the oven to 375°F (190°C). Lightly spray a nonstick baking sheet with oil.
   Cut the pizza dough into four equal pieces and roll with your palms into little balls.

2. Place the dough balls on the baking sheet, cover with a towel, and allow to rest for
   15 minutes. With your fingertips, press each ball out into a 4-inch (10-cm) round.
   Or, if using the pop-out dough, cut into four equal squares and transfer to the pan.

3. Using a sharp knife, slice the apples crosswise about $1/4$-inch (5-mm) thick. Fan
   $1/2$ an apple in a circle on each of the dough rounds (or squares), leaving a $1/2$-inch
   (1-cm) border. Sprinkle the sugar and the cinnamon evenly over the apples.

4. Cook for 20 to 25 minutes, until the edges of the crust are just starting to brown.

5. While the pizzas are cooking, combine the preserves and the liqueur in a small
   saucepan and heat through over medium-high heat, stirring constantly, until they
   cook down into a syrupy mixture. Drizzle the mixture over the warm pizzas and
   serve at once.

**Nutrition:**

Calories: 190

Protein: 5.07 g

Carbohydrates: 40.4 g

Fibre: 2.95 g

Total Fat: .652 g
 Sat: .109 g
 Mono: .125 g
 Poly: .172 g

Cholesterol: .493 mg

Vitamin A: 22.2 mg RE

Vitamin B6: .103 mg

Vitamin B12: .109 mcg

Vitamin C: 3.2 mg

Calcium: 45.8 mg

Iron: 1.91 mg

Potassium: 216 mg

Sodium: 20.9 mg

Zinc: .56 mg

### Toothsome Tips

If you really hate ending dinner without a little jolt of sugar to finish off, find a lowfat cookie you like and have one after dinner. Dried fruits are also a good, healthy way to have a sweet treat, particularly dried cranberries and cherries, which also work well as a midafternoon snack.

## Grilled Peaches with Honey, Ricotta, and Balsamic Vinegar

Serves 4

*It's a little too much trouble to fire up an outdoor grill just for this dish, but it's a natural if you've used the grill to cook the main course. Put the peaches on while the main course is resting, remove before you sit down, and garnish with the sweetened ricotta and allspice just before serving.*

2 ripe peaches, halved and stoned

1 tablespoon (15 mL) balsamic vinegar

$1/4$ cup (50 mL) lowfat ricotta cheese

1 tablespoon (15 mL) honey

Pinch ground allspice

1. Use a grill that has recently been used for cooking the main course, or preheat a ridged cast-iron griddle pan to medium heat. The peaches should not go onto a very hot grill.

2. Place the peaches cut side down on the grilling surface and grill for about 5 minutes, or until marked by the grill and golden. Turn right side up, brush the cut side generously with the vinegar, and grill for 3 minutes more. Transfer to a platter or individual plates and set aside.

3. When ready to serve, whisk together the ricotta and honey. Dollop a tablespoon (15 mL) into the centre of each peach and dust the tops with a little allspice.

**Nutrition:**

Calories: 59.4

Protein: 2.09 g

Carbohydrates: 10.8 g

Fibre: .809 g

Total Fat: 1.27 g
 Sat: .762 g
 Mono: .37 g
 Poly: .06 g

Cholesterol: 4.74 mg

Vitamin A: 40.7 mg RE

Vitamin B6: .012 mg

Vitamin B12: .045 mcg

Vitamin C: 3.04 mg

Calcium: 45.3 mg

Iron: .196 mg

Potassium: 108 mg

Sodium: 20.4 mg

Zinc: .28 mg

## Berries in Warm Vanilla Foam

Serves 4

*This dessert gives the luxurious mouth feel of whipped cream with a fraction of the fat and calories. Use fresh berries in season for their unbeatable taste. The pinch of chocolate on the top isn't enough to do any harm and it adds a scent of decadence to the dish.*

2 cups (500 mL) mixed berries (any variety)

1 vanilla pod, split, or $^1/_2$ teaspoon (2 mL) pure vanilla extract

$1^1/_2$ cups (375 mL) nonfat milk

1 tablespoon (15 mL) honey

$^1/_2$ teaspoon (2 mL) chocolate shavings

1. Wash the berries and let them drain.

2. In a small saucepan, scrape the vanilla seeds from the pod, if using and scald with the milk and honey by heating to just below the boiling point. Pour sweetened milk into a stainless steel foamer and add vanilla if using extract. Pump foamer until maximum volume is obtained, then put aside and the foam will firm up.

3. Portion berries into four cocktail glasses and top with a generous dollop of foam. Sprinkle a pinch of chocolate shavings over each serving. Serve with the foam still warm.

### Nutrition:

Calories: 377.4

Protein: 15.0 g

Carbohydrates: 70.7 g

Fibre: 10.0 g

Total Fat: 6.6 g
 Sat: 3.3 g
 Mono: 1.9 g
 Poly: 0.6 g

Cholesterol: 7 mg

Vitamin A: 938 RE

Vitamin B6: 0.29 mg

Vitamin B12: 1 mg

Vitamin C: 107 mg

Calcium: 495 mg

Iron: 1.6 mg

Potassium: 1046 mg

Sodium: 198 mg

Zinc: 2.3 mg

### Toothsome Tips

When serving fresh berries or other soft fruits, make a deceptively simple sauce by combining lowfat yogurt with brown sugar to taste and a splash of Grand Marnier, Cointreau, or whatever fruit liqueur is on hand. Candied ginger is a great pantry item for livening up fresh fruit or store-bought frozen yogurt. Finely chop just a few pieces for a tasty and beautiful topping.

## Toothsome Tips

Frozen juice concentrates make easy solutions for desserts and breakfasts in the lowfat kitchen. They save you the work of boiling down a quart of fruit juice to achieve the intense flavour and slight syrupy consistency that are so useful to lowfat bakers and smoothie enthusiasts. Thaw a large can, then refreeze in smaller quantities so you won't need to waste the whole thing when you only need a little.

## Strawberry and Rhubarb Crepes

Serves 4

*Strawberry rhubarb pie is a great Canadian classic. The best ones are home baked but the pies that Pamela buys at her local Mennonite farmers market really are in a class by themselves. These crepes have the same spring-fresh filling of fresh strawberries and rhubarb but they are cooked down in unsweetened juice and served in very thin crepe shells.*

For Shells:
$^1/_3$ cup (75 mL) all-purpose flour
Pinch baking powder
Pinch salt
1 tablespoon (15 mL) canola oil
2 tablespoons (25 mL) applesauce
$^1/_3$ cup (75 mL) nonfat milk, room temperature
1 large egg, room temperature, beaten
Vegetable oil spray

3 stalks rhubarb, chopped
12 strawberries, sliced
1 cup (250 mL) unsweetened cranberry-apple juice
1 tablespoon (15 mL) Grand Marnier
Garnish: $^1/_4$ teaspoon (1 mL) icing sugar

1. For crepe shells, sift together flour, baking powder and salt. Make a well in flour and add the oil, apple sauce, milk, and egg. Whisk together, gently, until smooth. Let the batter rest for about 45 minutes. Place a nonstick or seasoned crepe pan over medium heat and spray with oil. Spoon 2 tablespoons (25 mL) of batter into pan and swirl to get an even coating. Let cook until the shell is lightly coloured on the bottom and set on the top—about 2 to 3 minutes. As each shell is removed from the pan, drop 2 even tablespoons (25 mL) of filling into centre and fold into an envelope shape. Note: If making the shells ahead of time, place a layer of waxed paper between each of them and store in the refrigerator until ready to use. This recipe will make five shells in case one tears or gets eaten.

2. While batter is resting, make filling by combining in a medium saucepan, the fruit and the juice. Heat over a medium high heat until the juice has reduced to a syrupy consistency, about 15 minutes. Add Grand Marnier and cook for an additional 2 minutes. Dust with icing sugar and serve warm.

**Nutrition:**

Calories: 299.5

Protein: 7.5 g

Carbohydrates: 53.8 g

Fibre: 13.4 g

Total Fat: 7.5 g
 Sat: 0.7 g
 Mono: 2.6 g
 Poly: 2.0 g

Cholesterol: 46 mg

Vitamin A: 430 RE

Vitamin B6: 0.35 mg

Vitamin B12: 0 mg

Vitamin C: 274 mg

Calcium: 277 mg

Iron: 2.7 mg

Potassium: 1361 mg

Sodium: 77 mg

Zinc: 1.0 mg

## The Least You Need to Know

➤ High-fat desserts are out unless you've paid your dues, i.e., kept fat and calorie intake low for 2 or 3 days, so learn to love fruit. If you need a shot of sugar to finish the meal, find some lowfat cookies you like and keep them on hand. Have one after dinner.

➤ Poaching fruit in wine makes a luxurious dessert, and any soft fruit that doesn't require peeling will do. Save some of the poaching liquid to make an elegant cocktail when added to sparkling wine.

➤ Frozen fruit juice concentrates are a valuable tool for adding flavour and a pleasant texture to lowfat baked desserts, and for breakfast smoothies.

# Chapter 27

# Buoyant Breakfasts

> **In This Chapter**
>
> ➤ Kick–start the fat burner
>
> ➤ Super smoothies
>
> ➤ Golden polenta

If you eat breakfast, studies show you will experience fewer cravings during the day and have less trouble following a common-sense eating plan. By eating within 1 hour of waking, you turn on the fat-burning engines and kick-start a metabolism that's been asleep for 8 hours. Many people work in offices and have less control over what they can eat for lunch, so it becomes even more important to have a good lowfat breakfast. That way, you'll be less hungry at lunchtime and more capable of making sensible food choices. Eating small amounts several times during the day is much better for you than trying to restrict yourself to one or two meals, when you are more likely to overindulge because you are so darned hungry. Small meals throughout the day also keep your energy high, and your metabolism continues to work faster, meaning any calorie intake is likely to be burned off more quickly, not stored, as fat, for later.

We both have a pet peeve against many nonfat and some lowfat dairy products, but lowfat cottage cheese and yogurt are standbys we couldn't do without. If you are pushed for time, there's nothing better than a substantial bowl of either one topped with fresh fruit, berries, or a sliced banana. On weekends, however, the bad breakfast genie may visit your home, particularly if you have kids or a nondieting spouse who looks forward to a festive weekend breakfast. Bacon is definitely out, as are whole-egg omelettes (egg-white-only omelettes benefit from the addition of 1 yolk for 2 omelettes and are great as long as you use lots of flavourings). Watch out for excessive calorie intake at breakfast, even if there is no fat—you need to leave enough calories left over for the rest of the day. As always, fruit is a great option.

## Mango Yogurt Smoothie

Serves 2 generously

*Giving a recipe for a smoothie is almost like providing instructions for a game of catch. Whatever is around gets involved. Add fresh fruit just past its prime, drained canned fruit (buy the kind packed in fruit juice concentrate, not syrup), and ice cubes if you like a frozen smoothie. Experiment and find a few you like, then keep the ingredients on hand so you're just a flick of the blender switch from a healthy, fibre-rich breakfast. Here's a basic smoothie to get you started.*

1 fresh mango

1 banana, peeled and cut into 1-inch (2.5-cm) pieces

3 slices canned or fresh pineapple, quartered

$1/2$ cup (125 mL) plain lowfat yogurt

1 tablespoon (15 mL) finely chopped fresh mint

Peel the mango with a sharp vegetable peeler and then core it by making long slices about $1/4$-inch (5-mm) thick from top to bottom. Slice crosswise to release the flesh from the difficult, woody pit.

In a blender, purée the mango, banana, pineapple, yogurt, and mint until smooth, scraping down the jar as necessary. If desired, you could freeze the smoothie until almost firm, about 2 hours, and scoop into small bowls.

### Nutrition:

Calories: 211

Protein: 4.72 g

Carbohydrates: 48.9 g

Fibre: 4.63 g

Total Fat: 1.58 g
 Sat: .791 g
 Mono: .397 g
 Poly: .156 g

Cholesterol: 3.72 mg

Vitamin A: 420 mg RE

Vitamin B6: .562 mg

Vitamin B12: .345 mcg

Vitamin C: 42.6 mg

Calcium: 138 mg

Iron: .603 mg

Potassium: 636 mg

Sodium: 3.15 mg

Zinc: .765 mg

## Creamy Polenta with Bananas and Raisins

Serves 4

*This is a variation of a recipe that appeared in Brigit's first book,* Polenta. *It didn't take much alteration to make it lowfat. This creamy, comforting dish is equally good in any season, but it is particularly suited to chilly fall weekends.*

2 $1/4$ cups (550 mL) water

2 cups (500 mL) 1% milk

$1/2$ teaspoon (2 mL) salt

$1^1/2$ tablespoons (20 mL) sugar

$3/4$ cup (175 mL) polenta or coarsely ground yellow cornmeal

$1/2$ cup (125 mL) golden raisins

1 ripe banana, peeled and sliced $1/4$ inch (5 mm) thick

2 tablespoons (25 mL) honey

$1/2$ teaspoon (2 mL) ground allspice

1. In a large heavy saucepan, bring the water, milk, salt, and sugar to a boil over medium-high heat. Reduce the heat and, when the liquid is simmering, drizzle the polenta over in a slow, thin stream, whisking constantly in the same direction until all the grains have been absorbed and the mixture is lump-free.

2. Reduce the heat to very low. Switch to a wooden spoon and stir thoroughly every 1 or 2 minutes for 20 to 25 minutes, depending on how soft you want the polenta to be (the longer you stir, the softer the grains will be). Add a little more hot water or hot milk if it gets too stiff—this should be a very liquid mixture.

3. Stir in the raisins and ladle into four warm bowls. Distribute the bananas over the top and drizzle with the honey. Sprinkle a hint of allspice over each bowl and serve.

### Nutrition:

Calories: 280

Protein: 7.43 g

Carbohydrates: 60.8 g

Fibre: 3.04 g

Total Fat: 2.54 g
 Sat: 1.11 g
 Mono: .655 g
 Poly: .487 g

Cholesterol: 5.49 mg

Vitamin A: 95 mg RE

Vitamin B6: .363 mg

Vitamin B12: .505 mcg

Vitamin C: 4.93 mg

Calcium: 185 mg

Iron: 1.38 mg

Potassium: 555 mg

Sodium: 347 mg

Zinc: 1.09 mg

## Scrambled Parmesan Tofu

Serves 2

*Low carbohydrates and high protein are the perfect combination for a high-energy start to the day. The turmeric gives the tofu a rich, yellow, eggy look but can be omitted if unavailable.*

$^1/_2$ teaspoon (2 mL) or a 2-second spray olive oil

1 clove garlic, minced

2 scallions, white, and 2 inches (2.5 cm) of green, thinly sliced

2 large white button mushrooms, sliced

$^1/_2$ red bell pepper, cored, seeded, and diced

2 cups (500 mL) washed and dried spinach leaves, loosely packed

1 (10 $^1/_2$-ounce/294-g) container firm tofu, cut into $^1/_2$-inch (1-cm) crisscross sticks (this is easiest if done while tofu is still in the container)

1 tablespoon (15 mL) grated Parmesan

$^1/_4$ teaspoon (1 mL) ground turmeric

$^1/_2$ teaspoon (2 mL) salt

1. Heat a large nonstick or cast-iron skillet over medium-low heat and add the olive oil. Sauté the garlic, scallions, mushrooms, and bell pepper for 3 to 4 minutes, stirring frequently, until golden.

2. Add the spinach and cover the pan. Cook for 1 or 2 minutes more, until wilted.

3. Add the tofu, Parmesan, turmeric, and salt and stir, breaking up the tofu, for about 2 minutes, until warmed through and crumbly. Serve immediately on warm plates.

### Nutrition:

Calories: 262

Protein: 26.4 g

Carbohydrates: 11.2 g

Fibre: 1.89 g

Total Fat: 15.3 g
 Sat: 2.67 g
 Mono: 3.99 g
 Poly: 7.54 g

Cholesterol: 2.46 mg

Vitamin A: 364 mg RE

Vitamin B6: .300 mg

Vitamin B12: .044 mcg

Vitamin C: 58.6 mg

Calcium: 385 mg

Iron: 16.9 mg

Potassium: 653 mg

Sodium: 636 mg

Zinc: 2.80 mg

## Cucumber and Salmon Breakfast

Serves 2

*There's no denying the appeal of smoked salmon and capers. The cucumber adds a welcome crunch to this elegant breakfast.*

2 slices whole wheat bread

1 tablespoon (15 mL) light cream cheese

4-inch length cucumber, peeled, halved, and seeds scraped out

2 slices smoked salmon or lox

1 teaspoon (5 mL) capers, rinsed, patted dry, and coarsely chopped

Toast the bread until golden on both sides and transfer one slice to each of two plates. Spread $^1/_2$ tablespoon (7 mL) of the cream cheese evenly on each slice.

Slice the cucumber $^3/_8$ inch (9 mm) thick lengthwise and place over the cream cheese, and top with a slice of the salmon. Scatter half of the capers over each and serve.

**Nutrition:**

Calories: 119

Protein: 5.89 g

Carbohydrates: 18.2 g

Fibre: 2.55 g

Total Fat: 3.17 g
  Sat: 1.24 g
  Mono: 1.1 g
  Poly: .502 g

Cholesterol: 5.83 mg

Vitamin A: 30.6 mg RE

Vitamin B6: .112 mg

Vitamin B12: .280 mcg

Vitamin C: 3.01 mg

Calcium: 42.3 mg

Iron: 1.49 mg

Potassium: 195 mg

Sodium: 263 mg

Zinc: .876 mg

## Egg White and Salsa Omelette

Serves 2

*Unless you have a use for egg yolks, it is probably more economical to buy an egg substitute for dishes like this. Most of those egg substitutes are just egg whites, anyway, but read the label to make sure that's what you're getting. This omelette has a lovely, golden look—and with the pungency of the salsa to compensate, we never miss the yolks at all.*

6 large egg whites (or 4 tablespoons/50 mL egg substitute)

$^1/_4$ teaspoon (1 mL) salt

$^1/_4$ teaspoon (1 mL) ground white pepper

$^1/_2$ teaspoon (2 mL) lemon juice

1 teaspoon (5 mL) finely chopped fresh basil

1 teaspoon (5 mL) finely chopped fresh cilantro

$^1/_3$ cup (75 mL) bottled mild salsa

1. Beat the egg whites until frothy and add the salt, pepper, and lemon juice. Beat again briefly, then stir in the basil and cilantro.

2. Heat a medium nonstick skillet over medium-high heat. Add the egg mixture and cook for a minute or two, until you can lift the edges up intact. Tilt the skillet so the uncooked eggs run underneath as you lift the edges all around.

3. When the omelette is just firm, place half of the salsa on the lower half and spread it a little, keeping away from the very edge. Fold the top half down to cover the filling, forming a half-moon shape. Slide the omelette out onto a waiting, warmed plate, top with the remaining salsa, and serve.

**Nutrition:**

Calories: 39.4

Protein: 5.31 g

Carbohydrates: 3.47 g

Fibre: .75 g

Total Fat: .014 g
 Sat: .003 g
 Mono: .003 g
 Poly: .006 g

Cholesterol: 0 mg

Vitamin A: 15.4 mg RE

Vitamin B6: .003 mg

Vitamin B12: .1 mcg

Vitamin C: 5.43 mg

Calcium: 5.26 mg

Iron: .11 mg

Potassium: 79.6 mg

Sodium: 573 mg

Zinc: .013 mg

## The Least You Need to Know

➤ Breakfast sets you up for the day—it gets the metabolism going, burning fat. If you consume some protein, vitamins, and minerals but not too many calories, you'll get off to a good start and be less likely to overeat throughout the day.

➤ At home, you control what goes on the plate. If you eat lunch out, or at a work or school cafeteria, you won't know what's in the dishes that are offered. Instead, make a nice, filling egg-white omelette for breakfast and opt for fruit and lowfat cottage cheese with a cracker for lunch.

➤ Smoothies are a ridiculously easy, fun, and healthy option for breakfasts. Keep lots of canned fruit (packed in fruit juice concentrate, not heavy syrup) on hand and buy fresh fruit and lowfat yogurt regularly. If you are a vegetarian or want a protein punch in the morning, add $1/4$ cup (50 mL) of wheat germ or powdered soy protein per blender-full.

➤ If you need a little "mouth feel" before starting your day, choose one of the yogurt-based butter-flavoured spreads and indulge in a teaspoon (5 mL) on a piece of toast. It tastes pretty good for half the fat of butter.

# Index

## A

acid, 54

acorn squash, 172

adapting non-lowfat recipes,
43–44, 130, 179

aerobic exercise, 47

age, 14

Alaskan king crab, 44
*see also* shellfish

alcohol, 14, 48–49

aluminum foil, 136–137

American pantry, 74

anaerobic exercise, 47

anchovies, 71, 210

appetizers
Bruschetta with Tomato-
Basil "Salsa," 196
Crab Quesadillas, 198
Frozen Shrimp Cocktail, 195
Homemade Mini-Pizzas,
200–201
Hot and Smoky Hummus
Wrap, 193
Smoked Mackerel with Spicy
Garlic Foam, 197
Stuffed Mushrooms, 199
Sun-Dried Tomato Tapenade,
192
Tzatziki (Greek Cucumber
Dip), 194

Apple Pizza, 296

artichoke, 88

arugula, 55

Asian Noodles with Chicken
and Scallions, 268

Asian pantry, 74–75

Asian restaurants, 78–79

asparagus, 88, 110, 117, 187

Asparagus and Tofu with
Sesame Dressing, 187

Avocado and Grapefruit Salad,
148

avocados, 147–148

## B

Baby Greens with Raspberry
Vinaigrette, 178–179

Baked Fideo, 207–208

Baked Polenta with Not-Your-
Own Tomato Sauce, 248–249

balance system, 19, 42

balanced diet, 38

balsamic vinegar, 54, 71

Basic (Medium-Hot) Curry
Powder, 68

basil, 55–56

basting, 105

beans and legumes, 30
Garbanzo Bean (Chickpea)
and Spinach Soup, 166
Hot and Smoky Hummus
Wrap, 193
Lentil Soup for the Soul,
174–175
Spicy Lentil Salad, 250–251
White Bean and Watercress
Salad, 184

beef. *See* meats

Beet and Apple Cole Slaw,
180–181

beets, 88, 117, 180–181

bell peppers, 107, 117

Berries in Warm Vanilla Foam,
298

blanching, 228

boiling, 116

bok choy, 89

Braised Lamb Shanks with Pearl
Onions, 287–288

Braised Turkey Legs with
Lemon, 132–134

braising
adapting non-lowfat recipes,
130
Braised Turkey Legs with
Lemon, 132–134
browning first, 127
defined, 114, 125–126
equipment, 126
liquid, 127–128
Ratatouille, 131
*repére*, 127
skimming, 129–130
stocks, 128
stove-top, 126
suitable foods, 127
using wine, 127–128
*vs.* roasting, 126
*vs.* stewing, 129

bread, 170

breakfast
Creamy Polenta with
Bananas and Raisins, 303
Cucumber and Salmon
Breakfast, 305
Egg White and Salsa
Omelette, 306
Mango Yogurt Smoothie,
302
Scrambled Parmesan Tofu,
304

breast-feeding, 28

British Columbia-Style White
 Potatoes and Green Beans,
 223
broccoli, 89, 117, 173, 174,
 224–225, 235
Broccoli and Parmesan Stuffed
 P.E.I. Potatoes, 235
Broccoli-Cheddar Soup, 173
broccoli rabe, 89
Brown, Basil, 25
Bruschetta with Tomato-Basil
 "Salsa," 196
brussels sprouts, 117
Bulgur in Savoy Cabbage
 Leaves, 244
butter
 cholesterol, 94
 as garnish, 92–93

**C**

cabbage, 89, 117, 170–171
calcium, 27
calories
 balance, 19
 counting, 18, 19
 and energy, 18
 non-fat, 23
 in various foods, 7
Canada's Food Guide, 15, 29
Canadian Pork Council, 108
Canadian weight statistics, 34
capers, 71
caramel, 220
carbohydrates, 23–24, 79
Carmelized Winter Vegetables,
 219
carrots, 89, 119
cast-iron, 100–101, 155,
 157–158

cauliflower, 89, 117
Celery Root and Potato Gratin,
 231–232
ceviche, 149
cheese, 186
chervil, 55, 56
chicken. *See* poultry
Chicken Breasts Escabeche, 269
chicken broth, 73, 74
Chicken Paillard with Salsa
 Fresca, 271
Chicken Scallops with Dijon
 Sauce, 272
Chicken Yakitori, 267
Chile Vinegar-Marinated Skirt
 Steak with Onion Cilantro
 Relish, 280–281
Chinese broccoli, 89
Chinese Egg Drop Soup, 167
Chinese Five Spice, 68
Chinese food, 79
chives, 55, 56
cholesterol, 12
 blood, 12
 causes of high, 13–14
 dietary, 12
 and fat, 21–23
 HDL, 22, 61
 high cholesterol level, 12–13
 LDL, 23, 61
 olive oil, 69
 and soy products, 61
chutney, 80–81, 94–95
cilantro, 54–55, 56
Cinnamon Applesauce, 294
cirrhosis, 48
citrus fruits, 145
citrus juices, 54
citrus zest, 249
colon cancer, 30
common sense, 7

complex carbohydrates, 23–24
convection ovens, 115
cooking spray, 70
coriander, 56
corn, 107, 117, 221–222, 225
Corn and Garlic Confetti, 225
Cornish game hens, 266,
 276–277
cottage cheese, 73, 301
covered kettle grills, 98–99
crab. *See* shellfish
Crab Quesadillas, 198
crayfish, 44
cream cheese, 73
Creamy Polenta with Bananas
 and Raisins, 303
Cucumber and Salmon
 Breakfast, 305

**D**

dairy products, 73–74, 301
desserts
 Apple Pizza, 296
 Berries in Warm Vanilla
 Foam, 298
 Cinnamon Applesauce, 294
 Grilled Peaches with Honey,
 Ricotta, and Balsamic
 Vinegar, 297
 Pears Poached in White
 Wine, 282
 Pineapple Frozen Yogurt
 with Banana Rum Salsa,
 293–294
 Pink Grapefruit Granita, 295
 Strawberry and Rhubarb
 Crepes, 299–300
diabetes, 35
diet, 13

meats, 109–110
Medium-Hot Grilling Rub,
60
open grills, 98
outdoor, 99
overcooking, 107–108
pork, 107–108, 284
resting time, 109
safety tips, 104–105
and salt, 102
smoking, 98, 104
suitable foods, 105–107
touch test, 107
grinding spices, 67–68

**H**

Hargrave, Shirley, 42
Health Canada, 8, 28, 34, 35
herbs, 54–58
crumbled, 237
as garnish, 92
steamed foods, 93
*vs.* spices, 55
Homemade Mini-Pizzas,
200–201
Hot and Smoky Hummus Wrap,
193
Hot Summer Tomato Soup, 168
hydrogenation, 15

**I**

Indian food, 79
indirect grilling, 101–102
indoor grills, 100–101
insulin, 35
iron, 27

**J**

Japanese food, 78, 266
juices. *See* fruit juices

**K**

King Crab with Kuta Beach
Dippin' Sauce, 258

**L**

lamb. *See* meats
Lamb Loin with Shallot Jus, 289
Latin American pantry, 74
Latin American restaurants, 80
"layering" flavour, 54
leeks, 89
legumes. *See* beans and legumes
lemon juice, 54
lemons, 95
Lentil Soup for the Soul,
174–175
Linguine with Spicy Bread
Crumbs, 209–210
lobster, 44
see also shellfish
lowfat dairy products, 73–74,
301
lowfat pantry. *See* pantry items

**M**

magnesium, 27
Mango Yogurt Smoothie, 302
marjoram, 55, 56–57
A Mash for All Seasons,
233–234
mayonnaise, 74
McGill University, 10, 23, 63

meats
beef, 108, 109, 279, 281
Braised Lamb Shanks with
Pearl Onions, 287–288
Chile Vinegar-Marinated
Skirt Steak with Onion
Cilantro Relish, 280–281
interior temperatures, 108
lamb, 108, 109–110, 280
Lamb Loin with Shallot Jus,
289
Mom's Flank Steak from the
1970s, 282
pork, 107–108
Pork and Fresh Ginger Sauté,
286
portion sizes, 282
as protein source, 288
room temperature, 283
steak, 103
Steak Kebabs with Yogurt
Sauce, 283–284
trimming fats from, 116, 128
Wine-Braised Pork Chops,
285
Mediterranean Chicken Salad,
185
Mediterranean diet, 23, 30,
38–39
Mediterranean food, 80
Mediterranean Orange Salad,
188
Mediterranean pantry, 74
Mediterranean Potato Gratin,
232–233
Medium-Hot Grilling Rub, 60
metabolism, 47
Mexican food, 80
Middle Eastern food, 80–81
Middle Eastern pantry, 74

**313**

**314**

Garam Masala, 69
grinding your own, 67–68
steamed foods, 93
*vs.* herbs, 55
Spicy Lentil Salad, 250–251
spinach, 226
Spinach with "Rustic Salt," 226
spring menu, 46
Stale Bread and Garlic Soup, 169
steak, 103
Steak Kebabs with Yogurt Sauce, 283–284
Steamed Broccoli with Gremolata, 224–225
Steamed New Potatoes with Butter and Chives, 230
Steamed Whitefish with Salsa Fresca, 261
steaming, 116
artichoke, 88
benefits, 85–86
chicken, 87
equipment, 86–87
fish, 87, 90-91
and herbs, 93
liquid, 88, 91
overcooking, 87
shellfish, 90
and spices, 93
vegetables, 87, 88–89
and vinegar, 94
water level, 86
when to steam, 86
stewing, 129
stir-frying, 156
Strawberry and Rhubarb Crepes, 299–300
stress reduction, 49
studies. *See* research studies
Stuffed Mushrooms, 199

substitute low-fat ingredients, 43–44
sugar, 10, 291
sulphur, 27
summer menu, 45
summer squash, 89
Sun-Dried Tomato Tapenade, 192
surimi, 198
sushi, 79, 149–150
Sushi-Dipping Sauce, 150
sweet potatoes, 89
Swiss chard, 89

**T**

Tabbouleh Salad, 181–182
tapenade, 239
tarragon, 55, 58
tempura, 80
Thai food, 79
thyme, 55, 58
tofu
Asparagus and Tofu with Sesame Dressing, 187
firm, 62, 107
Scrambled Parmesan Tofu, 304
silken, 62
Tomato-Barley Risotto, 245
Tomato Couscous, 243
tomatoes
Bruschetta with Tomato-Basil "Salsa," 196
Hot Summer Tomato Soup, 168
Oven-Roasted Tomatoes, 120
roasted, 119–120
Sliced Summer Tomatoes with Balsamic Vinegar, 183

Slow-Roasted Tomatoes, 220–221
Spaghetti with Barely Cooked Tomato Sauce, 204–205
Tomato-Barley Risotto, 245
Tomato Couscous, 243
trans-fatty acids, 15
trichinosis, 107–108
Tuna Teriyaki, 259
turkey. *See* poultry
Turkey-Stuffed Vine Leaves with Yogurt, 275–276
turnips, 89
Tzatziki (Greek Cucumber Dip), 194

**V**

Vegetable Gratin, 218
vegetables
Asparagus and Tofu with Sesame Dressing, 187
baby, 143, 231
Beet and Apple Cole Slaw, 180–181
British Columbia-Style White Potatoes and Green Beans, 223
broth, 171
Carmelized Winter Vegetables, 219
Corn and Garlic Confetti, 225
Grilled Asparagus with Lemon Dressing, 110
Grilled Corn on the Cob with Vegetable Medley, 221–222
grilling, 107

# About the Authors

Chef Pamela Steel is a Contributing Editor for *President's Choice® Magazine*, where her column, *Nice Timing*, has been a popular feature since the magazine's inception. Her previous cookbooks include a book of her columns, *Nice Timing, Recipes for Homemade Love*, a lovely book of memories and homespun recipes, as well as four books in the "mania" series, *Pasta, Casserole, Soup* and *Cookie Mania*. She has also written *The Complete Idiot's Guide To Cooking Soups, Canadian Style*. Pamela worked as a consultant on *Modern Woman Magazine's Family Favourites For EveryDay* and *The Urban Peasant*, James Barber's, latest cookbook, *Cooking For Two*.

Brigit Légère Binns is a food writer and consultant based in Venice, California. Her first solo cookbook, *Polenta*, was published by Chronicle Books in January 1997. It has been featured by the Book-of-the-Month Club, and was chosen as one of the 15 best cookbooks of 1997 in the Food Section of *The San Francisco Chronicle*. Her second solo book, *The Jody Maroni Sausage Kingdom Cookbook* (Rizzoli), was published in September of 1997. She was co-author of *The Rockenwagner Restaurant Cookbook* (Ten Speed Press, 1997), and food consultant on *The Patina Cookbook* (Harper Collins, 1995). She has done recipe testing, editing, and/or recipe development on the following nine books: five books in the Williams-Sonoma collection (including *Stir-Fry* and *Simple Fresh Appetizers, Soups, and Salads*), also *Casual Cuisines: Pizzeria, Casual Cuisines: Diner* (both Weldon Owen), *The California Cook* (William Morrow, 1995), and *The Angeli Restaurant PastaPizzaCalzone Cookbook* (William Morrow, 1997).